THE BIRTH OF A TEXAS GHOST TOWN

T0282781

Number Twenty-two:
Tarleton State University Southwestern Studies in the Humanities
William T. Pilkington, General Editor

THE BIRTH OF A TEXAS GHOST TOWN

Thurber, 1886–1933

MARY JANE GENTRY

Edited and with an Introduction by
T. Lindsay Baker
Foreword by Larry Gatlin

Texas A&M University Press
College Station

∞ This paper meets the requirements of ANSI/NISO Z39.48–1992 (Permanence of Paper). Binding materials have been chosen for durability.

Library of Congress Cataloging-in-Publication Data

Gentry, Mary Jane, 1912–1996.
  The birth of a Texas ghost town : Thurber, 1886–1933 / by Mary Jane
  Gentry ; edited and with an introduction by T. Lindsay Baker ; foreword
  by Larry Gatlin. — 1st ed.
      p. cm. — (Tarleton State University southwestern studies in the
      humanities ; no. 22)
Includes bibliographical references and index.
  ISBN 978-1-58544-629-2 (cloth : alk. paper)
  ISBN 978-1-62349-909-9 (book/papberback : alk. paper) | ISBN
  978-1-60344-397-5 (e-book)
      1. Thurber (Tex.)—History. 2. Ghost towns—Texas—History. 3. Immigrants—
Texas—Thurber—Social life and customs. 4. Thurber (Tex.)—Social life and
customs. 5. Thurber (Tex.)—Ethnic relations. 6. Coal miners—Texas—Thurber—
History. 7. Coal trade—Texas—Thurber—History. 8. Brick trade—Texas—Thurber
—History. 9. Thurber (Tex.)—Economic conditions. I. Baker, T. Lindsay. II.
Gatlin, Larry. III. Title.
F394.T48G46 2008
976.4'551—dc22

                                                        2007026465

Contents

Illustrations

Foreword

When I was sixteen and seventeen years old in Odessa, Texas, I was in Mary Jane Gentry's American history class. That was at Odessa High School in 1964–65.

As a teacher, she was hard; I mean, really hard. It was difficult to make an A. And for those who didn't want to work, it wasn't really very pleasant. She made it uncomfortable for the ones who didn't want to study. She believed that just doing the regular work was not enough.

On the other hand, I like history, and I studied hard. In my class, I was her pet, but we were all afraid of her. She would take no crap—no crapola. It was all businesslike. In Miss Gentry's class you had to learn all twenty-five articles of the Treaty of Versailles that ended World War I, and you had to learn the eight causes and effects of the Western movement. It was hard work, but she made it come alive. Her incredible sense of humor just bubbled out.

One day we were talking about the Spanish American War. She was discussing the Spanish ambassador, Enrique Dupuy de Lôme, and his letter that criticized Pres. William McKinley. She said that de Lôme declared McKinley did not have the backbone of a chocolate éclair. I popped off and asked, "Miss Gentry, what is an éclair?" She knew that I was just being a smartass and went on with the class.

The next day when class began at two o'clock in the afternoon, this sweet lady brought in a box with thirty chocolate éclairs. She had them baked at an Odessa bakery. You know, in Odessa in those days, no one just happened to have chocolate éclairs; she had them specially baked. She made history fun.

Even so, there were the reading assignments. We all know history can be pretty dull and dusty. We had to do the readings, because she taught by asking us questions; she used the Socratic method. Miss Gentry brought it to life. She put flesh and blood into the teaching of American history.

After I left Odessa in 1966 to go to the University of Houston, I stayed in touch with Miss Gentry for many years. I went to see her when I came back to visit my family. One time, she invited me in and showed me her library. I held her thesis on Thurber in my hands, and now it is reaching a much wider audience through the pages of this book. I am pleased that people who weren't fortunate enough to know her in person will be able to share in Mary Jane's passion for learning about the past.

LARRY GATLIN
Austin, Texas
March 29, 2007

Editor's Preface

In 1975, when I was a graduate student about the age that Mary Jane Gentry was in the 1940s, I discovered her never-published history of Thurber. As a research associate in the History of Engineering Program at Texas Tech University, I was helping undertake a statewide inventory of historic engineering works as part of a contract the school had with the Texas Historical Commission. This survey necessarily included Thurber, the best known coal mining community in nineteenth-century Texas.

Even before I had read the "Gentry thesis," as this work is known among Thurber researchers, I had begun stopping in the abandoned town to dine at Randy Bennett's family restaurant called "The Smokestack." As a native of Cleburne, I passed back and forth through the town site driving to school in Lubbock. Eventually I included sketches of Thurber history in my *Building the Lone Star* and *Ghost Towns of Texas* guidebooks to historic sites in the state. Like most other researchers, I found Mary Jane Gentry's thesis from 1946 to be the most reliable source available at the time.

Then in summer 2002 Tarleton State University selected me to serve as the founding director of its W. K. Gordon Center for Industrial History of Texas, a museum and research center located at Thurber. Created through the generosity of Mrs. W. K. Gordon Jr., the institution collects, preserves, and interprets the industrial history of Thurber and the state of Texas. Losing no time, I re-read Mary Jane Gentry's history of Thurber as a "refresher course" on its past. Quickly I decided that one of my goals as the director of the new institution would be to make the Gentry thesis available to more readers than just a handful of fuzzy old professors like me and a handful of grass-roots historians passing around "bootlegged" photocopies.

Here the editor-in-chief of the Texas A&M University Press entered the story. After discussing the project with me for some time, she suggested that the Gentry manuscript might find an appropriate place in one of the publisher's series, in particular the Tarleton State University Southwestern Studies in the Humanities. Dr. William "Tom" Pilkington of Tarleton, who edits the series, read the typescript and became as convinced as I was that it should reach print. The editorial staff at the university press in College Station then reviewed the manuscript, they agreed, and I began preparing the sixty-year-old work for modern readers.

Users of this book will be reading Mary Jane Gentry's history just as she prepared it. Only inadvertent misspellings and typographical errors have been amended. The scholarly notation is that of 1946, so it varies slightly from current style. The manuscript includes some 1940s racial terminology that current writers would not have chosen. Gentry originally illustrated the thesis with photocopies of documents and photographs. With the exception of her portrait, I have chosen the current illustrations from the images that she actually used and later donated to the Special Collections Division at the University of Texas at Arlington Libraries. There, archivists Brenda McClurkin and Gary Spurr greatly facilitated access to and reproduction of the interesting images.

In writing the introduction to this book, which sketches the life of Mary Jane Gentry and attempts to place her into the context of other mid-twentieth-century women historians in Texas, I traveled to all of the places she lived and worked. At every turn librarians and archivists did all they could to facilitate my research. In Odessa Carolyn Petersen, director of the Learning Resources Center at Odessa College, opened the invaluable historical files of the school to my investigation, while at the same time she placed me in touch with numerous individuals who gave oral interviews. Cheri Dalton at the Office of Media Relations and Publications at Odessa College provided Gentry's old college news service file and shared her remembrances of being one of her pupils. In the Southwest History and Genealogy Department of the Ector County Library, Rita Wilson and Doris Baker similarly made available materials that proved to be essential.

At the San Angelo Independent School District, Interim Superintendent Joanna Rice gave permission for me to undertake research in historic manuscript records of the district, while Joan Hartung and Marta Turney located the necessary volumes and brought them to me for examination and note taking. Suzanne Campbell and Shannon Sturm, archivists at the West Texas Collection at Angelo State University, provided very helpful manuscript and printed materials, as did Tatyana Shinn, reference librarian at the Tom Green County Library. In Austin reference staff at the Austin History Center assisted me with research in city directories and high school yearbooks, while Margaret Schlankey at the Center for American History at the University of Texas moved mountains to provide access to the papers of Walter Prescott Webb and the records of the Texas State Historical Association. Claudia Rivers, head, and Anne Allis, library assistant, made available the highly important file of Mary Jane Gentry's correspondence with book publisher J. Carl Hertzog in the C. L. Sonnichsen Special Collections Department in the University of Texas at El Paso Library.

Mary Jane Gentry's family, friends, colleagues, and former students provided the human perspective on her life that would have never appeared in documentary records. These invaluable interviewees included Dan R. Gentry, Joe Connally, Dr. Judy Cornes, Cheri Dalton, Truett L. Hilliard, Carol L. Horton, Dr. Paul Johnson, Mary Nell Johnson, Mary Manitzas, Debbie Morris, and Kay Thomas.

Colleagues and administrators at Tarleton State University played a major role in making publication of this volume possible. Provost Gary Peer, Deans Donald L. Zelman and Dean Minix, and Social Sciences Chair Michael Pierce have all supported and encouraged this project. Dr. William "Tom" Pilkington, who coordinates the Tarleton State University Southwestern Studies in the Humanities for Texas A&M University Press, could not have been more helpful. My colleagues at the W. K. Gordon Center for Industrial History of Texas have tolerated me as I have rattled on and on about the book project and its author, and they generously offered their helpful editorial suggestions for the introduction. These patient co-workers have included LeAnna S. Schooley, Bethany Kolter, Gene Tucker, Stephanie Winnett, and Rhonda Rucas. My wife, Julie P. Baker, assisted by holding down the fort while I gadded about the state on the trail of Gentry, not to mention critiquing my introduction.

Most importantly I wish to express thanks to the members of Mary Jane Gentry's family, who have provided continuous assistance and encouragement in this project. Her surviving brother, Dan R. Gentry, gave Tarleton State University permission to publish his late sister's history of Thurber. With interviews, letters, and copies of unique documents, he has been the key to the success of this project. We all owe him a debt of gratitude for his efforts to ensure the survival of Mary Jane Gentry's legacy to all Texans.

T. LINDSAY BAKER
W. K. Gordon Center for Industrial History of Texas,
Tarleton State University

Editor's Introduction

Mary Jane Gentry and Her History of Thurber

B orn in Boston, the daughter of a Texan father and a Canadian mother, Mary Jane Catherine Gentry became the historian of Thurber, perhaps the best known Texas ghost town. Her narrative, completed in 1946 though never published during her lifetime, served as the foundation on which all later studies of the notable town were built. It remains the most readable of all the histories of Thurber.

Mary Jane Gentry's father, Guy Jonathan Gentry, was born in Texas in 1887. He grew up on a farm northwest of Stephenville in Erath County, Texas, in a home filled with brothers and sisters. Deciding to escape a life of raising cotton, he joined the U.S. Marine Corps. In 1910 a census taker noted his service on the battleship U.S.S. *Missouri* in Boston Harbor in Massachusetts. It was in the Bay State that he had met pretty Florence Jessie McDonald, who had come from Nova Scotia. Family tradition holds that they met on the Boston Common. The couple married and on 24 March 1912 Flora delivered their first child, a daughter named Mary Jane Catherine.[1]

Guy Gentry received a military transfer to Grand Rapids, Michigan, to serve as a Marine Corps recruiter. On leaving the armed service, he brought Florence and their new daughter back to Texas, where a son, Daniel, was born. Then the young family returned to the Northeast, where Guy spent at least part of World War I working as a machinist in a munitions plant at Erie, Pennsylvania. There another daughter, Isabel Rita, joined the family. Following the close of the conflict and the cancellation of military contracts for artillery shells, Guy took his family and his machinist skills back to Texas.[2]

*Mary Jane Gentry about the time that she wrote her history of Thurber.
Courtesy of Dan K. Gentry.*

Guy Gentry found work in the booming coal mining town of Thurber in the northwestern corner of Erath County. The Texas & Pacific Coal Company had established an industrial enterprise there, with the company owning the town of Thurber, its mines, and its brick kilns. However successful the place might be, Florence balked when she arrived there in the fall of 1919 and saw the hot, dusty town with smokestacks belching dirty smoke. Mary Jane remembered her mother's first remark on seeing Thurber: "We'll stay and put the children in school, but as soon as the school term is over, we are leaving." Little did she imagine that her family would stay for the next seventeen years. Four more children followed: Angus, Ann, James, and Flora. Guy worked part of the time at the central machine shop, but often duties took him to the coal mines and brick plant, where he made field repairs on equipment. After the mines closed in the 1920s, the company shifted Gentry to become the assistant superintendent in the brickyard, which operated until 1931. When the census taker visited the Gentry home on 3 April 1930, he found them living on Marston Street, where their neighbors were white-collar workers with jobs like paymaster, manager, and physician, so the Gentry family clearly constituted part of the Thurber elite.[3]

Mary Jane Gentry began her formal education in the first grade of Hunter's Academy at Thurber in the fall of 1919. The influence of this schooling and the disposition of her family gave the girl a lifelong thirst for learning. The classrooms in Thurber, where most pupils were the children of families that had immigrated from overseas, exposed Mary Jane to other people's ways of thinking and acting, leading to an openness that friends observed for the rest of her life. Gentry remembered that before the first day was over, "I had quite a list of new friends. They made no objection to my Yankee ancestry, and I certainly did not object to such surnames as Bida, Galik, Biondi, Maletski, Marchoni, Vietti, Zinnani, Buffo or Chyz." For little Mary Jane they were no different from the Smith, Jones, and Carr children she had known in other places.[4]

From Hunter's Academy, a private school with classes taught by Catholic nuns, Gentry moved into the public schools of Thurber. She graduated as valedictorian of the class of 1930 at Thurber High School. Perhaps because of her own desire to learn and possibly due to parental encouragement, she next attended the nearby junior college in Ranger. Convenient passenger trains of the Texas & Pacific Railway moving east and west between Mingus (Thurber Junction) and Ranger helped facilitate her first steps into higher education. She graduated from Ranger Junior College with an associate of arts degree in May 1932. After another year Gentry received the first of several Texas teaching certificates, a temporary license based on two years of approved college work that permitted her to teach for up to three years.[5]

Gentry came back to her hometown to begin her teaching career. Thurber had had public schools for decades, but by the time she returned, the town and its schools had begun the decline from which they never recovered. The coal mines closed in the 1920s, and the brick kilns ceased operating in the early 1930s. With few jobs left, people moved away from Thurber, and the company began moving its offices to Fort Worth. Still, a four-teacher elementary school remained at the town site, and the local school board hired "one of their own," Mary Jane Gentry, to teach there during its last few months of operation. Minutes from the board meeting on 6 September 1934 recorded, "Voted to employe [sic] Miss Gentry. No salary decided at this time." After the Thurber school consolidated with the schools in the town of Strawn at the end of the academic year, Mary Jane moved to a two-teacher country school known as Springer Gap, just across the county line in Palo Pinto County. The rural school served the Dodson Prairie community six miles north of Strawn. Boarding with local families, Gentry became a favorite in that partly German settlement, which was her home for the next five years.

During the summer Mary Jane traveled to Austin, where she took undergraduate courses at the University of Texas with the goal of completing her baccalaureate degree. The contrast between rural Palo Pinto County and the urbane and refined university campus must have made a strong impression on the young woman, for she continued returning to and enjoying visits in Austin for much of the rest of her life. After multiple summers of study, Mary Jane on 5 June 1939 received a bachelor of science degree in education. After completing this degree, on 25 August 1939 she received her second Texas teaching license, this time a permanent elementary certificate.[6]

Mary Jane Gentry's world expanded during her studies in Austin. Once she completed her degree and earned a permanent teaching certificate, she could escape the confines of poorly paying country-school jobs where she had been trapped. Even though she had a contract to spend 1939–40 back in the Dodson Prairie country school, during summer 1939 she accepted an offer to teach in the public schools of San Angelo, Texas. The pretty town beside the tree-lined Concho River on the Edwards Plateau appealed to Gentry, who first had to secure a release from the three trustees of the rural school board. They agreed on a Saturday, and the next day Mary Jane boarded a bus to San Angelo, arriving about a month after classes had begun. The San Angelo school superintendent had held the job for the twenty-seven-year-old teacher with a newly signed diploma from the University of Texas. For a monthly salary of $81.81, she went right to work at San Jacinto Elementary School, a handsome two-story masonry school still operating nearly seventy years later at 814 Spaulding Street on the east side of town.[7]

While completing her degree at the University of Texas, Mary Jane Gentry made the acquaintance of one of the most prominent members of the history faculty, Dr. Walter Prescott Webb. She became his protégée, maintaining the relationship for years to come. Already Webb was nationally known for his book, *The Great Plains* (1931), and had lectured abroad. He had spent his childhood partly in Eastland County and attended Ranger High School, so the professor identified with his student who came from the same part of the state. With Webb's encouragement, Mary Jane in 1939 decided to continue study toward a master's degree in history at the University of Texas with plans to write her thesis on the history of Thurber. As early as the summer of that year, Webb, director of the Texas State Historical Association, announced in the *Southwestern Historical Quarterly* that "Miss Mary Gentry . . . is writing a history of Thurber, the Texas and Pacific coal mining town, in which she spent her childhood," adding that he himself had "spent two summers in Thurber when it was in its heyday." He concluded his report on Gentry's forthcoming work with the declaration, "The time has come to write the history of Thurber."

Webb not only promoted Mary Jane Gentry through the state historical association's scholarly journal but also placed her on the program as a speaker for its annual meeting in Austin on Saturday, 27 April 1940. Traveling from San Angelo, she spoke on "Thurber: Texas Ghost Coal Town," eliciting favorable responses from listeners. One member of that audience was journalist and author Boyce House, who reported to W. K. Gordon Sr., the former general manager of coal company operations in Thurber, that he found the talk interesting and that it had prompted him to write a newspaper column about it. Mary Jane Gentry seemed well on her way to undertaking graduate study and the history of Thurber, but events across the sea modified her plans.[8]

Throughout World War II and the immediate postwar years, Mary Jane Gentry taught in San Angelo while wartime rationing of gasoline and automobile tires slowed her thesis research. Each summer, though, she continued to travel to Austin, now to take graduate courses. Anytime she could manage it during the war years, she conducted documentary research and oral interviews for her history of Thurber. In San Angelo she transferred from the elementary school to San Angelo Junior High School in March 1942. There she was able to teach history classes with more intellectual substance.[9] Gentry always lived close to her schools, first at 312 Koberlin, in a mixed neighborhood of Victorian residences and twentieth-century bungalows six blocks from the elementary school and only one and a half blocks from the junior high, and then starting in 1944 she lived at 527 Pulliam, in another bungalow district still only about a six-and-a-half-block walk from the junior high school. She could walk to work throughout the wartime years.[10]

American entry into the conflict had an immediate effect on Gentry's life as a San Angelo teacher. Two months after the attack on Pearl Harbor, she began making monthly payroll deductions toward the purchase of war bonds, starting at $6.25 in February and in September increasing these regular purchases to $12.50 monthly. In June 1943 Gentry paid an additional "victory tax" that started at $7.60 per month but quickly rose to $11.60 and then increased in stages to $18.20. This meant that by the end of the war, when her monthly salary was $135.33, Mary Jane was contributing almost 23 percent of her earnings to the war effort through bond purchases or war taxes.[11]

The young teacher had a very personal connection with the war effort and was pleased to play her role on the home front. Brother Dan R. Gentry served with an armored unit in Europe, brother James Edward Gentry sailed in the U.S. Merchant Marine on both the Atlantic and the Pacific, sister Ann Hannah Gentry was a nurse for the U.S. Navy, and another brother, Angus L. Gentry, was a pilot with the U.S. Army Air Corps. After surviving an aircraft crash while moving P-47 planes between Florida and Massachusetts, Angus received thirty days' leave to come home to visit with his parents, then living in McCamey, Texas. On his way back to his base in Massachusetts, the aviator caught a ride on a plane that was going from Fort Worth to South Bend, Indiana, but was diverted by bad weather to the Chicago Municipal Airport. While attempting to land there on 20 May 1943, the plane struck a huge gas tank and all aboard lost their lives. Angus was buried in the family plot at the Mount Marion Cemetery in Strawn, Texas.[12]

Despite restricted travel and reduced funds for research because of her contributions to the war effort, Mary Jane Gentry continued summer coursework in Austin while doggedly pursuing interviews and documents for her thesis. When not attending classes or teaching, she spent time with her family in McCamey. Feeling physically isolated from her professors while in San Angelo, she sometimes questioned her work on a graduate degree. In response to a letter expressing some of these frustrations, mentor Walter Prescott Webb commiserated on 31 August 1943: "I can well understand how difficult it is for you to work on Thurber when you have heavy school duties and the general psychological difficulties incident to the war. . . . I also am finding similar difficulties in my own work." A year later Gentry wrote to Webb from

San Angelo: "I have been unable to write a thesis that does justice to Thurber." She elaborated, "You were anxious for me to make Thurber 'live' on those pages. . . . I have a world of information—most of it interesting—but when I write it down, it seems to be so factual." Finally, at the end of summer in 1945, Gentry completed a preliminary draft for her history of Thurber. After mailing it to Webb on 1 September, she wrote a week and a half later that "no sooner was it in the mail than I wished I had it back so that I might re-write several passages." The early draft must have at least partially satisfied Webb, for he marked it up, returned it to Gentry in the winter, and asked her to begin sending him revised chapters one at a time. Realizing that his student could not gain access to the corporate records of the Texas Pacific Coal & Oil Company, in early summer 1946 he advised, "If financial information is not available, then it cannot be used by the historian." He encouraged Mary Jane in her work: "Let's get this finished before the end of summer school." Gentry did indeed complete the thesis, submitting it to her master's degree committee consisting of Walter Prescott Webb, Rudolph L. Biesele, and William N. Peach. They approved the work, and Mary Jane Gentry received her master of arts degree on 29 August 1946.[13]

"Thurber: The Life and Death of a Texas Town" was a very substantial volume. Although it was a master's thesis, at 237 pages it was longer than some doctoral dissertations. Mary Jane Gentry drew her raw material in part from oral interviews with nineteen informants, most of them people who were active in the historical events they described. Because it was difficult for Gentry to travel during the war, she also resorted to writing letters to secure remembrances from an additional eighteen individuals. Undertaking this research in the late 1930s and 1940s allowed her to gain significant insights from living resources unavailable to later Thurber historians. She carefully sifted information from all the known surviving Thurber newspapers, while also seeking data from other newspapers published in Austin, Dallas, Fort Worth, Ranger, Stephenville, and Strawn. The Texas Pacific Coal & Oil Company chose not to open its corporate records to her, so Gentry employed published annual reports to fill in gaps when possible. To illustrate the thesis, the author included more than two dozen positive photocopies of photographs, documents, and a map of downtown Thurber businesses. The work was masterful. Since its completion in 1946, the Gentry thesis has formed the cornerstone for subsequent scholarly investigations of Thurber and its industries.[14]

Mary Jane Gentry had a knack for choosing good places to live. When she located in San Angelo in fall 1939, it was a town that was prospering despite the lingering effects of the Great Depression. With a population of approximately twenty-five thousand, the community had weathered hard times thanks to its proximity to the Permian Basin oil fields that opened in the 1920s. Gentry had been in the small city only a short time when the Department of War opened a military flight training facility that became known as Goodfellow Field. Another facility, the San Angelo Bombardier School, followed after the American entry into World War II. Both of the military bases brought families to the town, and Gentry's classrooms bulged with increasing numbers of pupils.[15] When her teaching shifted from the elementary school to the junior high in March 1942, the move was not to a new facility with spacious classrooms. Instead it was to the old community public school, converted years before into a middle school. Its core had been built in 1884 from stones transported to the site of a former courthouse damaged in a Concho River flood two years before. She would teach there through May 1948.[16]

It was at the cramped, old San Angelo Junior High School where Mary Jane Gentry became involved in a history-related activity that she pursued for a decade and a half—the Junior Historian organization created by the Texas State Historical Association. Gentry's mentor, Walter Prescott Webb, founded the program in 1939 in his capacity as director of the association. As developed by Webb and H. Bailey Carroll, who became its first director, the Junior Historian organization helped train pupils in the sixth to twelfth grades to become bona fide grass-roots historians. As part of their activities in extracurricular clubs within schools around the state, young people under their teachers' supervision conducted research and wrote articles on Texas history topics for their own journal, *The Junior Historian*. The magazine became one of the first in America to be written by and for young people.[17]

Junior Historian chapters had already operated in both the junior and senior high schools of San Angelo.[18] Gentry became an active club sponsor at the junior high in fall 1944. The next spring she submitted several articles written by her seventh-grade pupils for consideration by the editors of *The Junior Historian*. She wrote to H. Bailey Carroll, whom she already knew personally as a university history faculty member, reporting that the articles were written by "boys and girls. . . . just twelve and thirteen years old." She added that they "did their own research . . . checking newspaper files and interviewing the 'old timers.'" As a teacher Gentry was gratified the next fall to see the work one of her pupils published in the November 1945 issue. This success led the editors in Austin to solicit submissions for a special issue of the magazine consisting solely of articles written by San Angelo pupils. The idea worked, and the special issue appeared in May 1946.[19]

In February 1947 H. Bailey Carroll asked Gentry if one of her seventh-grade pupils could speak at the yearly gathering of Junior Historians scheduled to take place concurrently with the annual meeting of the state historical association. The teacher suggested Bill Marschall, who was preparing a paper on San Angelo architect Oscar Ruffini, and Carroll proceeded to invite the young man to address the group. Gentry subsequently made the first of what became several trips to Austin chaperoning pupils. Yet another honor came to her chapter of the Junior Historians that same school year. Kenneth Lee Schlaudt in May 1948 received the Folklore Award for his article submission, "Legends of the Rocks," which then was published in the November 1948 issue of *The Junior Historian*. It should be noted that other mid-twentieth-century Texas women historians employed as teachers also guided their pupils' participation in the Junior Historian organization. Llerena B. Friend, known in later life as author of *Sam Houston, the Great Designer* (1954) and as the founding director of the Barker Texas History Center at the University of Texas in 1950, during the 1940s taught at the high school in Wichita Falls, Texas, and sponsored a Junior Historians chapter.[20]

Just as Mary Jane Gentry was building a reputation as the author of the Thurber history and as a "star" sponsor for a Junior Historians chapter, she took advantage of another opportunity. She traveled across the Atlantic to spend a full academic year teaching in Wales. Gentry participated in an exchange program, conducted by the National Educational Association, that had operated at San Angelo for at least one year. In 1947–48 a local teacher traveled to Ireland, while an Irish teacher took her place in Texas. Under the guidelines of the exchange program, each teacher continued to be paid in his or her home country. Taking Mary Jane's place in Texas for 1948–49 was Miss Gladys Cowles, the headmistress of the Secondary Modern Girls School in Bargoed, Wales, where Gentry would teach.

Gentry sailed from New York on 24 July 1948, arriving in Bargoed on 1 August. Her destination was a coal mining town with approximately fifteen thousand inhabitants situated about sixteen miles from Cardiff, the capital. Finding a green landscape and rainy weather all year, Mary Jane later mentioned that she felt cool enough in early August to wear a wool suit and to be grateful for a coal fire in the grate. After making arrangements to live in Bargoed in the home of a schoolmaster, she left for a month of travel in the Netherlands, Belgium, and Luxembourg combined with orientation meetings arranged by the exchange coordinators. She began teaching in Bargoed on 6 September 1948, closing the school year in late July 1949. School days started at 9:30 A.M. and ended at 4:10 P.M. Because the Welsh school calendar included lengthy holidays, Mary Jane was able to take several extended trips both to Ireland and to Europe during her academic year abroad. Among her school-holiday trip destinations were Switzerland and France at Christmastime, Italy during the Easter holiday, and Scotland during the Whitsunday (Pentecost) school break. In Britain she attended two receptions hosted by the American ambassador in London and was presented along with other American exchange teachers to Queen Elizabeth at Lambeth Palace, the London residence of the Archbishop of Canterbury. Among the highlights of Gentry's travel were viewing world-famous art in the Louvre at Paris, looking up at Michelangelo's ceiling of the Sistine Chapel in

Rome, and floating past masterpieces of Renaissance architecture in a gondola on the canals of Venice. After a cold, wet winter in Bargoed, she especially enjoyed the warm Italian sunshine in spring 1949.

The experience of living abroad only made Mary Jane want to travel overseas even more. When she returned to Texas in late summer 1949, she regaled her family, friends, and colleagues with her adventures. A story she liked to tell dealt with a spectator who sat behind her at an international rugby match that pitted Wales against England. "A big, strapping man who sat behind me kept jumping up and down shouting, 'Lovely! Lovely!' when a play pleased him," she laughed. Always careful about grooming and appearance, the educator from across the sea was surprised by the response of her Welsh pupils to her "daring" red fingernail "varnish" and cosmetics, as no students and few British teachers at the time used very much of either. The Texas teacher reported continued food rationing in Britain, as supplies remained limited even though World War II had ended three years before. Gentry related that the average individual received only one egg and just one and a half ounces of cheese weekly. She explained to colleagues that an American homemaker would find a week's supply of meat for four persons in Wales to be about the same amount one Texan would eat in a single meal. There were, however, plenty of cold-climate vegetables. "I think I can never look at another Brussels sprout or cabbage," she quipped.[21]

While Mary Jane Gentry taught in Wales, the San Angelo Independent School District completed construction of a new building, the brand new Robert E. Lee Junior High School at 2502 Sherwood Way on the newer southwest side of the city. Wartime prosperity persisted in San Angelo, with more and more people moving to the city on the banks of the Concho, and space was needed for increasing numbers of schoolchildren. It was in the new facility that Gentry began teaching in September 1949. Still residing where she had before at 527 Pulliam Street, this was the first time she had lived so far from her school that she had to use an automobile.

Seeing a need, she began encouraging students in the new school to organize their own Junior Historians chapter. In April one of the student officers in the club formally applied to the Texas State Historical Association for a charter, which the members duly received. In April 1950 Gentry traveled with three of the pupils to attend the gathering of Junior Historians at the annual meeting of the state historical association in Austin. There she was able to breathe the air of the capital city she enjoyed so much while at the same time visiting with friends and fellow historians in the association.[22]

After a year at the new junior high school, Mary Jane Gentry changed schools again, this time moving to San Angelo High School in September 1950. Teaching there for three years, she really came into her element as a teacher and historian. The older pupils grappled with more complex issues in social studies classes. Gentry inherited sponsorship of a Junior Historian chapter that already had an established reputation as a source of articles for *The Junior Historian* magazine. Being comfortable chaperoning pupils to the annual gathering, she organized participation in the springtime meetings in Austin at least in 1951 and 1952. One of Gentry's students, Loretta Stewart, presented a talk about the restoration of Fort Concho to the assembled Junior Historians at the gathering in 1951.[23]

Many of Mary Jane Gentry's students agree that she was a superb teacher. Employing a variety of instructional methods to achieve her twin goals of imparting information and inspiring students to want to learn more, she changed teaching styles depending on the subject matter and the abilities of students. Some pupils remembered Gentry conducting classes in seminar fashion, emphasizing discussion. Joe Connally, a student in 1952–53, remembered her use of the Socratic method: "She would ask, 'What do you think about the Battle of the Alamo?' You did not dare not be prepared in there. She did not yell at you; she would be disappointed, and that was worse." One pupil related, "There was great fear of her as a teacher," as all the young people knew that her in-class questions and assignments were demanding. Other students, like Cheri Dalton, remembered Gentry using traditional lectures: "Miss Gentry lectured standing in front the class and commanding your attention. She stood upright, dressed nicely. It was basically a lecture and questioning students to respond." Debbie Morris recalled, "She was such a storyteller. Everything was a story in her class. She would stand in the class, fold her hands, and tell stories." Former student Larry Gatlin added, "She put flesh and blood into teaching American history." Paul Johnson found Gentry's lectures "as good as any first-run movies," adding that "she was one of the most astonishingly accomplished lecturers that I have ever heard. She was mesmerizing."[24]

Students identified with their young, petite, well-dressed social studies teacher. "I felt like she was a personal friend. . . . She could relate to any age group," declared former pupil Debbie Morris. Joe Connally added, "There were about thirty of us in the class, boys and girls. Every boy had a crush on Miss Gentry." Cheri Dalton said that Gentry's students always wondered why she had not married. "There must be someone out there for her," they said to themselves, wondering, "Why hasn't someone snatched her up?" These pupils may not have realized that there had been "someone" out there for her. Mary Jane Gentry had an affair of the heart in San Angelo during the 1952–53 school year. She became romantically involved with a male teacher in the high school, but their relationship unexpectedly became public knowledge. Always a very private person, Mary Jane saw her professional reputation being placed in jeopardy. Breaking off the relationship, she decided to leave San Angelo completely after fourteen years. Knowing that she was planning to relocate, the senior class of 1953 recognized Miss Gentry by dedicating their yearbook in her honor. By 16 July 1953 she had moved to Austin and had received an offer to teach social sciences at Stephen F. Austin High School in the city.[25]

The state capital remained home for Mary Jane Gentry for the next two years. Not long after she moved, she wrote to El Paso bookseller and publisher J. Carl Hertzog. "At the present I am teaching in Austin High School and probably will stay here unless the rain runs me off," she wrote, in reference to the "drastic change in humidity for a West Texan." She resided in an apartment at 1209 Anderson Lane in the home of Henry F. and Maureen Gentry, a couple who shared her surname but were not related. When the students assembled the 1955 annual, they chose a picture showing Mary Jane with two girls in her classroom and wrote in the caption that she "put reality into her history classes." West Texas, however, called Gentry. When a colleague from Odessa told her about an opening in the high school there, the now forty-three-year-old submitted an application even though she had been offered a three-year contract to stay in Austin. On 5 August 1955 W. T. Barrett, the superintendent of schools, formally welcomed Gentry by letter as a new teacher of social studies in the town of Odessa.[26]

For the next thirteen years Mary Jane Gentry taught social studies, mainly history, at Odessa High School. These were happy years for Gentry, who devoted nine months a year to teaching in her favorite field and spent summers either taking courses in subjects of interest or traveling to Europe and beyond. Odessa boomed economically, attracting more and more residents, so her classrooms remained full. The teacher lived modestly in the then-new McDonald Apartments in the 200 block of West Seventeenth Street. She occupied one or the other of two smaller north-facing units until moving into a larger, east-facing apartment, number 217, in 1958. She remained there for eight more years, filling the space with books not just on the American West but also on the history of the Old World. In 1966 she wrote to publisher Carl Hertzog, "Tonight I am browsing through books (as I frequently do)," noting some of her favorite titles. The historian of Thurber reflected, "The Renaissance has long been the most interesting period of history to me." Musing about history and books in general, one Monday night she penned a four-page handwritten letter to the El Paso publisher, noting in closing, "it is long past midnight and tomorrow is a full day." In addition to teaching, Gentry initially worked with the Odessa High student council, but then in 1960 she became involved in reactivating the Junior Historians chapter at the school, sponsoring it for several years.[27]

The intellectual stimulation of teaching, reading, travel, and summertime study led Mary Jane Gentry to coauthor a textbook for seventh-grade Texas history use. Her longtime associate in the Texas State Historical Association, H. Bailey Carroll, received a contract to provide this text, but his responsibilities in the organization and teaching at the University of Texas prevented him from preparing the work himself. As was common during the mid-twentieth century, Carroll found two women historians he could hire to do the "grunt work" of putting the book together. He read their text, gave it his approval, and then essentially claimed credit for the work. The two women who actually wrote the book were Mary Jane Gentry and Frances Nesmith. The latter had earned degrees from the University of Houston and Columbia University, taught in junior and senior high schools in Austin and Houston, and, like Gentry, nursed along Junior Historian chapters. For personal satisfaction Nesmith wrote book reviews for the *Houston Post*. She and Mary Jane Gentry made an easy working team as they divided up the Texas past; each wrote half of the book. Given the time when *The Story of Texas* was released in 1963, the two women could not effectively protest that its title page had the name of H. Bailey Carroll in large letters while theirs, as the coauthors who in reality had done the work, appeared in much smaller letters below. Despite the situation, the women knew they had written the 360-page book. Perhaps as her own small protest against the discrimination, later in life Mary Jane Gentry made certain that she was identified as "coauthor" of the textbook and that her former professor and mentor was not mentioned at all.[28]

Many students and fellow teachers had recollections of associations with Gentry at Odessa High School. Former student Cheri Dalton listed her strongest memories of Mary Jane Gentry in the following words: "Caring. Compassionate. Intelligent. Classy. A mature single woman." She remembered that her teacher was very attractive, but that her appearance did not mean that she tolerated misbehavior: "You didn't buck her. You could not get away with messing around." Other teachers enjoyed her company. From being one of Mary Jane Gentry's former pupils in San Angelo, Mary Manitzas later became her colleague in Odessa. She remembered exclaiming, "Oh, Mary Jane! I can't believe I'm calling you that instead of 'Miss Gentry.'" Manitzas enjoyed walking around the running track at the school with Gentry after school, and she remembered that Gentry "would wear a dress, even when walking. . . . She was always so prim and proper." Several people recalled that about 1960 Gentry won a new Cadillac at the Bill Sears supermarket in Odessa. A longtime driver of Chevrolet cars, the thrifty teacher sold the luxury vehicle and put the money in the bank. Paul Johnson of Odessa remembered Gentry as "urbane, scholarly, and adventurous." [29]

It was while in Odessa that Mary Jane Gentry began traveling to more distant parts of the world that were not necessarily so safe as Europe. She often selected university summer school courses that had a topical link to interesting overseas travel destinations. Among her destinations were most of the countries in Europe, the Soviet Union, Turkey, Egypt, Iran, India, China, Japan, Australia, and New Zealand. She went on a shoestring budget and even gave public programs in Odessa on what she termed inexpensive travel. According to former student Paul Johnson, inexpensive was no exaggeration. She traveled "on the cheap." In a private conversation about bargain hotels where she had stayed, the teacher remarked to Johnson, "I think the one in Paris was a whorehouse." She always preferred individual travel. Judy Cornes remembered Gentry going to China "right after it opened up," adding, "She complained that the authorities had organized the trip and she had to stay with a group. She wanted to go off on her own." Mary Jane's most adventurous trip, however, took place in the 1970s. As an individual traveler, she followed the route of the historic Silk Road from Turkey across Iran and Afghanistan to Pakistan. Though she successfully made the trip, it was not easy, especially for a woman traveling alone. She told one of her pupils that she lost fourteen pounds of body weight on the Silk Road. "It was hard to find anything I wanted to eat, and I knew that I would have to eliminate it in one of those Asian toilets," Gentry explained with distaste. "She is the only person I know who went over the Khyber Pass," remarked fellow teacher Truett L. Hilliard of Odessa. He remembered his colleague saying that along the Silk Road some of the old Muslim men would walk over to her and gently pinch her arms when they thought she was exposing female skin that they thought, for the sake of modesty, should be covered.[30]

The coauthor of the seventh-grade textbook for Texas history, a traveler to the four corners of the earth, a person characterized by an

Odessa High School student as "far above anyone else on the faculty," Mary Jane Gentry chafed at the increasing paperwork and nonacademic duties required of teachers in the public schools. The 1968 yearbook pictured her in a nicely tailored dress and gloves standing at her assigned place during a football pep rally. She must have disliked such distractions from the teaching that she loved so much. Eventually the annoyances grew too great, and Gentry at age fifty-six escaped the routine of public school teaching in 1968 to join the faculty of Odessa College, a community college founded in 1946 that at the time had about twenty-eight hundred students. In a typical semester at the college she taught five classes of American history and kept office hours both mornings and afternoons five days a week. Other than serving on occasional committees, she was able to focus on teaching. Of the thirteen faculty members in the Social Science Department in 1969–70, only one had more years of teaching experience. Just before joining the faculty, Gentry had moved from her old apartment on West Seventeenth Street to a brick duplex at 1301 North Lauderdale Avenue. In 1967 she occupied one of the four units in a pair of duplex residences that an absentee landlord had recently built as rental property. She occupied an east-facing brick-veneer unit. At the time homes like Gentry's, with air-conditioning and tiled kitchens and bathrooms, were considered very nice housing.[31]

As Gentry traveled farther and farther afield during the summers, she became increasingly interested in Asian and Middle Eastern culture. She continued taking university courses on various topics. During summer 1969, at fifty-seven years of age, for example, she attended lectures at the University of Oregon on the histories of Russia and China. She spent summer 1970 at the University of Virginia listening to lectures on the history of China and on medieval civilization. More study on Asia followed in summer 1974 at Arizona State University, where she attended classes on the geography of the Middle East, the diplomatic history of East Asia, and the history of the Soviet Union. Professor Fred Giffin, who taught the course on the Soviet Union, later wrote Gentry to say, "It was a pleasure having you in class and visiting with you in the office. I hope you'll return." Gentry grew especially interested in

Islam and in Middle Eastern cultures. She eventually visited Turkey a total of three times. Her office at 234 Wilkerson Hall became a haven in predominantly Christian Odessa for the college's Muslim students. For a time Dr. Judy Cornes occupied an adjacent space, where she observed that Iranian students, then numerous at the school, "would come by her office and visit for hours." Colleague Truett L. Hilliard remembered that because Mary Jane had had such positive experiences traveling across the Middle East and South Asia, she felt at ease with the many students who came from that part of the world. "She probably spent more time with the Muslim students than any of the rest of us did," he reflected.[32]

Even as one of the older faculty members at Odessa College, Mary Jane Gentry continued teaching her full load of classes. In spring 1974 she applied for and received tenure at the school. She continued a role she had occupied for years as one of the faculty speakers the college made available to local and regional organizations. In October 1976 she drove forty-five miles from Odessa to Kermit, Texas, to address its retired teachers on the subject of Texas folklore, one of her favorite topics. Drives like this, however, became more difficult as Mary Jane aged, and she gradually reduced her obligations outside the classroom. Even so, she gained energy from her students, and she taught until she was sixty-seven, well past the expected retirement age. About this time she wrote that she hoped that she had been able "to influence a few students to look beyond the sterility of a pure utilitarian existence." She decided to retire from active teaching in spring 1979. Gentry told a friend, "After 45 years of teaching I retired . . . and I am thoroughly enjoying my new way of life—doing things I enjoy and doing them at my own pace." At the time she was planning a springtime 1980 trip to Egypt.[33]

For a while Gentry's colleagues and former students from Odessa High School and Odessa College maintained contact with her. Former high school pupil Paul Johnson continued to seek her out because of their shared interest in the past. "She lived in a duplex over on North Lauderdale," he remembered, adding that "it had one room that was solid books, all the way to the ceiling." Inspired by Gentry, he declared that knowing her had led him "to a lifelong fascination with history."

Her friend Judy Cornes, a fellow social science instructor at Odessa College, recalled, "After she retired, I would see her from time to time. We would have dinner together." Kay Thomas was Gentry's next-door neighbor, and she remembered, "Her favorite guest was Larry Gatlin, who was her student. Every time he came to Odessa, he would come to her house to see her." The nationally known country-and-western music star had been her pupil at Odessa High School in 1964–65. On one occasion in the classroom, Gentry referred to a politician as not having the backbone of a chocolate éclair, to which Gatlin popped off, "Miss Gentry, what is an éclair?" The next day she brought a box of éclairs from a bakery and let everyone sample them. Years later Gentry attended one of Gatlin's concerts in Odessa, and before the show she sent a box of éclairs to his dressing room. After the performance began, he announced from the stage that he wanted to make a special introduction and asked his high school teacher to stand in recognition of his esteem for her.[34]

The years forced Mary Jane Gentry to narrow her world, and with age she became less able to do the things that she loved. She found comfort in her library of beloved books. Next-door neighbor Kay Thomas found her constantly in her house reading. "Alright, Miss Gentry, stop reading and come out to talk with me," she would say. Thomas related that after Gentry retired, despite continuing overseas trips for several years, "She was a very lonely person. I would sit for hours and listen to her. I guess I was lonely too." Thomas observed that the childless former teacher lived a Spartan existence: "She had tons and tons of books, but otherwise not very many other things." The younger woman had painted the inside of Gentry's house and had to move everything, so Thomas knew exactly what Mary Jane used on a day-to-day basis: "She had two or three pots and pans to cook in, but she simply ate because she had to live." Mary Jane reduced her daily wardrobe to garments that were easy to keep clean. The highlights for her yearly routine became visits from younger brother Dan R. Gentry, who lived in Dallas.

In time Mary Jane's bright mind that had inspired countless pupils suffered from the effects of Alzheimer's disease. She became so forgetful that she could no longer care for herself. Brother Dan in 1993 helped her to move to Dallas so that he could help provide care. Despite her illness Mary Jane recognized the importance of her early work on Thurber, and in 1993 she donated most of her files of Thurber-related photographs, newspapers, and other research materials to the Special Collections Division at the University of Texas at Arlington Libraries. Gradually declining further, Mary Jane Gentry passed away in Dallas on 4 December 1996. A rosary was said at St. John Catholic Church in Strawn, Texas, followed by celebration of a mass on Saturday morning, 7 December, and the Texas historian was laid to rest in the family plot near her brother and parents in the nearby Mount Marion Cemetery. To this day native Texas bluebonnets live in the hardscrabble soil of the plot, and every spring they cover Mary Jane's grave in a blanket of blue.[35]

THE BIRTH OF A TEXAS GHOST TOWN

Preface

For nearly fifty years, Thurber was known as one of the most color-ful towns in the Southwest. It was noted for its coal mines, enor-mous horseshoe bar, badger fights, and grappo. Immigrants, from all parts of Europe, came to Thurber and successfully transplanted much of their European culture to this unusual coal mining camp.

The purpose of this study has been to collect and record, at least in part, the history of this unique town. Thurber no longer exists, and it is becoming more and more difficult to find accurate historical data relating to it. The old timers are scattered to all parts of the world, and even when they are located, it is difficult to persuade them to write of their experiences in Thurber. This reluctance is often caused by lack of education or from an insufficient command of the English language.

Since Thurber was owned by the Texas Pacific Coal & Oil Company, the official records of Thurber are in the possession of this company and were not available at the time this study was made. Probably someday, the company officials will allow the records to be studied, and when this is done, a more detailed history of Thurber can be written.

So far as I know, there is no complete file of Thurber newspapers; in fact, I have located very few issues and those to which I had access are falling to pieces and will soon be useless. County records would have been used more extensively if it had been possible to secure them, but many of the Erath County records have been packed into boxes and these boxes are stacked to the ceiling and almost to the four walls of a room which was once used as a coal bin. Lack of available working space in the room made it impossible to examine the material.

Although it is impossible for me to list the names of all persons who contributed information to this study, I wish to acknowledge their willingness to help me at all times. I am especially indebted to Gomer Gower who wrote many long, interesting descriptions of life in Thurber, and I have found these letters to be a valuable source of historical data. To Hazel Miller, I wish to express my appreciation for the use of her collection of Thurber pictures, Thurber newspapers, and personal papers of her husband, Mose Miller.

I am deeply grateful to Dr. Walter P. Webb whose patient supervision, advice, suggestions and words of encouragement made this study possible.

MARY JANE GENTRY
The University of Texas
August 1946

CHAPTER 1

Introduction

As one travels eastward from Ranger, Texas, along Highway 80, the scenery is rather commonplace until one reaches the eastern edge of the mountain, overlooking a great valley which is divided among three counties—Eastland, Palo Pinto, and Erath. From this high point, one's attention is immediately drawn to the conical and rectangular formations to the south and east. Against a background of mesquites, oaks, and cedars, the mottled appearance of the formations is without a doubt the dominating feature of the landscape. These red, black, and blue-gray mounds are coal dumps built from the refuse of the coal mines that once made Thurber the largest coal mining camp in the state of Texas.

Thurber was located in the extreme northwestern corner of Erath County—32° 30' north latitude, 98° 25' west longitude. It was approximately 75 miles west of Fort Worth and about 90 miles east of Abilene. Thurber was in that portion of Erath County which may be described as "broken country." It lay within the confines of an encircling chain of low hills, and as one looked down upon the town from any one of these higher levels, he was impressed by the air of protectiveness lent by these hills as they stood guard over all entries into the place.

The town seemed secure within the lowest part of this cup-like formation for, with the exception of a few slight nicks and one narrow break, the rim of the cup was unbroken. Those minor chips or nicks in the rim afforded the best means of entering or leaving the town; hence, all roads into Thurber, with the exception of one, came "over a hill." This exception was the road to Mingus which passed northward through the only complete break in the encircling chain.

Those hills which lay closest to the heart of Thurber seemed to have spurned all attempts to achieve individuality and had conformed to the conventional lines of flat-topped, elongated structures. Only the hills lying to the east and slightly beyond the inner rim impressed one as having striven to gain attention by casting aside the conventional forms accepted by their neighbors. These hills to the east dotted the landscape as isolated cones, squatty knob-like structures, and one hill of rectangular proportions stood out above all the rest.

The hills which overlooked the town from the north, south, and west were not covered with excessive vegetation, but on all of these hills there were dwarfed mesquites, an occasional live oak, and a substantial amount of grass. Once again the hills to the east struck the discordant note by supporting an even smaller amount of vegetation, and in this state of near nakedness, they stood in further sharp contrast to their more modest neighbors.

When one looked down upon the town, he could hardly fail to note the air of serene self-satisfaction which seemed to hang over it. It would be hard to say whether this complacent air was the result of the protectiveness of the ever-watchful circle of hills, or whether it was due to the instinctive knowledge that nowhere else in all the Southwest or perhaps in the world, was there another Thurber.

One somehow felt that the town itself, as well as its population, sensed the unusual forces which characterized the founding of it. For years the area had been looked upon as having practically no value. Suddenly the demand for coal brought prospectors, and the discovery of a workable vein of coal encouraged hundreds of miners to come in. The Europeans who came in numbers brought with them and firmly established their native customs in this West Texas setting. As if this were not enough to make Thurber unique, Colonel Robert Dickey Hunter organized the camp "on a plan that closely resembled a socialistic state."[1] Every building and every inch of ground was Company owned. A four strand wire fence was put around the camp and this fence served to keep out those elements to which the authorities objected, such as peddlers, labor agitators, and union organizers.

The natural resources were limited to coal and clay, both of which existed in quantity. The demand for coal was the economic factor which brought Thurber into existence, and the discovery of the nearby Ranger oilfield doomed it to extinction.

For years, the owners and residents lived in the hope that some new stimulus would again stir Thurber into an active life. Their hopes were not to be realized, and as the years went by, they saw Thurber dwindle away—the victim of a hopeless economic situation. Eventually the pulse of Thurber ceased to throb. The town was dead, and the only monument to its existence is the memories which live in the minds and hearts of all its people.

In Erath County and adjoining counties, there are numerous outcrops of coal, some of which can be traced for miles before they "dip" below the surface. The presence of these outcrops was known to the Indians, who, in all probability, occasionally burned some of this coal. Beyond a doubt many early settlers did use its fuel and many more told of finding coal whenever a water well was being dug or drilled.

For years little thought was given to developing these coal beds and a potential industry was ignored until the early 1880s. The first commercial interest in Thurber coal appeared as the result of the decision of the Texas & Pacific Railroad officials to extend the railroad west of Fort Worth. Thus when there was a demand for coal along the line west of Fort Worth, attention was focused on the coal deposits on or near the route.

Geologically these coal deposits are known as Seam Number One of the Strawn Division.[2] W. F. Cummins in his "Report on the Geology of Northwestern Texas" located this coal seam as follows:

The outcrop of Coal Seam No. 1 is first seen on the north, near the town of Bridgeport, in Wise County, and passes thence through the western edge of Parker County, between Millsap and Mineral Wells, and through Palo Pinto County, passing Gordon, and into Erath County, passing Thurber, to a point about ten miles south of Strawn, where it passes beneath the newer strata and does not appear again any where to the south-ward. This gives a line of outcrop about eighty miles long . . . [3]

The coal in this seam is bituminous and varies in thickness from eighteen to thirty inches. Near the middle of the seam there is a thin parting of slate. Since this coal was suitable for locomotive fuel, almost all coal mined from Seam Number One was used by the railroads.

One of the first mines to be operated along this seam was the Lake Mine,[4] located about three miles north of Millsap. At this mine the coal was from eighteen to twenty-six inches thick. When the coal was removed from the mine, it was loaded into wagons and moved to Millsap where the operators sold it to the Texas & Pacific Railroad. Eventually the owners closed the mine because the coal vein was thin and the cost of mining and transporting the coal was prohibitive.

In 1884, work on the Carson and Lewis mine was begun. This mine was one mile north of the Lake Mine, and was developed by putting in an "incline" to the coal. This mine, like the Lake Mine, was not a success because the lack of transportation facilities made marketing too expensive.

Four miles northeast of the present town of Gordon in Palo Pinto County was the Gordon Mine. This mine gave promise of becoming more important than the other mines in the area. The Texas & Pacific Railroad built a spur to the mine, and within a short time, a thriving settlement sprang up there. The mine was in operation for only a few months when the operators decided that the project was not profitable. Dumble in the "First Report of Progress" discussed the reasons for its failure as follows:

A short time spent in examining the locality convinced me that the mine had not been well located, as the coal at this locality had been too much exposed to atmospheric influences. . . . The coal had a large percentage of sulphur in it and in burning made a great amount of clinkers. The coal mined here was mostly used by the Texas and Pacific Railroad in their locomotives. There was a great deal of complaint among the engineers about the poor quality of the coal. I am of the opinion that a better place can be selected for working this seam in this locality; one where the coal has not been so much subjected to atmospheric influences, and consequently will not be so highly impregnated with the sulphuret of iron.[5]

This Gordon Mine is more interesting than the other mines because several hundred miners lived around it and the output of coal was more than six hundred tons per day.[6] When this mine closed in 1885 or 1886, the first thriving mining town in the Central Coal Field was abandoned. This was the beginning of the pattern that was to be followed by other settlements in the area—the outstanding conformer being Thurber.

The most important mine of the entire area was the Johnson Mine which was sunk by William W. Johnson and his brother, Harvey, in 1886. This was the mine around which Thurber was to develop. Unlike all other mines along Coal Seam Number 1, the Johnson Mine provided the ground work for a thriving camp that was to become the largest mining settlement in the state, and a camp that was to exist as a profitable enterprise for nearly fifty years.

C. S. Wilkins in "Thurber: A Sociological Study of a Company Owned Town" accounts for the beginning of this mine as follows:

The credit for locating the first profitable mines went to W.W. Johnson, a young capitalist and geologist from the East. While riding in the cedar breaks in the edges of Palo Pinto and Erath Counties seventy-four miles west of Fort Worth, he stopped at a farm house for water. He was telling the farmer of his diffi-culty in finding the proper kind of timber to fulfill his cross tie contract for the new railroad when the farmer began to tell him of his trouble in digging a well through the hard strata of black rock, which he thought might be coal. Johnson studied the structure and found what he thought were indications of a good supply of coal. He bought the land immediately.

The first shaft was sunk in 1886 to a depth of one hundred and twenty feet where a twenty-six inch vein of coal was found.[7]

Many miners from the old Gordon Mine came to work in the Johnson Mine; however, upon their arrival at the Johnson Mine, they refused to work for about two months because Johnson announced that his wage scale would be somewhat lower than the scale they had received at Gordon.[8] While the deadlock between Johnson and the miners was on, the miners set up tents and built a few crude shacks and huts.[9] After the wage-scale problem was settled, Johnson built a few structures which served as offices and homes for his "white collar" workers, and around the Johnson Mine, a small camp came into existence.

The Johnson Mine became a good producer with a capacity of four hundred tons daily.[10] Officials of the Texas & Pacific Railroad Company built a spur from the main line to the Johnson Mine and locomotives on the western division of the Texas & Pacific Railroad used almost the total output of coal.

After the settlement of the wage-scale dispute, the Johnsons expe-rienced no serious difficulties with the miners until they made the an-nouncement in September, 1888, that they would be unable to meet the August payroll. The miners refused to work until they received their pay and thus the Johnsons' first attempt to mine coal in Texas ended as it had begun—in a deadlock with the miners. It was probably with a sigh of relief that Johnson sold the entire mining enterprise to the newly-formed Texas & Pacific Coal Company, and in November, 1888, the new owners took possession of the Johnson mines.[11] The Johnsons later opened several mines in the vicinity of Strawn and Lyra. Today, this is the only area in which coal is being produced.

In October, 1888, a group of eastern capitalists met at the old Mansion House in Fort Worth and organized a company which they named the Texas & Pacific Coal Company. Among the organizers were three men whose names came to be synonymous with Thurber. These were Colonel R. D. Hunter, president of the Texas & Pacific Coal Company and beyond a doubt the most colorful character associated with Thurber; Edgar L. Marston, Hunter's son-in-law who succeeded him as president of the company; and H. K. Thurber, for whom the town of Thurber was named.

Erroneous stories have long been prevalent with regard to the manner in which the Texas & Pacific Coal Company received its name. The coal company was not given its name because it was part of the Texas & Pacific Railroad Company. Marston explained the company name as follows:

> Mr. Gould doesn't own a dollar of stock in the company neither
> does the T.P.R.R Co., nor have they ever owned any interest
> in it. When we were organized at the old Mansion House in
> Fort Worth in 1888, we reached the question of a name. It was
> suggested that since the property was on the T.P. line we might
> name it the T. & P. Coal Co. The suggestion was adopted.[12]

The Texas & Pacific Coal Company purchased from the Johnson Coal Company "all its rights, title and interest in what is known as the Pedro Herrera Survey, and the improvements thereon, comprising two thousand, three hundred and two and one-half acres located in Erath and Palo Pinto Counties. . . . This property and an additional twenty thousand acres adjoining was bought by your company."[13]

Colonel R. D. Hunter went to Thurber to develop the mining interests of the new company, and during his years as president, he managed the mines to suit himself. Hunter was born in Ayreshire, Scotland,

April 3, 1833, and he accompanied his parents to America when he was nine years old. The Hunter family settled in Bunker Hill, Illinois. When he was twenty-five years old, he married Janet Webster of Bunker Hill.

Hunter had a longing to go West so he moved his family to the state of Colorado. He had developed an interest in mining, and while he was in Colorado, he engaged in various phases of that industry. In 1872, he became interested in livestock, and he moved to St. Louis where he was a partner in Hunter, Evans and Company, a livestock commission business. As a partner in this business, Hunter made a fortune.[14]

Hunter leased land in the Cherokee Strip, Indian Territory, and stocked it with thousands of head of cattle. The Cleveland decree which required cattlemen to move their herds from the Indian Territory brought destruction to the herds of Hunter, Evans and Company, and Hunter's personal fortune was depleted. In an effort to recover his lost fortune, Hunter turned his attention to the coal fields of Texas, and it was through his efforts that the Texas & Pacific Coal Company was formed. When Hunter took over the Johnson Mine, he made it quite clear to the Johnson miners who were still on the property that his favorite motto was, "I will run my business or run it to Hell."[15]

The Johnson miners immediately felt his antagonistic attitude toward organized labor, and this knowledge did much to aggravate the difficulties that existed. The miners refused to accept his wage-scale which was lower than the Johnson scale and they declared that they were striking against the Texas & Pacific Coal Company.

Throughout the next nine months, Hunter stood as an impregnable wall against the miners and their attempts to keep the mines closed. His life was threatened, and in December, 1888, someone attempted to make good the threat and fired a shot into his living quarters.[16] Unable to cope with the lawless element alone, he called upon the county officials who in turn called for a detachment of Texas Rangers. Eventually in July, 1889, Hunter won his battle against the strikers.

Hunter was an interesting and colorful personality, but he was not the type of employer who inspired a feeling of friendliness among his employees. As one former sheriff remarked, "People feared Colonel Hunter and he usually had his way in all things."[17] Hunter admitted that he did not always have to have a legitimate reason to become angry with people when he testified as follows: "About the 10th or 12th of June I recollect having an interview in my office with Lawson in which I gave him a very severe cussing. Lawson did not insult me on that occasion. I just voluntarily gave him a cussing."[18]

Hunter resented interference and he attempted to make Thurber self-sufficient. To accomplish this, he put a wire fence around the camp. According to him, "Thurber had about 900 acres in it and that is enclosed with a wire fence."[19] The Colonel may have had several reasons for fencing in Thurber, but his foremost reason was to keep out former Johnson employees who still continued their strike against him. Even though these men did not work for Colonel Hunter, they did receive their mail at the post office within the enclosure. Since the Colonel kept locks on all the gates, these men had to receive permission to enter the camp.[20]

Such a situation was intolerable to those "strikers," and even the company employees resented being fenced in the "Bull Pen" as Thurber was then called by those who disapproved of the Colonel's policy. On May 11, 1889, an indictment was filed at Stephenville against Hunter for "obstructing a public road."[21] All legal papers regarding this indictment have been lost due to the carelessness of county officials, but in the Minutes of the County Court there is this notation:

This June 5th AD 1889. This day a case was called for the trial
and both parties appeared and announced ready for trial
and the Defendant Col. R.D. Hunter pleaded not guilty to
the indictment and waived trial by Jury and submitted to the
decision of the cause to the court and the court having heard
the Indictment read and the Defendant's plea of not guilty
thereto finds that the said Defendant is not guilty of the offense and adjudged by the court that the said Col. R.D. Hunter

be immediately discharged from all further liability for office of which has herein been tried and he may go hence without delay." [22]

If it were possible to read the indictment and the testimony, we would probably learn that Hunter agreed to remove the locks from the gates and to allow a free passage lane to the post office. "After he removed the locks from the gates, the guards kept watch . . . to see that anyone entering the inclosure for the purpose of going to the post office did not have an opportunity to mingle with non-union employees . . . However, public opinion became so outspoken against the arbitrary rule of the Colonel's that he finally removed the gates and provided lanes inside the inclosure to and from the Post Office." [23]

By the time Colonel Hunter resigned as president of the Texas & Pacific Coal Company in 1899,[24] the fence was little more than a reminder of the Colonel's desire to "run his business in his own way," but the miners hated the fence and in their minds it conjured nothing but bad memories. One of their demands in the 1903 strike was that the fence be removed. The company granted the request.[25]

Hunter was once described by one of his miners "as a feudalist of old who dreamed of a strictly monopolistic empire." [26] This same miner wrote: "As he relaxed his dictatorial attitude, conditions grew to be much better and still better as old age advanced on him and he went to his grave a much more tolerant man than when he first crossed swords with the miners from the old railroad mines." [27]

In spite of his disagreeable attitudes and actions, there was much to be admired in Colonel R. D. Hunter. He was a man of vision—a rugged individualist who believed in the industrial future of Texas. He aspired to set up a coking industry near his mines and he attempted to promote the construction of a railroad from Thurber to "the iron mines of Llano, Mason, and San Saba Counties." [28]

Hunter resigned as stated in 1899 and was succeeded by his son-in-law, Edgar L. Marston. Hunter did not live to see Thurber become the only "little city wherein every worker was a dues-paying member of his respective union." [29] He died on November 8, 1902, still confident that there was no place for organized labor in Thurber.

After the death of Colonel Hunter, the responsibility of overseeing the development of the town of Thurber and the management of the fifteen mines [30] that there were to be in operation during Thurber's lifetime rested upon the shoulders of William Knox Gordon.

W. K. Gordon was born in Spotsylvania County, Virginia, on January 26, 1862. Until he was twenty years old, he studied in the schools of Fredericksburg, Virginia. Upon the completion of his engineering studies, he began working on railroad surveys in Virginia, North and South Carolina, Georgia, and Mississippi. His work brought him to Texas, and from June 1, 1889, to November 1889, Gordon helped to survey a proposed railroad from Thurber to Dublin.

Hunter met Gordon while he was surveying the proposed line and he was favorably impressed with the young Virginian. He had need for a young man of Gordon's caliber and offered him a position as mining engineer in the Thurber mines. Gordon accepted the position and he immediately gained the respect and admiration of those with whom he worked.

The miners soon learned that the new mining engineer was outspoken, honest, and willing to fight for what he considered to be just. Even though he possessed more culture, refinement, and tact than the miners, they were well aware of the power in his fist should he find it necessary to exercise his authority by brawn instead of brains. Gordon, always fond of athletics, kept himself in A1 condition, and a daily workout with the punching bag was a routine matter with him.

Within a short time, Gordon gained the respect and confidence of Hunter's employees, and it was largely through his diplomatic and engineering abilities that Thurber grew and prospered. Gordon later became general manager of Thurber, and he maintained that position until he moved to Fort Worth in the middle 1920s. [31]

During the years in which he managed the mines and the town of Thurber, Gordon lived in Thurber, knew his employees personally, and was not above accepting suggestions from those whom he employed.

The miners had a feeling of affection for him that few "bosses" ever enjoy. The lowest miner felt no hesitancy in approaching Gordon, and regardless of how unimportant his story might be, he always found "the Boss" ready to listen. Neither color, nationality, nor creed stood as an obstruction between Gordon and his men. Even when the miners had called a strike against the company and were moving from the town, many of them embraced Gordon and with tears in their eyes told him good-bye.

Although Thurber no longer exists and the mines have been closed for many years, Gordon still prides himself in being able to say, "and even today should an old miner meet his old time 'Boss' it would do your tender heart good to see the warmth and kindly feeling of the meeting." [32]

Fate decreed that Gordon who was largely responsible for the prosperity of Thurber would be the one to discover and develop the Ranger oil field which eventually was the economic force that destroyed Thurber. Today, William Knox Gordon lives in Fort Worth, and he has the satisfaction of knowing that his personal interest in Thurber and in his employees had paid many dividends—the chief ones being lasting friendships and pleasant memories.

The Johnsons, Colonel Hunter, and W. K. Gordon had the vision and the courage to industrialize the rugged, semi-barren northwestern corner of Erath County. For 30 years[33] the few farmers who attempted to eke out an existence from the area complained of the presence of coal whenever they drilled a water well. They probably would have complained for many more years had not the Johnsons had the foresight to realize the value of the coal deposits. Although the Johnsons met with only limited success, they must be recognized as pioneers who had the courage to attempt the industrialization of a section of a county that seemed destined to remain an agricultural area.

Hunter, as president of the newly formed Texas & Pacific Coal Company, acquired the Johnson coal mines and from then on the growth of the mining camp and the development of the coal mines progressed at a rapid pace. Immigrants from all parts of the world flocked to Thurber;

labor troubles disturbed the peace and quiet of an agricultural community, and Hunter made good during his day his threat to "run his business" as he saw fit.

When W. K. Gordon assumed management of the town, he was able through his diplomacy and tact to develop a feeling of good will toward the Texas & Pacific Coal Company not only within the town itself but throughout the county. Thurber's prosperity was contagious and soon the entire county was deriving financial benefits from the new industry. Today, Thurber is gone, and Erath County has once again settled down to the business of growing crops and livestock and remembering the days when Thurber provided an excellent market for many of the county's agricultural products.

CHAPTER 2

Coal and Brick

Thurber coal and Thurber brick were well known throughout the state of Texas, and even though coal mining was the chief industry of the area, the production of brick was of importance too. Both industries were developed by the Texas & Pacific Coal Company, and by far the greater part of Thurber's population derived a livelihood from one or the other of the two industries.

As already stated, it was in 1886 that Harvey and William Johnson decided to mine coal in the northwestern corner of Erath County, and within a few months after they made this decision, they sank the first shaft less than one-half mile southeast of Thurber. Prior to this, the mines of the Indian Territory, Arkansas, and Alabama supplied Texas with fuel. A large amount of capital had been spent in prospecting and rewards had been offered by the Texas railroads for the discovery of coal along their lines.[1] The Johnsons located their mine within three or four miles of the Texas & Pacific Railroad, and this railroad bought almost all coal taken from the Johnson Mine. After the Johnson Company had sold about thirty-five thousand tons of medium grade bituminous coal to the Texas & Pacific Railroad Company, labor difficulties arose and the Johnsons sold the Pedro Herrera Survey, a tract of 2,312 ½ acres, and all improvements to the newly-formed Texas & Pacific Coal Company.

The new owners continued to develop the two mines which had been sunk by the Johnsons, and in addition opened thirteen other mines in Erath, Eastland, and Palo Pinto counties. All mines were designated on company records by numbers; that is, Mine #1, Mine #2, etc. Numerically speaking, the last three mines to be developed should have been Mine #13, Mine #14, and Mine #15, but in order to avoid the use of the number 13, these three were known as New #1, New #2, and New #3.

The following chart shows when each of the fifteen mines was opened and the location of each:

TABLE 1

Mine	Date	Location
#1	1886[1]	About one-half mile southeast of Thurber. Erath County.
#2	1888[2]	Less than one mile northwest of #1. Erath County.
#3	1888[3]	About 600 yds. west of New #3. Erath County.
#4	1890[4]	Less than one mile north of #1. Erath County.
#5	1892[5]	One mile west of Thurber. Erath County.
#6	1893[6]	About one mile south of #5. Erath County.
#7	1894[7]	Less than one mile north of #5. Palo Pinto County.
#8	1896[8]	About one-half mile west of #7. Palo Pinto County.
#9	1898[9]	About one mile south of #8. Erath County.
#10	1900[10]	About one-half mile northwest of #8. Palo Pinto County.
#11	1903[11]	About one-half mile south of #10. Palo Pinto County.
#12	1907[12]	About one mile south of #11. Erath County.
New #1	1908[13]	One mile south of #12. Eastland County.
New #2	1910[14]	Two miles west of #11. Eastland County.
New #3	1911[15]	Less than one-half mile west of Thurber Quadrangle. Erath County.

1. *Annual Report of Texas & Pacific Coal Company, 1889*, p. 4.
2. *Ibid.*
3. *Annual Report of Texas & Pacific Coal Company, 1890*, p. 3.
4. *Annual Report of Texas & Pacific Coal Company, 1892*, p. 8.
5. *Annual Report of Texas & Pacific Coal Company, 1892*, p. 8.
6. *Annual Report of Texas & Pacific Coal Company, 1894*, p. 3.
7. *Ibid.*
8. *Annual Report of Texas & Pacific Coal Company, 1896*, p. 3.
9. No definite date for the opening of this mine is available; therefore, 1898 is an approximate date.
10. *Annual Report of Texas & Pacific Coal Company, 1900.*
11. Gomer Gower to M.J.G., July 22, 1946.
12. *Ibid.*
13. *Ibid.*
14. *Ibid.*
15. *Ibid.*

Coal Mine Number 10 at Thurber. Courtesy, AR 88, Special Collections, The University of Texas at Arlington Libraries, Arlington, Texas.

Occasionally a name would be given to a mine, but names never became as popular as the numbers. Mine #9 was named "Warfield" in honor of Mary Warfield Ward, a cousin of Wallis Warfield, the present Duchess of Windsor.[2] At the time Mine #11 was being sunk, Edgar L. Marston and his small daughter, whom he called "Little Sister," visited the site of the new mine. When Marston introduced the child to Ben Matthews, the pit boss, Matthews promptly said, "In your honor we will name the mine 'Little Sister.'" Today the child for whom the mine was named is the wife of the opera singer, Lawrence Tibbett.[3]

Since the coal vein tended in a westerly direction, the newer mines were west of the town, and it became necessary in 1895 for the company to purchase seven passenger cars to carry the miners to and from their work.[4] For this service the miners paid one dollar each month whether they rode the train or not.

At 5:30 A.M. each day, the blast of a whistle pierced the stillness of the morning and in every miner's home the rush to get to work began. The sound of the whistle told the miner that everything was in readiness for work and that the Black Diamond would leave the downtown station at 6:00 A.M. While the miner hurriedly dressed in his work clothes—usually blue overalls, shirt, and jumper—his wife prepared his lunch pail. During the winter, when all was in readiness for his departure, the miner lighted the oil-burning or carbide lamp on his mining cap, put it on his head, and started out to catch the mine train, for to miss the train usually meant the loss of a day's work.

Just before six o'clock on a dark, winter morning, the flickering lights of these pit-lamps moving swiftly from all directions reminded one of giant fire-flies making their way to a central meeting place. Those miners who lived below Stump, Polander, and Italian Hills boarded the train at the downtown station, while those who lived on the above named hills boarded the Black Diamond at the "Lizard," a saloon located on Number 3 Hill.

Coal Mine Number 11 at Thurber. Courtesy, AR 88, Special Collections, The University of Texas at Arlington Libraries, Arlington, Texas.

"The distance between these points being roughly one-half mile, many a belated miner living on the hills welcomed indications of a stalling of the train when climbing the tortuous railway reaching from the downtown station to the 'Lizard' on a continuous up-hill grade. When the 'All aboard' signal was given at the 'Lizard,' the train now being on a level track, proceeded westward."[5] At each mine, all miners and other workmen assigned to that particular station left the train, which then proceeded to the next mine. After all the workers had been distributed, the cars were placed on a siding at the last mine where they remained until the work day was over.

Not all men who worked at the mines were miners. There were many workers above the ground and it was their job to provide for the welfare of the men in the pits; hoist and weigh coal; credit each miner with the amount of coal he mined; keep his tools sharpened and bring the miner to the surface at the end of the working day. As in any other industry, there were foremen to oversee the various phases of the work. The engineers, boilermen, and firemen kept the hoisting machinery in working condition and were responsible for keeping a current of fresh air circulating throughout the mines. The checker, or check puller as he was sometimes called, removed the miners' checks from the loaded cars of coal, dropped the check down a tube to the weigher, and dumped the car so that the coal would fall upon the screen. The checker also dumped the loads of slate and rocks as they were hoisted. By means of signals, he knew in advance whether the car on the way up contained coal or slate—the signal came from below—one blast of the whistle meant coal and two blasts meant slate. There were two weighers—one paid by the company and one paid by the miners. The one hired by the miners was known as the check-weigher, and it was his job to check with the company weighers on the weight of all coal taken from the pits. He was the miners' assurance that the coal was weighed correctly and the proper weight credited to the miner.[6]

The miners descended into the pits by means of cages or elevators. The height of the elevator shaft varied according with the depth of the coal vein—the deepest coal in the Thurber field being mined about five hundred feet below the surface. Upon reaching the bottom of the shaft, the miners proceeded down the main arteries, into the lateral entries, and finally into their assigned rooms which consisted of thirty-six feet of coal face. The Thurber mines were developed on the "long-wall" plan which W. K. Gordon described as follows:

> At the bottom of the shafts, entries like spokes in a wheel were driven inwards and as the coal was mined and sent back over the spokes or entries to the shaft bottom, the spokes or entries were extended to a distance of perhaps one-half mile. Then the shaft would be abandoned and a new start made. At the inside end of the entries or spokes 36 feet of coal face was allotted to each miner and this arrangement extended entirely around the mine—again resembling the rim or tire of a wheel. Along this rim, or along the coal face, air was forced by big ventilating fans, thereby giving the miners a fresh current of air at all times.[7]

Gomer Gower was somewhat more specific in the following description of the development of "long-wall" mining in the Thurber mines:

> In the four main entry system of longwall mining, all entries turned at an angle of ninety degrees from the main shaft and were designated as the Main South, Main North, Main East, and Main West, and do in a manner form the spokes of a four spoked wheel. Each of the mines at Thurber was developed according to this plan with the exception of "New #1" at which mine the entries were turned at an angle of sixty degrees from the main shaft and was pretty well imitative of a six spoke wheel, each spoke diverging from the hub, or shaft, forming a circle at the outer ends of the spokes. The advancing coal face formed the rim. These spokes were continually being lengthened as they advanced into the coal body. Obviously, the distance between

the spoke ends was being lengthened thus creating a circular working face, the production from which was served by the main entries.

These main entries served two purposes: haulage ways and intake airways. Lateral entries turned off these main entries at the angle of sixty degrees, and from these lateral entries, rooms turned off at sixty degree angles. Thus you will see that provision was made for the ever expanding space between the ends of the spokes so that a uniform circle is maintained throughout the mine, a condition essential to successful long-wall mining.

To make it more plain. Let us consider mine #10 with its four main entry system. A circle drawn in conformity with the ends of its four spokes will show that the diameter of the circle is two thousand seven hundred and twenty yards (2720), and its circumference practically eight thousand one hundred sixty yards. This circumference represents the outer rim of the coal face to which all the coal between it and the comparatively small pillars immediately surrounding the mine shaft proper, has been mined.[8]

The greatest handicap in working the Thurber mines was the thinness of the coal vein. Those miners who came from eastern coal fields where the vein was high enough to allow them to work standing up found it difficult to work in a limited space of twenty-seven to thirty-six inches. The coal vein was described as low coal not only because it was thin but because, in order to mine the coal, the miner had to lie on his shoulder and hip and keep his arms free to swing his pick above him. He often loosened coal by setting off a charge of dynamite, and as he removed the coal, he threw the dirt and slate into the vacancy caused by the removal of the coal and in this way many of the openings were filled.

Empty cars were available for each miner, and as he filled each car, he fastened his tag on the front of the car so that the weight of the coal would be credited to his account when it was weighed. Men responsible for the movement of coal from the rooms to the cages would pick up the loaded cars and move them through the tunnels. Before the installation of electric locomotives, mules pulled the loaded cars through the tunnels to the cage at the bottom of the shaft. One writer in 1898 described the mules as follows:

> The coal cars used hold [*sic*] about a ton each, and are drawn by demure looking, ducklegged little mules, which are splendidly trained to trot along without bit or driver, and are as tractable and obedient as any other part of the complicated mechanism of a coal mine. Once transplanted to the bowels of the earth, they never see daylight again until their working days are over. They seem to thrive on the work and enjoy it . . . [9]

When the car of coal reached the cage, it was placed in the cage. The person in charge of the cage was known as a cager, and when he was ready for the cage to be hoisted, he signaled the hoisting crew—one blast of his whistle told them that coal was in the car, two blasts meant slate and rock. This signaling was necessary because when the cars reached the dumping area those loaded with coal were tipped in one direction and those loaded with refuse were tipped in another.

The company operated the mines on a screened basis which meant that as each car of coal was hoisted, the coal was poured onto an inclined screen, six feet wide, twelve feet long, with one and one-fourth inch spaces between the bars. The miners received pay only for whatever coal slid down the full length of the screen and fell into the railway car which was placed below the lowest part of the inclined screen. The coal which passed through the screen was graded pea or nut coal depending upon the size. Although this type of coal had practically no commercial value, it reduced the miners' earnings by about twelve or thirteen percent. In other words, he mined the pea and nut coal free.[10]

A thirty minute lunch period gave the miners little time to loaf so the majority of them ate their lunches in the pits. Occasionally a miner would find that the rats had eaten his lunch while he worked. As long as mules were stabled in the mines, rats were numerous and they often removed the lids from the lunch pails and helped themselves to the lunch they found therein. In order to protect their lunches, the miners would either tie the pails to the overhead timbers or place heavy rocks on them.[11]

At 5:30 P.M. the miners put away their tools and made their way toward the elevators. When miners were to be hoisted, the cager sounded three blasts on his whistle and the hoisting crew knew that men and not coal would be coming up. Should the Black Diamond not be at the mine, the men would have to wait until it did arrive. These delays were often long and tiresome to men who had spent long hours mining coal. Not only were they tired and hungry, but they were covered with coal dust and could not relax until they had a bath.

Much of this delay was due to the fact that the train crew which took the miners to work also served as the coal-switching crew to take the loaded cars to Thurber Junction (Mingus), pick up empty cars, and distribute these empties to the various mines before quitting time. Delay in accomplishing any part of this assignment disrupted the entire schedule, and a message would be telephoned to the mines that the evening train would be anywhere from one half hour to one hour late. Such an announcement to the tired, hungry miners brought forth "a cursing in all the known languages of the earth . . . and the blue tinge of the atmosphere could be seen."[12] Sometimes in retaliation after an unusually long wait, some of the miners would not report to work the next day.

These delays in the evening schedule continued until May, 1905. A regular evening schedule was brought about in this manner. The company decided to discontinue at noon the services of cagers, motormen, and some of the men who worked on the surface. No arrangement was made for these men to return home at noon. They either had to walk or wait for the evening train. Naturally this lack of planning disgruntled the men, and they were justified in feeling as they did, because they still had to pay one dollar train fee each month.

The miners were also displeased because they often had to stop digging coal early in the afternoon owing to a lack of empty cars. Finally, in May, 1905, the miners selected a committee to confer with Gordon regarding a plan by which it would be possible to provide a sufficient number of empty cars each day, and also to provide transportation for the men if circumstances made it necessary for the working day to end earlier than the usual quitting time. No satisfactory agreement was reached and the miners decided to solve the problem in their own way.[13]

The check-weighman received instructions to check each evening to see that there was an ample supply of empty cars to enable the miners to work the next day. They announced that if there were not sufficient cars, the miners would not report for duty. Company officials looked upon the announcement as an idle threat and made no attempt to provide the required number of cars. On two successive mornings the miners met the train only to be informed by the check-weighmen that there were not enough cars. The entire group of men returned to their homes, and on the third morning the check-weighmen announced that there were enough cars to enable them to work all day.

A second committee met with Gordon and together they decided that each day it would be announced whether the miners would work a full or half day. A train to bring the miners home would be provided to fit each day's schedule.[14]

Beyond a doubt the Black Diamond and its engines, "Calamity Jane" and "Rain-in-the-Face"[15] will linger long in the memories of those who rode to and from the mines. In many ways the Black Diamond was Thurber's melting pot. Men from all nations sat in those cars and through the years, they learned to share in the joys, sorrows, and tragedies that came to all regardless of nationality, race, or creed. They learned to understand the strange habits and customs of those from other parts of the world, and they were sympathetic with the feeling of homesickness that sometimes overwhelmed their fellow miners. Strong friendships grew out of these daily rides, and even the despised periods of waiting for the return trip home in the evenings strengthened the bonds of comradeship.

The Thurber mines were among the best equipped in the state, and the company took many precautions to prevent accidents. The mines were dry and free from gas, and mine fires were few. In 1897 there was a fire at Mine #5 which probably is among the most serious fires in the Thurber mines. The following description of the fire is taken from *The Texas Mining and Trade Journal:*

The tipple and engine house licked up by the fired fiend. The night shift at work in the mines brought safely out by courageous friends—eleven mules suffocated.

It was 5:30 A.M., Wednesday, at that hour when sleep is sweetest, at that hour which, when one is aroused, one feels they would exchange their dearest treasure for "just another nap," when the appealing shrieks of the steam whistle at No. 5 shaft was heard, and at a glance in that direction showed the heavens lighted by reflection from a raging blaze. While those in the vicinity of the shaft, one and a half miles from town, were hurrying to the scene, the townspeople were none the less active, for Nightwatchman Singleton was busying himself giving the alarm and arousing the company officials and other employees, who responded with that promptness so characteristic of our people in answering distress calls. In a remarkably short time the livery stable was emptied of horses and vehicles, and an army of determined men were on their way—determined if possible to rescue and preserve the lives of men whom they felt sure were entombed in the bowels of Mother Earth, doubtless unaware of their danger. Scores of men followed this cavalry on foot, and soon one of the locomotive engines was thundering over the hill drawing a number of coaches filled with miners and others anxious to risk their own lives for those of their friends and comrades. On this train was Col. R. D. Hunter, president and general manager, who at the first alarm, though unwell, hurriedly prepared to go. Not knowing the nature of the trouble, he felt his presence was needed, feeling, too, solicitous of the welfare of his employees.

It was the tipple over the main shaft on fire, which soon spread to the engine and boiler houses and fan house, the blaze originating in the top of the tipple in the weigh room, and it is supposed, from a torch, carelessly placed by one of the slate-dumpers too near the cinder-like woodwork.

It was within fifteen minutes of time to sound the whistle for a change of shift, when the Night Engineer Brewster discovered the fire, and immediately ran up in the tipple, but so rapidly had the flames taken hold, he could do nothing, and he at once realized the place was doomed, and hurried to give the alarm by putting all the power that steam could exert into the huge steam whistle, and with remarkable presence of mind started his pumps a-going, setting every fire-fighting apparatus at hand to play on the flames.

At the first glance from those rapidly arriving the picture of certain death, and destruction sprung up, more vividly than can be described, and the fate of those fifty human souls in various portions of the mines, ignorant of the death-dealing flames raging above them which threatened to shut off their every means of escape was problematical.

Every structure on top was doomed, the flames shooting high into space, and seemed with demon-like hilarity to mock the very efforts of those who would attempt to check them, but the fan-house over the air-shaft and man-way adjoining the engine room was the last to ignite, from the intense heat, and this, as the only means of escape for the entombed miners, MUST BE SAVED EVEN AT THE SACRIFICE OF THE LIVES OF THOSE WHO WOULD ATTEMPT IT. The fan-house was the only salvation, and (the) fire fiend was rapidly eating its way into it.

Ass't. Supt. J. H. McLure was among the first to arrive, Supt. Gordon being out of the city. The heat about the structure was so intense that it was almost beyond human endurance to stand it, but "Mac," standing at the man-way, shouted out: "This fan-house must be saved; these men in the pit must be warned; who'll follow me to deliver this message of life or death!" To this responded the voice of Robert McKinnon, Ben Matthews, Robert Beveridge,

James McLeary, Tom Coulson, Ben and Harry Bookman, James Blackwell, and Jimmie Nickol who said, "We'll go!" The crowd by this time numbered several hundred, was paralyzed by their admiration for the courage of the daring men who were taking one chance in a thousand for their lives, but the thought of those poor souls underground urged them to sacrifice. These men gathered around the man-way, and Mac called out to the crowd: "Men save the fan-house, or we perish—God help us," and they were lost to view, and the prayers from hundreds of hearts went up in their behalf while the demonstration of human endurance from the fire fighters was admirable, yet it seemed as though it was a fight against Fate.

Col. Hunter was in the midst of the workers and his encouraging words urged them to superhuman efforts. Piece by piece the burning woodwork was torn away, and as the pumps and fan had stopped, a bucket brigade of a hundred or more was quickly formed from the tank and a deluge of water was hurled down the air shaft and thrown upon the burning fan-house, this water down the air shaft being the only means of forcing air and keeping it fresh throughout the pit for the salvation of the men therein.

The woodwork of the main shaft was burning to the bottom of the pit, and none save those on the bottom knew the extent of the fury, and this apparently unsurmountable condition of things confronted the brave little party of rescuers who had gone down. The miners were scattered at various places throughout the mine for a distance of three-quarters of a mile in different direction and in intimation of their peril could reach them until the lack of air warned them, unless the rescuers could reach them. To go through this firey furnace was apparently certain death, and to go around by any other route was over 1000 feet one way and three-quarters of a mile the other. To act, and to act quickly was imperative. McLure, McLeary, Beveridge, and Coulson decided to go through, and, placing sponges in their mouths, they did so, while the others taking a southern route, went on their errand of mercy. The air was yet good, but smoke was filling the roadways, and the rescuers had to grope their way as best they could till they were far back in the entries, where the miners were peacefully digging away, and were loath to believe that peril was so near. Most of them being foreigners, it was difficult to make them understand the situation, as the smoke and lack of air had not yet reached them. They were corralled, about forty of them, and the journey, and a difficult one it was, was taken up by an old "return" way, not shorter than three quarters of a mile, and finally the "bottom" was reached, and the miners formed into a line at the mouth of the "Man-Way," but the rescuers, almost exhausted, knew not the condition of things, above, knew not whether the fan-house has been saved, or whether, now that they were at the mouth of the "man-way," they were doomed not to ever see the light of day. For had the fan-house burned, the "man-way" and air shaft would have been filled with burning debris, shutting off their only means of escape.

At this time the encouraging voices of another party composed of Capt. Eddy, John Murphy, Thos. Armstrong, and others whose names we have been unable to get, were heard descending the man-way, through smoke and heat, which told to the now almost thoroughly exhausted party of fifty or sixty that life was yet in reach, but that an effort was necessary to obtain it, and soon the slow progress of ascent was begun, only two or three being allowed to proceed at a time. Everyone escaped. . . .

The scene at the top can't be described. As the smoke-begrimed miners emerged from the "man-hole," they fell exhausted upon fathers, mothers, wives, brothers, sisters and friends, and were borne away in love's arms, and not until the last one was safe on terra firma did the rescuers come up, and by many were the words "thank God" uttered, who perhaps never before called His name in reverence.

During the entire time the bucket brigade worked heroically, and right here we must mention a scene seldom witnessed on an occasion of this kind—the fact that some 15 or 20 young ladies were in the line, working with a determination. Among the entombed men were their fathers, brothers, sweethearts and friends, and their devotion to the effort to save their lives was admirable. . . .

On the "bottom" there were 22 mules, and of this number eleven died from suffocation. Their quarter is near the main shaft, and so dense was the smoke, heat, etc., there that those nearest could not survive it, and gives the reader an inkling of what the rescuers and miners were compelled to pass through.

While everything on top was destroyed, except the fanhouse, and much damage resulted to the timbers in the main shaft and near the pit bottom, it will in no way interfere with the output of coal, generally speaking for No. 8, the new shaft which the Company has been holding in reserve for a year, was at once put in operation. . . . [16]

The miners continued to remove coal from the Thurber mines until 1921. In that year the company was forced to abrogate its contract with the union, because it was unable to withstand the decrease in the demands for coal and the lower prices at which coal was being sold. The officials of the Texas & Pacific Railroad had decided to use oil-burning locomotives and the major market for Thurber coal disappeared. In the meantime the Texas & Pacific Coal Company held highly productive leases in the Ranger oil field and had become so interested in the development of these leases, that it was decided in April, 1918, to change the name to Texas Pacific Coal and Oil Company.[17] When the officials announced that the company could not pay the wage scales demanded by the union, the miners refused to work and in consequence, the company closed the mines. With the exception of a few feeble attempts to operate with "scab labor," the mines remained closed.

The Texas Pacific Coal & Oil Company removed all the buildings on the surface, but did not remove all the materials within the mines. Although this material is still in the mines, there is too much danger and risk involved to make its removal worthwhile. "The shaft bottoms are badly caved. The ventilating system is utterly destroyed with the result that miles and miles of mine entries are filled with the deadly black damp, a substance which requires a strong current of free air to remove."[18]

Today the mines that once produced 3000 tons of coal each day[19] have left little evidence of their existence. The fan houses, tipples, and other buildings are gone and many of the dumps have been sold as cinders. At the present, grass, woods, and mesquites are rapidly reclaiming the land that once was snatched from them, and soon there will not be a single visible remnant of the industry that made Thurber the greatest mining camp in the state of Texas.

Although Thurber owed its existence to coal, a second industry in Thurber, one that outlived coal production, was brick making. In many respects the brick industry might be called the step-child of the Texas & Pacific Coal Company, in that it provided a use for the otherwise useless pea and nut coal. Then in 1917 when the company developed the nearby gas fields and there was a surplus of gas, coal was replaced by gas as fuel for the brick plant.

James Green and L. M. Rumsey, St. Louis friends of Hunter, visited in Thurber during February, 1897, and became interested in the shale clay deposits there. Green owned the Laclede Fire Clay Works in St. Louis, and he sent Thurber clay to St. Louis to be tested. The tests proved that the clay was suitable for drain pipes, roof and floor tile, pressed and vitrified brick.[20]

These excellent testing results and the decision of the government to use only brick made from shale clay in government work were strong factors in Hunter's decision to build a brick plant. The Green and Hunter Brick Company was incorporated in March, 1897, with a capital stock of $100,000.[21] Before the summer was over, the new brick plant was producing brick from the best equipped plant of its kind west of the Mississippi River.[22]

Originally, Hunter's interest in the brick plant was a private business interest and the brick company was not a part of the Texas & Pacific Coal Company. But in 1900, the Texas & Pacific Coal Company acquired 1820 shares of the 2000 shares of the Green and Hunter Brick Company's capital stock. The cost of this purchase was $91,233.21, and the coal company amended its charter so as to permit it to engage in the manufacture and sale of brick.[23]

The brick plant, or brick yard as it was more often called, was less than one-half mile southeast of the business section of Thurber, and the shale deposits were about one mile north of the plant. At first mules pulled the wagons loaded with clay to the plant, but this mode of transportation did not last long. Small engines with electric motors pulled the loaded cars until the 1920s when gasoline motors replaced the electric motors.[24]

Thurber brick became popular in all parts of the state, and large orders kept the plant running day and night. This brick was used in many Fort Worth and Dallas buildings, and millions of Thurber bricks went into Texas highways. "The longest brick highway in Texas joins Ranger, Olden, Eastland, and Cisco and is paved with Thurber brick."[25] Beneath the asphalt of Congress Avenue in Austin is the old pavement of Thurber brick. Probably the most noted project handled by the Thurber Brick Company was the Galveston Sea Wall. This wall required a special dry-pressed block instead of the usual brick, and the Thurber brick tested out as best suited for this project.

Eventually the only type of brick manufactured in Thurber was paving brick, and in order to make a well-baked vitrified brick, it was necessary to change from the up-draft type of kiln to the down-draft type. There were twenty-five of those new kilns in actual use. These kilns varied from sixty-five to one hundred and ten feet in length; were about eighteen feet wide; approximately twelve feet high, and the average kiln held about one hundred thousand bricks.

When the clay was brought to the brick plant, it was crushed and screened until it became a very fine dust. Conveyors then carried it to the mixing trough where electric mixers combined the clay dust with water, and after a thorough mixing, the wet clay was forced into a mold the width and thickness equivalent to that of a finished brick. As the shaped clay emerged, there was no break in the length—just one continuous stream of molded clay, and from this mold, the clay slid onto a moving belt which carried it to the cutting table. A series of thin blades cut the clay into brick lengths as it passed along the belt. After the wet bricks passed from beneath the saws, they were removed by workers who placed them on cars which would take them to the drying rooms.

The purpose of the drying rooms was to remove excessive moisture, and from these rooms, the wet bricks went into the kilns to be burned. G. J. Gentry, who was associated with the Thurber Brick Company, described the burning process as follows:

> It took about 30 days to process a kiln of paving brick. The first step in the processing was to place the "green" brick in the kiln. This was followed by the water smoking period during which time the heat was applied and gradually increased. When the temperature reached between 1500° and 1600° F., the period was referred to as the "blue smoke."
>
> At this heat the carbon and sulphur were driven off. The last step in the actual baking process was the application of the high heat—about 1960° F. This heat was maintained for approximately five or six days or until the brick settled. This was the period of vitrifaction. The burning time for kiln was about ten days. It required several days to cool a kiln before men could begin emptying it.
>
> In about 1926, the installation of Leeds Northrop Indicating and Recording Pyrometers at a cost of $10,000 made the Thurber Brick Plant one of the most modern in the nation.

This installation made it possible for the management to
keep a check on the exact operation of the burning of
each kiln.[26]

In 1930, the company closed the brick plant and Thurber's last industry ceased to function. Probably the chief reasons for closing this plant
were: (1) there was no longer a need for a brick plant to consume useless
pea and nut coal, or surplus gas, and (2) paving brick was unable to
compete successfully with other paving materials.

Liquidation of the plant began in 1933, and a Breckenridge salvage
company bought the entire plant with the exception of the machinery
which another salvage company bought. Workmen wrecked all brick
structures including the kilns, and anyone who wished to buy brick had
an opportunity to do so.

The last structure of any importance to go was a giant red brick
smokestack which had been erected in 1898. This smokestack was one
hundred and sixty feet high and during the years when coal was burned,
it had furnished a draft for many of the kilns. Later when gas replaced
coal, each kiln had an individual stack and the smokestack stood idle.
Its role in the brick making industry was to stand as a reminder of the
days when Thurber depended almost wholly upon the coal industry.

Newspapers carried advance notices that dynamite would topple
the giant smokestack on March 29, 1937.

> Forty sticks of dynamite were placed in the base of the chim-
> ney under the direction of C. C. Hamilton of Mingus. Mr.
> Hamilton pushed a plunger. The base of the great chimney
> shot out with a dull roar, ballooning red dust. The giant shook,
> tilted and crumbled. Thousands of persons had come for miles
> around to see the spectacle. They cheered, and then for some
> reason began running toward the pile of brick that had been
> the chimney. . . . the construction of the chimney had required
> about sixty days. It came down in six seconds.[27]

Among the spectators who watched the dynamiting on that Sunday afternoon were many who viewed the scene through tear-filled eyes. A stranger might wonder what there was about an old brick smoke stack that could arouse so much sentiment. To him, the toppling of this plant was an interesting if not an awe-inspiring spectacle, but to the ex-Thurberite, it was proof that a town could be obliterated so completely that nothing except the memory of it survived.

CHAPTER 3

Labor Difficulties

I t was in December, 1886, that the Johnson Company opened Mine #1 on the site later known as Thurber. The working force for two years was composed principally of men who had been at Coalville[1] where the Gould system had operated two mines for the purpose of supplying locomotive fuel.[2] The Johnsons attempted to lower the wage scale from $1.95 to $1.50 per ton, and the miners refused to work for such wages. After two months of idleness, the Johnsons agreed to pay the demanded scale and work was resumed.

Amicable relations existed between the Johnsons and their employees until September, 1888, at which time the Johnsons announced that they were unable to meet the August payroll. Although many of the miners felt that this inability to meet the payroll was caused by too large a part of the company's profits being invested in the sinking of a second mine, they continued to mine coal during September. After having worked seven weeks without pay, said Gomer Gower, "the miners gave the Johnson Brothers five days grace and continued to work until September twenty-fifty with the hope that the Johnson Brothers would find some way out of the difficulty. At the expiration of the five days grace, in the absence of the much looked for pay, there was nothing for the miners to do but stop until they did receive their hard-earned wages."[3]

Since the coal operators saw no possibility of being able to meet the payroll, they decided to sell out to a newly-formed company, the Texas & Pacific Coal Company. Not only did the new owners purchase the Johnson mines and additional property, but on November 12, 1888, the Texas & Pacific Coal Company became the sole owner of a strike that was to cause it a great deal of trouble and expense for a long period of time.

Colonel R.D. Hunter, president of the new company, described the situation as follows in his *Annual Report* for 1889:

> Possession was taken of the property November 12, 1888. I found at this time three hundred men of all nationalities in control. On the twenty-second of September, the miners had struck on account of non-payment of wages. They were receiving at that time one dollar and ninety-five cents per ton for coal-mining.
>
> My first action was to post notices that any employees of the old company would be given work on personal application to the superintendent at one dollar and forty cents for coal-mining. We did not have an applicant. They took the advantage of having been on a strike with the Johnson Company and published to the world that they were on a strike on account of reduction of wages by the Texas Pacific Coal Company. Steps were immediately taken to secure new men, and the second greatest battle with the Knights of Labor in the state of Texas began.[4]

As stated in the *Report* of Hunter, not only did the miners refuse to accept the reduced wage scale, but they refused even to consider the other demands made by Hunter. These demands are adequately described by Gomer Gower, one of the Johnson miners at the time Colonel Hunter took possession.

> The Colonel demanded that the miners renounce their allegiance to the Knights of Labor and promise to refrain from

joining or otherwise affiliating in the formation of a union of any sort. This latter condition had the same effect on the miners as the shaking of a red shawl in the face of a bull. A committee of miners was selected to confer with the Colonel who received this committee cordially, yet with an ill-concealed belligerency and finally dismissed it with the admonition: "I'll make a dollar look as big as a wagon wheel to you before I get through with you." He very decidedly made his word good in this respect. . . . Another condition submitted by the Colonel to the idle miners was that the mining rate be on a screened coal basis.[5]

The miners very promptly and emphatically rejected all the conditions proposed by the Colonel and more particularly the condition that they forever renounce the union and make a YELLOW DOG pledge and they forthwith declared a strike against the company.[6]

No sooner had the miners refused to accept the company demands than the Knights of Labor organization through the columns of its official organ, the *National Labor Tribune,* began publishing items in which miners in other parts of the country were warned not to accept employment from the Texas & Pacific Coal Company.

During the month of December, 1888, conditions continued to grow worse, and in his *Annual Report,* Colonel Hunter wrote:

The miners decreed that the mines should not be worked. To enforce this, resort was had to fire arms with the intention of killing myself and two others. Our superintendent and pit boss arrived December 20th, on the night of which, for purpose of intimidation and murder, the so-called strikers made an attack on the store and office where we were staying. This state of affairs continued until Christmas, when the County judge called upon the adjutant-general for a company of Rangers acknowledging the inability of the county to protect life and property at the mines.[7]

Adjutant-General W. H. King responded by ordering Ranger Captain S. A. McMurry to report to the Johnson Mines. McMurry arrived at the mines on December 20, and he remained in the vicinity of Thurber until July 6, 1889.[8] During his assignment at the mines, McMurry and his men kept an ever-watchful eye on the situation and thus they exerted enough influence on the striking element to prevent any serious outbreak. The entire set-up resembled a tug-of-war—the miners pulling in one direction and Hunter straining with all his physical and financial might in the opposite direction. The Rangers acted as referees to see that no foul punches were administered.

Hunter commented upon the presence of the Rangers as follows:

While the presence of the State Rangers preserved order at the mines, no immunity could be had from the misrepresentations and threats made by the striking element which prevented new men from going to work. At this time five hundred men were ready to leave Pittsburg for the mines, but the day before their departure, the streets of that city were littered with circulars of a character which kept all at home except a few laborers, who on arriving at Fort Worth, refused to go to the mines. The Knights of Labor threatened expulsion of any member who would accept work from the company. The Pittsburg experience was repeated at every place where we tried to employ men.[9]

The following paragraph taken from the *Fort Worth Daily Gazette* confirms Hunter's charge that "no immunity could be had from the misrepresentations and threats made by the striking element."

The Texas and Pacific coal miners are still on a strike. One hundred Mexicans arrived a few days ago but have all quit and refuse to go into the mines. Several old miners came in from the north yesterday but as soon as they found it was a brother miner strike "on account of low wages," they refused to do any work. Captain McMurry and his rangers are still at the mines, but have had no trouble with the miners as yet, for the men seem to want wages and not "blood" and it is hoped their wages will be restored to what they were.[10]

After several such unsuccessful attempts to secure miners, company officials requested that the *National Labor Tribune* send one of its staff to Texas to investigate the situation at the company's expense. This periodical was chosen because it was the "leading labor publication of the East, and a journal of high repute among all classes." [11]

William Rennie who came to carry on the investigation reached Fort Worth on December 20, 1888, and arrived at the mines two days later. The following excerpts are from the report which he made to the *National Labor Tribune* on December 25, 1888:

I arrived at Fort Worth, Texas, on the morning of the 20th, and met Mr. Edgar L. Marston, treasurer of the company, and Messrs. McLauchlan and Clinton, a committee representing the miners who used to work for the Johnson coal company. After some conversation with Mr. Marston, and making arrangements to visit the mines next day, I spent most of the day in company with the committee. The representations made to me by the committee were the same as have appeared in the *Tribune* over the signatures of Mr. McLauchlan and others . . .

During the day I met nine young men who had arrived from Pittsburg a week previous, who were awaiting the arrival of a large delegation of miners from Pennsylvania, which was expected, but failed to come on account of having read the circular distributed by Mr. McLauchlan and others, a copy of which was printed in the *Tribune.* . . .

On Saturday morning . . . I took the Texas and Pacific train for Strawn . . . After dining there . . . I was driven by the county road in a conveyance . . . I first heard the statement of the president and a number of other gentlemen connected with the company. I then attended a meeting of the miners, assembled in their lodge, and I learned from the men at the meeting the following facts:

1. That not one of them had ever worked for or had been in the employ of the Texas and Pacific Coal Company.
2. That the Texas and Pacific Coal Company was a new one and had possession of the property for about five weeks past.
3. That they, the men, had quit work for the Johnson Company about the 26th day of September on account of that company not being able to pay them their wages.
4. That they had received their wages in full from the Johnson coal company prior to the date of the transfer of the mine to the Texas and Pacific coal company, and at that time no one was in the employ of the Johnson company.
5. That the Texas and Pacific coal company had posted a circular a part of which read as follows: "A schedule of prices and a code of rules can be had by calling at the office. Any person wishing employment with the company must apply in person to Mr. R. S. Weitzel, superintendent."

   I found that no one had made application for work. They say the reason why they did not was the great difference between the schedule of prices adopted by the Texas and Pacific coal company and that of the Johnson coal company— the prices for mining, according to the schedule of the Texas and Pacific coal company being $1.15 to $1.40, while that of the Johnson coal company was $1.75 to $1.95.
6. The rules adopted by the Texas and Pacific coal company differed from those in use by the Johnson coal company, for according to the rules of the Texas and Pacific coal company certain dead work was required from the men, which is not required by the defunct company, the Johnson coal company.

I then spent some time in investigating the truth of the representations made and circulated by Mr. McLauchlan and others.

1. I found the water to be good, and heard no reports of sickness by the use thereof. The company furnished water free, and is now sinking an artesian well to increase the supply and distribute it over the whole camp.

2. I found that the company had completed quite a number of two, three, and four-room houses, and had lumber, windows, and doors on hand for fifty, and I was told that fifty more would be built as fast as men and money could build them, the rent from these houses being from $4 to $8 per month.

3. I found that the company had paid a good consideration to the men who had houses on the company's property and in a number of cases showing mercy not usually shown in a mining camp in Pennsylvania.

4. I went into the mine with Superintendent Williams (who has been a miner since ten years ago) and found the mines perfectly dry. The vein at the places I visited I would think averaged twenty-three inches, but Mr. Williams tells me it runs above this and sometimes below. I was informed, however, that the company invested a very large amount of money here on the representations of five or six of the best experts and mining engineers of the country, who reported the vein to average twenty-six inches.

5. I was informed that no one would be compelled to trade at the company's store, and that wages would be paid twice per month.

I have to report that I found no instance in which the company has misrepresented anything, excepting that the roof is hard soap stone instead of slate.[12]

Evidently the *National Labor Tribune* was favorably impressed with Rennie's report, because it printed the declaration that under union rules no strike was in progress. Articles published in the *National Labor Tribune* advised union men not to neglect the opportunity to secure work in the

Texas field. As a final admonition to the so-called strikers at the former Johnson mines, this warning appeared in the *National Labor Tribune:*

> This paper will not give up excellent prospects for the employ-
> ment of some thousands of miners and mine laborers at the
> behest of men who are notoriously playing dog in the manger.[13]

Mere renunciation of the so-called strike did not solve the problem. The strikers refused to accept the decision made by the *National Labor Tribune.* They contended that the report was biased and that it in no way presented the true facts of the situation that existed. The announcement that no strike was in progress proved to be just another example of empty words. As so often happens, a condition or situation that does not exist theoretically does exist in reality. Here at the Texas & Pacific coal mines was a situation that bore all the earmarks of a strike, yet it was not accepted as a strike because the striking element had never been in the employ of those against whom it was striking.

In spite of the theoretical non-existence of the strike, the men who chose to be known as strikers were as successful in preventing the operation of the mines as any group of lawful strikers has ever been. In fact, it appears that the lack of proper credentials was an asset rather than a liability.

Each time Hunter tried to secure miners, members of the striking element would warn the prospective miners, and once again the company would be without employees. Not only were these failures exasperating, but they were expensive. The company paid the transportation of many who upon their arrival refused even to enter the mines.

On one occasion, Ranger Captain McMurry helped Hunter "slip in" a train load of miners. In January, 1889, Hunter went to Brazil, Indiana, to secure men to operate the two mines, and on his return requested McMurry to meet him in Fort Worth. On February 5, a trainload of miners was to arrive, and Hunter felt that McMurry should be on hand to prevent trouble should the strikers attempt to stop the train. About one half of the incoming miners were negroes, and since negroes were especially disliked by the strikers, McMurry went to Fort Worth. The subsequent happenings are best described by McMurry in his Monthly Report to the Adjutant-General:

> The Colonel asked me to ride down to the train dispatcher's office with him. There we learned that the train would arrive about 9 P.M. On coming out of the Dispatcher's Office I noticed lounging around the Union Dept Jackson, the Labor-Agitator, and four or five more of his kind. I told Col. Hunter that the presence of these men indicated no good, that they were waiting for the train to arrive and it was their intention to try to persuade and bull-doze the men and use every means fair or foul to prevent them from going further. To avoid stopping at Fort Worth or being delayed there as little as possible, Colonel Hunter, myself and two men went to Dallas and met the train containing the miners. On our arrival at Fort Worth the four special cars which had been chartered by the T and P Coal Co. were detached from the regular train a short distance below the Union Depot. Engineers were changed in a short time and we moved on through.
>
> I don't think Jackson and his crew "caught on" for quite a while, as they came down to our train just before it started, they walked to the rear of the train. I followed a short distance behind them. They did not speak to me nor I to them. It seemed that they were anxious to do some dirty work although they possess an unusual amount of "gall" they did not attempt to get on the train, and I imagine they were very much chagrined when the train did not halt at Depot to give them an opportunity to deliver themselves of their inflammatory speeches and distribute their lying documents.[14]

Even after this trainload of men reached the mines, most of the white miners refused to work. Many of them openly joined the strikers while others attempted to slip out of the camp under the cover of darkness. The majority of the negroes reported to work and thereby fulfilled their contract with Colonel Hunter. Among the strikers, there was a strong belief that these colored miners were professional strike breakers. If they were, the Colonel made no reference to them as such when he wrote:

> It was February before we succeeded in securing the services of a body of miners. During this month, I shipped one hundred and seventy-two white and black miners from Brazil, Indiana, at the expense of the company. Of this number fifty-four of the white men on arrival at the mines refused to work and joined the lodge of the Knights of Labor, which hold their daily meetings about one mile from our headquarters. The black men remained faithful to their work, and experience has shown they give less trouble and are easier to please than the foreign element which predominates among the white miners. We continued shipments of men under like conditions until our mines were equipped. This has cost the company a total loss of TEN THOUSAND EIGHT HUNDRED AND THIRTY-THREE DOLLARS AND SIXTY FOUR CENTS FOR TRANSPORTATION.[15]

Another account of this particular group of miners is given by Gomer Gower.

> This group of negroes were habitual and confirmed strikebreakers, having participated in the breaking of mine strikes first, in Iowa, then in Colorado and from there they were shipped to Indiana from which state they were inveigled by the Colonel's agents to continue their nefarious practice in Texas. With the arrival of this group of negroes the Colonel's hopes for a complete victory over the striking miners were bolstered considerably and the strikers' dream of unionizing the mines of the company began to wane. These negroes were all practical miners and as indicated had worked in the low-coal field in Iowa, which fact made them the more desirable as workers in the low coal mined at Johnson's Mines.[16]

On April 6 of the same year, Ranger Captain McMurry informed General King that:

> The T & P Coal Company is getting out about 200 tons of coal pr. day. There are about 35 or 40 of the strikers still hanging around the outside of the inclosure. They have been making a strong effort with the Farmers Alliance to work up a mob spirit, and to come to the Mines and try to stampede the Negroes. There is no doubt they have held several meetings in this neighborhood for the purpose of organizing a mob, but so far their hearts have failed them. I have understood also they sent a delegation to Comanche County to get assistance. I do not think under the circumstances it would be prudent to withdraw my company from here for a while yet.[17]

On May 23, McMurry wrote to King "that everything is getting along pretty well here, but is not in shape to have my men moved away yet, this is a hard case—something like 'slow fever.'"[18] In another letter, dated June 6, McMurry wrote, "there are still about 30 to 40 strikers on the outside. They are very much annoyed a/c of a number of them have been arrested for Rioting, Intimidation, Carrying Pistols, etc. I don't think they can hold out much longer. We arrested 5 or 6 of them this morning."[19]

On July 2, McMurry wrote, "the strikers still remain in force on the outside, praying for the Rangers to be moved away, they claim that they could soon get clear of 'Old Hunter' and the Negroes, were it not for the Rangers."[20]

When McMurry left Thurber on July 8, 1889, he left four or five men to maintain the order that the Rangers had established.[21] Although McMurry's departure did not signify the end of the strike, it did mark the end of a period of threatened violence. The strike would end only when the Knights of Labor gave such an order and eventually this did happen.

With regard to the end of the strike, Hunter commented as follows in his *Annual Report* for 1889:

The strike continued until the Fall when Mr. Powderly[22] sent his adjutant to see me. Finding us determined to maintain our position and seeing that we had succeeded in the face of their opposition, they abandoned the fight and declared the strike "off." The county is now interested in the success of your enterprise, and we are vigorously prosecuting some of the ringleaders of the murderous gang, a few of whom are serving their time in jail. The cost of this fight has been THIRTY THOUSAND DOLLARS cash, and FIFTY THOUSAND DOLLARS would not cover the loss of the company occasioned by the delay in operation.[23]

Adjutant-General King gave a good summary of these labor difficulties in his *Annual Report for 1889–90*. That part of the Report which describes the work of the Rangers in Thurber during 1888 and 1889 is as follows:

Captain McMurry and his company have rendered important services at widely distant points east and west along the line of the Texas & Pacific Railway and the detachments have been sent as far south as San Saba to aid the civil officers and against lawless combinations, or in aid of courts and witnesses. For more than a year a large part of this company had to be kept on duty at the coal mines in Erath County, to keep the peace and prevent violence and possible bloodshed by a large body of miners who claimed to be on a "strike."

As a matter of fact, these miners—those who claimed to be "strikers," and who were attempting by violence and threats to prevent others from working—have never been employed by the company which had then become possessed of these mines. In a technical sense these men could not "strike" against those who had never employed them, but it suited their purposes to put forth this claim to keep miners from other sections away from these mines, and the local trouble, violence, and threats kept up by those on the ground caused the coal company heavy losses and costly and vexatious delays in the management of their business. . . . These men were not in the employment of the new company, and because they were not consulted as to the rate of wages fixed by said company, they not only refused to work when offered employment, but combined to prevent others from working; who were willing to accept the rates offered. These men were members of the Knights of Labor organization and appealed to their brethren abroad for the means of support while engaged in the so-called strike. Col. R. D. Hunter, the president of the coal company, was on the grounds during all these troubles, and while he had no objection to the employment of Knights of Labor, and did employ them by the hundreds, he did object to putting in his service any of the men who had voluntarily and recklessly produced and precipitated all these troubles.

These discontented and idle men numbered several hundred, and from threats and efforts at intimidation, some of them proceeded to acts of violence, and then the State was called on to interpose its power to prevent bloodshed. I went to the mines in the winter of 1888 and 1889, and found affairs in a very threatening and dangerous state. I remained several days and had a long interview with six committeemen who directed the movements of the unemployed miners.

I had brought Captain McMurry and eight or ten of his men into the mining camp or village, and after giving the discontented spirits to understand that no further lawlessness or violence and no undue or improper interference with men at work would be permitted, I left the Rangers in charge to see that these orders were observed.

The task was a difficult and dangerous one, with such surroundings and in the midst of such a multitude of unemployed, ignorant and discontented men, but for more than a year a detachment from this company kept the peace in this camp, and gradually produced order and safety out of confusion and turbulence. The Knights of Labor organization, through their own delegates and agents finally got at the real facts of this

pretended strike, and the exceptionally good wages and condition of those who were at work in these mines and when this
was understood, support was no longer given to the idle, and
most of them were compelled to seek other fields for their mis-
sion of misrule.[24]

After the "so-called" strike was officially ended peace and quiet came to
Thurber for a short time. This new tranquility was short lived, because
on July 5, 1890, Colonel Hunter wired General King to send Captain
McMurry to Thurber at once. His appeal came as the result of threats
made by the old strikers who were still loitering in the surrounding
country. Immediately after sending the telegram, Hunter wrote the following letter to King:

Fort Worth, Texas, July 5th, 1890
General W. H. King
Austin, Texas

Dear General

As I have always called upon Gov Ross and yourself in my
troubles at these mines as your Rangers have been my only
Protection as against the unlawful element that has prevailed
against our enterprise in this Country with the Presence of
your Rangers we have saved bloodshed. And peace and prosperity has reigned, and we have built up a flourishing village
of some fifteen hundred souls, and our pay roll now amounts
to over $20,000 Dollars per month but a new trouble is now
threatening us the Knights of labor element finding that they
were defeated as an organization are now secretly trying to
get up a race war. We have about 800 Negroes in camp men
women and children and the rest are whites. And they have all
been very peaceable, and orderly until very lately. When this
new movement has been inaugurated and I cannot tell what
moment the flare may burst forth. I ask you again for a little

assistance if you can consistently give it. Please send me Capt McMurray and a few men. He as I before said has saved plenty of blood shed, and his presence here with a squad of men in my opinion will do it again. I am not an alarmist but I do not think there is any time to lose. There is a lot of bad men hanging around here with there arms on their saddles. Some of them well known horse thieves and exconvicts, who are friends of the old strikers. Who are ready to commit any crime at a moments notice. Platt arrested one of them yesterday for drawing a Pistol on a negro, and he gave bail. He has just been arrested today again for a like offense. Would you also please send John L. Sullivan a permit to carry arms. He is one of the Captains old men now in the employ of this Company in trying to preserve the Peace but not having the right to carry side arms he is in great danger. Please wire me at coal mines Junction, Texas my expense your conclusion, as I shall await it anxiously.

Thanking you and Gov. Ross for all Past Courtesys,

I am sincerely yours

R. D. HUNTER[25]

General King complied with Hunter's request and on July 10, Captain McMurry arrived in Thurber. Two days later he wrote: "There has been considerable disorder and there is a very 'hard' set in this community. After taking in the situation and consulting with Col. Hunter and Dept Sheriff Platt, have concluded it best to order 3 or 4 men to this place to remain 2 or 3 weeks."[26]

No serious outbreak occurred and before a month had passed, the Rangers left Thurber and the local authorities maintained order until June 1894. During the year 1894, there was a more or less universal discontent among the coal miners throughout the United States and the miners in the Thurber mines were no exception. However, upon a closer study of the 1894 labor difficulties, one finds that much of the trouble could be traced back to the personal differences between Colonel Hunter and the owners of a rival saloon in Palo Pinto County.

When Colonel Hunter appealed to Adjutant-General W.H. Mabry for aid, he wrote:

> Although our men have not struck, and are still at work, the striking miners from the Territory and else-where, are sending their walking delegates in here in a clandestine manner and are trying to create a strike. Three of the rascals have been arrested and put under bond, but they keep sending more, and while our people are trying to work, they have been terrorized in a great degree.[27]

Adjutant-General Mabry sent Captain William (Bill) McDonald of Company B to Thurber to investigate the trouble and to prevent violence. McDonald talked with all parties involved, and he learned that two men by the name of Bruce and Stewart had opened a saloon about three-quarters of a mile from Thurber. In order to encourage the men from the Thurber mines to come there, Bruce and Stewart would distribute circulars advertising free beer for all who would come for it. According to McDonald, while the miners were in the saloon, Bruce, Stewart, and anyone else who had a grievance against the company would encourage the miners to strike against the Texas & Pacific Coal Company.

So many of the miners took advantage of the free beer that their drunkenness was interfering with their ability to mine coal. Colonel Hunter issued an order forbidding his employees to patronize the Bruce and Stewart saloon. Bruce and Stewart retaliated by bringing a lawsuit against Hunter in which they charged that he had deliberately closed a public road because it passed within a few yards of their premises. McDonald wrote that:

> . . . on the 1st of m'ch wages was cut from $1.15 per ton to $1.00 and while they say they would like very much to have more for their labor yet they can make very fair wages and that they can get the cash for it and don't have to take any time checks but are promptly paid in cash, and that goods are cheap (which I find

correct). Some of them say they quit work on account of circulars being distributed and parties from the outside threatening to go to work, but when they found out that the state would not allow others to interfere with them, they very willingly went to work and are now getting out more coal than they have since the trouble began. There has been a bitterness engendered (as indicated in my last letter) on account of circulars being distributed in the camp. . . . Bruce and Stuart [Stewart] has a saloon and Bradford a dry goods establishment about three quarters of a mile from this town and adjoining the mining property and there is quite a Jealousy existing between them.[28]

Together with his report to the Adjutant-General, McDonald sent copies of several affidavits which were made in the lawsuit against Colonel Hunter. Among these affidavits was one made by W. K. Gordon. In spite of this fact that this affidavit is rather lengthy, it merits a place in this study, because it explains quite clearly the difficulties which existed between Colonel Hunter and his rival saloon owner.

The only men from whom I hear any dissatisfaction are the parties who have been frequenting Bruce & Stewart's saloon. A number of the miners who are not dissatisfied have expressed fear to me that the mines would be blown up. I have frequently been told by miners that parties would come to them in the mines and tell them that if they did not quit work they would be blown up with dynamite. They could not tell who these parties were because it is dark in the mines and everybody looked alike, and they would disappear as soon as the threat was made. They have also told me that parties would come to their houses at night and make similar threats. This has been going on since about the middle of May.

I know of a saloon that was formerly run by Grant, situated South-east from Thurber, and right adjoining the town. I know that during the time that saloon was run there, miners

from Thurber would congregate at the saloon and drink and
gamble. On returning to the camp they would yell, shoot off
guns, and create a disturbance in this manner which could
be heard plainly all over the town to the great annoyance of
the inhabitants of the town. The men who would get on these
sprees would be incapacitated for work several days afterwards
and thereby create inconvenience and delay the operations of
the mines. A man who has been on a spree is unfit for mining
work and it is very dangerous indeed to allow him to go into
the mines, because in handling powder and dynamite he might
cause an explosion, which would endanger the lives of his fellow workmen as well as destroy the property of the company.
Col. Hunter has given strict orders to allow no man to enter the
mines who is drinking or who is in a drunken condition. I have
standing orders from Col. Hunter, which I have given to all my
subordinates, who are in a position of trust and have control of
other men, to promptly discharge any of them who get drunk.
I know, as a matter of fact, that Col. Hunter has given orders,
and through me, to the saloon-keepers of the Co. not to sell
any liquors to any employee of the company who is drinking
to excess, and at all times to shut down on men who are drinking to excess. I also know that when men who are drinking
too much are refused liquors at the Company saloon, they at
once go to the Bruce & Stewart's where they continue to drink.
I have frequently passed Bruce & Stewart's and seen miners
lying around the saloon and drinking at the saloon in a state of
beastly intoxication. I remember the last of 1892 or first of 1893
when the saloon of Jimmie Grant in Erath Co. was raided by the
officers and a number of men were said to have been arrested for
gambling. Soon after this, the saloon of Grant was moved into
Palo Pinto County, just outside the town of Thurber. Thurber
is just on the line of Palo Pinto and Erath Counties. The saloon
was then placed on the road running from Thurber to the main
track of the T. & P. R. R. This wagon road was on the right of

way of the R. R., extending from the main line of the T & P tracks into the town of Thurber. It was so near the railroad as to make it dangerous on account of animals being frightened by passing trains. I have often had to drive horses out of the road into the brush myself until the train would pass. It has been determined by Col. Hunter and myself that it was necessary to change this road on account of its dangerous proximity to the railroad long before Grant opened his saloon. This was not a public road. There is, and has been, no county road leading from the T. & P. R. R. into or through Thurber. About two months after Grant opened his saloon on this road, it was changed and a new road was made by the company, and the old road was discontinued and abandoned. This new road passes within 400 yards of where the saloon stands. When the road was changed the saloon was still being run by Grant. Bruce & Stewart did not take actual possession of the saloon until nearly a year after the road had been changed. . . . Shortly after the road was changed, the following letter addressed to Col. R. D. Hunter was received at Thurber through the mails. [See Photostat]

. . . There are no fences, ditches or other obstructions between the new road and the saloon of Bruce & Stewart. The country is open and nothing to prevent persons from passing from the new road to said saloon. All bridges opened over said road are the private property of the Company. . . . About the middle of last week I found D.W. Stewart in Thurber distributing circulars advertising free beer at the saloon of Bruce & Stewart and calling on the miners to come down there. I told him that I considered it a trespass for him to come into the camp and distribute these circulars and that I wanted him to get out.[29]

No serious outbreak occurred and the credit for this lack of violence should be given to McDonald who displayed a great amount of courage and wisdom. When McDonald arrived in Thurber, Colonel Hunter

$200.00 REWARD!

I, the undersigned, hereby offer a reward of Two Hundred Dollars for the arrest and conviction of the party or parties guilty of writing the following letter. This letter was dropped into the postoffice at Thurber about May 27, last. Parties were too cowardly to sign their names to same.

R. D. HUNTER,

PRESIDENT TEXAS & PACIFIC COAL CO.

COL. R. D. HUNTER:

We have started an organization of avengers to kill tyrants, and if you do not open the road to Jimmy Grant's saloon we will kill you, you son of a bitch. And we have been chosen by the goodness of God to put down all monopolies, and if you do not discharge W. K. Gordon and that son of a bitch, Bob McKeinan, and that gray haired bitch, Ben Mathews, we will kill you anyway. Open the road to Jimmy's and discharge the three sons of bitches and we will not hurt you.

AVENGERS.

We are called by the Supreme Ruler to remove R. D. Hunter, F. Crouk, W. K. Gordon, Bob McKeinan, and Ben Mathews and Andrew Remage.

Do you understand.

Reward poster printed for Colonel Robert D. Hunter in response to threats against coal company employees. Courtesy, 93-44, Thurber, Texas, Photograph Collection, Special Collections, The University of Texas at Arlington Libraries, Arlington, Texas.

was very dubious about his ability to handle the situation alone, and he warned the Captain that he would have to deal with a group of desperate men intent upon violence.

One evening McDonald saw a great number of kegs of beer being moved to a hillside about one-half mile from the town. He asked where

FREE!!

COME ONE! COME ALL!!

Bruce and Stewart will give you all the beer you can drink for nothing and the best beer in the country at that.

Boys drink with us; we are among you; we are one of you; we treat you right.

We will give free beer to the public from twelve o'clock, noon, until 9 o'clock at night, on next Saturday, June 2nd, 1894.

Saloon just outside of the wire.

BRUCE & STEWART.

Poster advertising free beer at the Bruce and Stewart saloon just outside coal company property near Thurber in 1894. Reproduced from photostatic illustration in Mary Jane Gentry, "Thurber: The Life and Death of a Texas Town," 1946, courtesy of Dan R. Gentry.

the beer was being taken and some one told him that the miners were planning a mass meeting that night. After dark, McDonald decided to go and have a look at the meeting. When he arrived on the scene, he found several hundred men intently listening to a speaker. The speech was highly inflammable and the miners were on the point of agreeing with the speaker that the mines should be dynamited and the Colonel disposed of.

McDonald bided his time and silently worked his way to the speaker's platform which in this instance was a large log. When the speaker finally stopped for a breath, McDonald stepped upon the log and told the miners who he was; that he was along, and that the man to whom they were listening was asking them to commit a crime for which they would be imprisoned. The miners listened to him and believed him.

The next morning a messenger informed McDonald that a crowd of miners wanted to see him. McDonald picked up his Winchester and went out to see what was going on. When he appeared, the miners informed him that they were ready to go to work and asked if he could furnish them with protection while they were in the mines.[30]

McDonald assured them that he had nothing to fear, and within a short time, the men were working. In this way, the 1894 labor difficulties were eliminated through the willingness of one man to explain to the miners that desperate acts meant destruction to themselves as well as to their employers.

It might be well to stop here and consider the fact that the majority of these miners had little knowledge of our language—certainly not enough command of it to understand the real significance of all that was being said. Hunter was not the type of person around whom a miner, ignorant of our language and customs, could feel at ease. He was always the boss in the white silk shirt and the white pleated trousers. Men, such as Bruce and Stewart, who had few scruples, took advantage of these miners and by constantly expounding upon the worst features of the miners' work and existence, were able to arouse them.

The mob spirit is most active in men who are lacking in understanding, men who feel that they are mistreated, and in men who are dissatisfied. Ignorance is no real excuse for violence, but had violence occurred at the mines, the real criminals were the "walking delegates," as the agitators were called.

McDonald was a wise man when he stepped before the miners and explained to them in a simple manner that they were able to understand that they were being led into trouble by men who pretended to be helping them. He spoke a language that they understood and his confident manner inspired their confidence in him, and they returned to the mines with the feeling that the law was their friend.

In 1903, the United Mine Workers of America decided to sponsor the movement to organize the Texas miners. Local unions had been organized at Bridgeport, Wise County, and at Lyra in Palo Pinto County. It seemed inevitable that Thurber should also become a union camp. For several months, W. K. Gordon had expected Union representatives to attempt to organize the miners on Labor Day. He wrote to Governor S. W. T. Lanham and asked him to send a detachment of Rangers to Thurber just in case there might be disturbances which would lead to serious consequences. In response to Gordon's request, Adjutant-General John A. Hulen ordered Captain John E. Rogers to Thurber. The Captain sent men to Thurber in time to be there on Labor Day.[31] Gomer Gower has given the following account of the events:

> All efforts to organize the Thurber miners failed until September, 1903, when after careful, secret preparations, a spectacular walkout was effected on Labor Day. . . . Mr. Gordon had sensed the possibility of a move to organize his employees, especially so was he on the watch for a move to be made when the miners celebrated Labor Day. In order to accomplish the defeat of the miners' purpose, he threw the Club House and grounds formerly forbidden to the miners open and provided a lavish barbecue, with the usual trimmings, for the entertainment of the miners for their gala occasion. This was the chance for which the miners had been waiting. A miner's son, Harry Connors, now deceased, was provided with a saddle horse and instructions to ride around among the more than eleven hundred miners assembled at the club grounds and at the proper time give out the word that an organizer for the United Mine Workers of America was ready to receive them into that organization at Lyra, some eight miles distant. This ruse worked so well that practically every one of those who had been on pleasure bent at the beginning of the day fell into line and followed the intrepid Harry like rats following the Pied Piper to Lyra.[32]

Sixty of the Thurber miners joined the union at Lyra on Labor Day, and they received instructions to work quietly among the other miners and to get as many converts as possible. William M. Wardjon, International Organizer for the United Mine Workers, later said that these sixty men set the camp ablaze with the fire of unionism.[33] He went so far as to compare this attempt to unionize Thurber with the story of Sampson [*sic*] when he sent the foxes with burning tails through the wheat fields of his enemies and in this way destroyed them. Wardjon, determined to have the Thurber mines operated on a union basis, declared: "Before the miners could ever return to work under any terms other than unconditional surrender, he would let the grass grow over Thurber."[34]

The following account of the organization of the miners is taken from the *Fort Worth Telegram,* September 11, 1903:

> The manner in which the organization of the union was brought about is an interesting story and it is just now being told by the organization. It was planned by Wardjon and District President Hanraty who was personally known to Manager Gordon. Hanraty could not go into the place in his own identity. He bought a long beard with mustache and thus disguised he entered the Thurber vicinity. For two nights he slept in the woods and on the third day, he called at the company headquarters and asked Gordon for a situation at the brickyard. He did little work making brick, but he talked unionism and suddenly disappeared. He was followed into camp by Joe Finiolio, the Italian organizer. Later on Mexican and Polish organizers were sent in to talk with the Mexican and Polish employees.[35]

The sixty union miners found the majority of the miners ready to join the union, and the following demands were presented to W. K. Gordon on Wednesday, September 9, 1903:

> To W. K. Gordon, General Manager, Texas and Pacific Coal Company of Thurber, Texas: We, the duly authorized representatives of the employees of the above coal company, respectfully present the following demands:

1. Price of mining to be $1.35 per ton of 2000 pounds of coal to be mined on the same basis as heretofore. Cross entries $1.50 per yard, corner entries $1.50 per yard.

2. The inside day wage to be as follows: Timber men $2.50 per day, tracklayers $2.50 per day, airmen or ventilators $1.50 per day, drivers $2.35 per day, motor drivers $2.35 per day, cagers $2.35 per day, greasers and praggers $1.50 per day, trappers $1.20 per day.

3. Outside Day Work Scale—Car trimmers and slate dumpers $2.00 per day, slate pickers $1.50 per day, blacksmiths $2.75 per day, firemen $2.00 per day, engineers same as agreed to and paid in Arkansas and Indian Territory.

4. Eight hours to constitute a day's work.

5. That we be paid in full every two weeks.

6. We demand the right to organize into the United Mine Workers of America organization, and respectfully ask the Texas and Pacific Coal Company of Thurber to recognize said organization.[36]

Company officials refused to grant the demands and the miners again marched to Lyra where those who had not already done so joined the union. More than one thousand miners repeated the oath of the United Mine Workers of America.

During the forenoon of September 10, the miners held a meeting at the Rock Creek bridge about one mile below Thurber Junction and four miles from Thurber. "On one side of the creek, Mexican mine workers stood with bared heads and uplifted hands, repeated the oath of the United Mine Workers as it was administered to them in Spanish by one of their number."[37] On the other side of the creek, Wardjon spoke upon the subject of unionism to about five hundred men. He spoke through interpreters to the Italians, Poles, and Mexicans and without an interpreter to the English speaking element. He asked the men to remain away from the mines and not to get their tools or their pay until they heard from District President Hanraty.

After this speech, one old darkey was heard to exclaim, "We are going to have everything 'union' after this, union 'lasses, union batter-cakes, union steaks—everything will be union." [38]

The miners continued to make charges against the company and its employment policies. They stated that each miner paid a fee of one dollar a month to ride the train to and from the mines, and that even if the miner rode only once during the month, he still had to pay one dollar. The miners also contended that the following notes issued by Gordon prior to the strike had helped to precipitate the organization and the demands which they presented to him on September 10:

> To Mine Employees: In accordance with instructions received last July from our president, Edgar L. Marston, the following rates and changes will be in effect commencing October 1, 1903: Price of mining $1.05 per ton instead of $1.00. A bonus will be paid miners who have to their credit at the end of the month more than 30 tons. The minimum bonus 2¢ a ton; maximum 10¢ a ton for production of 70 tons or more a month. Trains (for miners) will leave Thurber at 7:00 A.M. instead of 6:30 and nine hours will constitute a day's work.

The second notice read as follows:

> For the information of all employees notice is given that Thurber will remain a non-union camp. Those who are unwilling, can get a settlement at any time.[39]

When W. K. Gordon was asked to comment on the Company's position with regard to this strike, he issued the following statement:

> We offered the miners an increase from $1.00 per ton up to $1.05 and bonuses based on their output running up to 10¢ per ton.
>
> We offered this advance thinking that we could double the output and thereby afford to cut our profit in two. The miners

have demanded $1.35 a ton straight and an increase in the wages of other employees, the whole amounting to about 33 per cent advance. The company cannot pay this scale. We were told that if we did not pay it they would tie us up. If we should agree to pay it we would be tied up through bankruptcy, so we might as well be tied up now.

In the fourteen years that this company has been in existence we have had no trouble with our men. Some of them belonged to the union, but we made no objection. When there was trouble elsewhere we permitted collections for relief to be taken up in the camp, and the company generally contributed fifty or seventy-five dollars to the fund. Our people during these years have been happy and prosperous. Some of them have saved considerable money and have deposits in the company bank; others have sent their earnings to Italian banks in New York. Now the men have joined the union. The union leaders tell them to make this demand upon us. They say that the company can afford to pay the scale, as the advance will cost it nothing, since we can raise the price of coal on the railroads and the public. We cannot do this, however. We are forced to compete with the mines of Indian Territory and Alabama, where the veins are thicker than here, and which mines enjoy interstate freight rates, often more favorable than those of the Texas Railroad Commission. If we were to ask the railroad people to share this advance with us, even to bear one-fourth of it, they would laugh at us, and tell us they would get their coal from Indian Territory.

These men will not believe that we are obliged to do business on an exceedingly close margin. Nevertheless, we are now getting 85¢ a ton less for our product than we received fourteen years ago, and yet the scale which we announced to take effect Oct. 1 was the same as the scale we paid at first.

I am sure the company will never grant the demand, that it will go out of business first, as it cannot operate at such prices.[40]

When Pete Hanraty spoke to the miners, he told them that they should vacate the company houses, and that they should withdraw the pay due them. The company paid off the single men first, because they did not have household furnishings to pack and they had no houses to vacate. The men very quietly lined up before the pay windows and waited their turn. When Hanraty learned of this, his comment was: "Now I understand they have laid the single men off and that they will pay the married men as soon as they vacate the houses. If they keep on doing business in that way I will think they are pretty fair fellows after all." [41]

On Friday, September 11, the miners withdrew pay due them to the amount of $10,000. The company officials brought in additional $15,000 in cash from Fort Worth and the miners continued to withdraw their pay throughout Saturday and up until noon Sunday. The amount paid to the miners on these last two days amounted to about $30,000.

Gordon suggested to some of the men that they should get their tools as otherwise they might be damaged. A few of the men in turn suggested that it would be impractical to carry the tools with them, and Gordon assured them that the company would purchase them at a reasonable price. Gordon also promised to run a train to the mines so the men could get their tools from the mines.

On the morning of September 12, Gordon ordered a train of seven coaches to take the miners to the mines so that they might get their tools.

All went out, the miners, the Sheriff, the Rangers, and the News correspondent on the train of seven coaches which were shunted onto the tracks that led to the four life shafts. The Rangers were not needed but as Capt. Rogers remarked, they went along just to be-a-going. At the "Old Girl," #10, Captain Rogers went below. The employees showed him the mule stable, the brilliantly lighted tunnels, then into the shafts hewn out of rock where one has to stoop and where the only light is from a tallow dip. From the tunnels, he was taken into the entries and finally to the rooms where the miners lie down to work in a space 26 inches

high. There were 500 men on the train. Others went out in
buggies and wagons. Some few depended on their "buddies." [42]

During all this time, a peculiar quietness settled over Thurber. The
activities of the place abated to such an extent that one wondered if
Thurber could ever again be brought to life. It was not natural for
1000 men to quit work because their demands were refused, and for all
of them to refrain from disorder, intoxication, and anger. Neither was it
natural for the big saloon to be almost deserted on Saturday night. Not
only did the company officials realize the seriousness of the situation,
but each and every miner conducted himself in a sober manner.

The union leaders had assured the miners that shelter, provisions,
and work would be given to them, and that there was no need for them
to worry about the welfare of themselves and their families. The majority of the miners were willing to go to Lyra and work in the mines
there. Others planned to go to California, and many planned to return
to Italy.

When the exodus from Thurber began, it was an orderly retreat. Day
and night one could see an endless stream of wagons, carts, and buggies
carrying the miners, their families, and their household goods away
from Thurber. Not only was this exodus an unusual way in which to
settle a strike, but it was pathetic within itself. There was no rowdiness,
no shouting, no hateful retorts, and certainly no destructiveness.

The Italians were an affectionate people, and the men kiss and em-
brace each other as we are accustomed to see women do. Those who
were departing kissed and hugged their friends and tears flowed freely.
For those who were returning to Italy, "prayers were uttered that the
blessed saints might watch over them during the long journey to their
native land." [43]

Dozens of the miners went to W. K. Gordon, and in their broken
English told him good-bye. It was not at all unusual for a miner to em-
brace Gordon, and with tears in his eyes remark that it made him sad
to be leaving Thurber. Gordon, too, felt sad and there were often tears
in his eyes as he told the men good-bye. "One young fellow, in bidding

his American friends good-bye, choked back incipient sobs, 'Hello! Hello!' were the words he used. That was his idea of the language of this country." [44]

An outsider may find it hard to understand why there should have been any feeling of sadness between the strikers and their former employers, but it is not strange to anyone who lived in Thurber. Of course it was only natural for the company officials to operate the coal mines in such a way that Thurber would be a profitable enterprise. In attempting to reap these profits, there were times when the employees were underpaid and their working conditions were not always as they should have been. But at the same time, in most instances, the company officials were quite thoughtful of those who worked for them.

People in Thurber were closely associated with one another and they felt a certain kinship that is rarely found in towns of Thurber's size. Most of those who made up the population of Thurber describe it as "being more like a family than a town." [45] It was this feeling for Thurber that made the strikers and the employers sad and unhappy as they looked upon the long lines of vehicles which were moving the population out of Thurber.

The reaction of the Italians to the strike has never been satisfactorily explained. They had listened to the union organizers and they had joined the union. With their membership cards in their pockets, they returned to Thurber, collected their tools, packed their personal effects, withdrew their pay, and departed for Italy. Some of them did not bother to take their union cards after they paid for them. They never explained just what they had anticipated in regard to the strike, but they seemed determined to get away from it as if it were a pestilence. "One enthusiast kissed his hand toward the town as the train pulled out and in his native tongue, he said, 'Good-bye, Thurber, forever.'" [46] "Although the Italians have a fondness for their native land, they have a penchant for American clothes and especially for American shoes. Many of them bought six pairs of shoes each before leaving." [47]

By September 14, a death-like silence had settled over the camp. The ice plant and the brick plant ceased to operate for want of coal, and

Thurber was an abandoned town. Quiet reigned throughout the place and the few Rangers stationed there found no occasion to quell disorders. Gordon gave Wardjon the credit for the order which prevailed during the removal of the miners.

No doubt Wardjon exercised a great influence over the miners, and he often counseled them to do no one wrong and to respect the company officers. But the real reason for the orderliness must be credited to the people themselves. They bore no ill will; they were not of a destructive nature, and many of them did not have a clear-cut knowledge of the principles of unions and their methods of securing their demands.

W. K. Gordon made a few attempts to secure miners from other sections of the country, but the union organizers threatened to organize even the "scabs." As a result of one attempt to secure workers, eighteen miners arrived from Pottsville, Pennsylvania. They were met at Thurber Junction (Mingus) by a special train from Thurber. On this train were the Texas Rangers and company officials. Men representing the union came from Lyra to meet the workers also. A consultation was held and the imported workers decided that they would refuse to work in the Thurber mines. They accompanied the union representatives to Lyra and on the next morning, September 18, they left for the pits in Kansas.

C. W. Woodman, who was the Secretary of the Texas Federation of Labor and who had organized all company employees other than the miners, wrote:

> Thurber found itself short of help. While the strike was in progress, the company brought in several train loads of strikebreakers, but only three reached the mines, others changing their minds after reaching Gordon, a nearby railroad station. Those three were finally admitted to the union and became known as the $30,000 men, being all [that was] left of a $30,000 shipment of strikebreakers.[48]

During all the troubles, Gordon had refused to agree that the company officials would participate in the labor conference which was to be held in Fort Worth on September 23. This conference was to meet for the purpose of settling a wage scale for mining coal in Texas. The following notice was sent to Gordon inviting the company officials to the conference:

> You are hereby cordially invited to attend a joint conference of coal operators and miners at Fort Worth, Texas, September 23, 1903. The purpose of the conference will be to formulate and agree upon a scale of prices and conditions to govern the mining of coal at the mines in the state of Texas.
>
> We believe that the fact has been established beyond successful contradiction that both the employer and the employee are materially benefited by the system of wage agreements, and where once tried, neither side has been willing to abandon it or return to the old unsatisfactory system of dealing singly with employees. When fairly discussed both sides are far more apt to arrive at an amicable understanding in regard to any differences that may arise than when both parties go around with a chip on their shoulders and refuse to consider the other side of the question.
>
> Trusting that you will receive this invitation with the kindly spirit that it is given and that you will see your way clear to comply with this request, we are, very respectfully yours,
>
> PETER HANRATY
> *President District No. 21,*
> *U.M.W. of Am.*
> *S. F. Brachney, Secretary-Treasurer*

P.S. A committee of miners will meet you at the Worth Hotel at 9:30 A.M. on the above date to arrange for a place of meeting.[49]

Gordon still made no statement as to whether or not the Texas & Pacific Coal Company would participate in the conference. Less than two weeks after the strike was called, Edgar L. Marston, President of the

Texas & Pacific Coal Company, arrived in Fort Worth. He came to Fort Worth in his private car Number 111, and immediately upon his arrival he requested that a conference be arranged between himself, Hanraty, and Wardjon.

On September 19, 1903, the *Dallas Morning News* carried the following statement which was made by Edgar L. Marston. This statement is interesting because it quite clearly sums up the feeling of the company officials toward the United Mine Workers' efforts to unionize the company mines.

> The present condition of affairs at Thurber, according to what I have heard, has been caused not so much by the recent demand by a committee of miners for an increase in wages, or for an eight-hour day, but a demand that the United Mine Workers of America receive official recognition in the management of the Texas and Pacific Coal Company.
>
> To fully appreciate the condition at Thurber, one must recall the experience of 1888, at which time Colonel Hunter and myself organized this Coal Company for the development of the Texas coal fields. We found a coal shaft with a capacity of 150 tons per day, and operated under the auspices of the Knights of Labor. This organization dictated the wages paid, the hours of work per day, the number of men employed, and to whom work should be given. They objected to or excluded all men not belonging to their association. They denied the right that a man has by the Constitution of the State of Texas to sell his labor in a free market, thereby sacrificing the rights of a non-union man. They opposed the introduction of labor saving machines, and, in fact, sought to limit the supply of labor and to control the fuel supply of the country. . . .
>
> The owners prior to our purchase had no control over this property, and while receiving from the railroads $2.75 per ton, lost money on every ton mined. Under such circumstances, we thought it best at the inception of our operations to enforce the

authority of the operator and have the same recognition of each employee. . . .

At no time had there ever been a refusal on the part of the officers to meet each and every employee and discuss the differences of opinion or adjust grievances which might affect the operation of the mines. Mr. Gordon has always been ready to meet one and all. There has been no dissatisfaction, grumbling, no upheaval nor strike between 1888 to September 1903.

Without any demand from the employees, the working day last fall was reduced to nine and one-half hours, and without any suspicion or intimation of discontent the management, having during the present summer secured a broader market for its production of the coming fall and winter, published two weeks ago a new schedule of increased wages and a reduction to a nine-hour day, to take effect Oct. 1, 1903. . . .

The miners, in the manner of leaving Thurber, have set an example to all other laboring men; they have left quietly, orderly, and without disturbance, recognizing the ownership of property. This feature is very gratifying, but any one acquainted with the beautiful spirit of citizenship predominating at Thurber would expect nothing else. . . .

Our employees left us after making demands which meant bankruptcy of the company. It is now the duty of the officers of the company to man our mines and continue operations, as we have done in the past. This is what will be attempted by publishing to the world our schedule of wages, and compensation for the various and many classes of labor employed in Thurber. . . . The company does not oppose trades unionism or organized labor, nor has it discriminated against its employees on account of membership or non-membership. . . . We have, however, always maintained that owing to our location and surroundings and the number of men employed that the interest of both parties could and would be best served by a personal meeting or a direct control between the employer and the employees. . . . I can see where this is impractical in many instances and owing to the nature of employment, individual meeting with employees is impractical. But at Thurber we have always encouraged the cultivation of an independent spirit. . . .

I do not look for any interference from the members of the United Mine Workers of America in the operation of the Thurber mines, provided the company secures men who are willing to work for the wages offered and 9 hours a day as proposed by the company.[50]

No immediate agreement resulted from the meeting between Marston, Hanraty, and Wardjon, but the union leaders agreed to ship no more miners out of the country. At the time of the agreement, the Texas & Pacific Railroad Company had several coaches in Thurber ready to take out two hundred men. Hanraty's telegram arrived in time to stop the movement, and the two hundred miners returned to Lyra to await further orders. Marston, who was president of the Green and Hunter Brick Company and also the Texas Coal and Fuel Company, agreed that those two companies would recognize the union, but an agreement on the union activities in the Texas & Pacific Coal Company was not reached until later.[51]

The reason for Marston's delay in recognizing the right of the union to organize Thurber was due to a technicality. He contended that the Texas & Pacific Coal Company had no employees at the time of the conference. In fact, he went so far as to say that the company had no union employees on whose account the company should recognize the union. Neither were there any other employees to be organized into the union. Someone at the meeting inquired whether if the employees returned to Thurber would the union be considered. Marston is said to have replied, "It might be that way." [52]

Marston realized that he would have to give permission to the union to organize employees of the Texas & Pacific Coal Company. He conceded to the union objection to the charge of $1.00 per month train fare. Marston also conceded to the right of outside purchases, but no decision was reached which would allow the men to select the physicians they used. He maintained that the company had the right to choose the physicians, because it was their duty to keep the camp clean and also because the company paid the expenses of those physicians while they attended eastern schools of medicine at specified periods. The fence which surrounded the town was discussed, but it never became an issue during the conference. The miners had no real objection to the check system so it was left in effect.[53]

During all the strike difficulties, union organizers had not been permitted to enter Thurber, and those who did came surreptitiously. But on September 20, 1903, for the first time in fifteen years a union labor meeting was held in Thurber. The meeting which had been held fifteen years earlier was in 1888 when there was a serious conflict between the Johnson operators and their employees who were members of the Knights of Labor. This second meeting occurred when Edgar L. Marston accompanied by Pete Hanraty and W. M. Wardjon entered Thurber in Marston's private railroad car.

About 2:30 in the afternoon, the miners marched from Lyra to Thurber. More than 1000 men entered the Opera House to hear Woodman [Wardjon?] and Hanraty speak. This meeting was definitely a celebration of a victory won, and the miners were told that bygones would be bygones. The organizers explained clearly that Marston and Gordon were willing and ready to deal fairly with the men at all times. The former employees of the company were told to remain around Thurber until after the labor meeting which would be held in Fort Worth the following Wednesday. The purpose of this meeting was to prepare contracts fixing the scale for work in the Texas coal mines.[54]

In his speech, Wardjon remarked, "We have been hobnobbing with a millionaire (referring to Mr. Marston)—not as a millionaire, but as a man with a heart. Every official of this company I have met is a gentleman."[55]

The miners at Rock Creek were told to keep mining coal so that the brick plant could resume operations. While he was in Thurber, Woodman organized the brickmakers and all employees other than the

miners. A.C. Woodall, representing the Brickmakers at the Sixth Annual Convention of Texas State Federation of Labor, spoke of Woodman's work as follows:

> This brings me down to the organization of the unions outside
> of the miners and to the work of Bro. C. W. Woodman, and
> right here I wish to say that I never saw a more untiring and
> ceaseless worker than he. He worked with and for the boys both
> day and night until now it is safe to say that he has the unique
> distinction of being the only man in the United States that has
> thoroughly and completely organized every branch of labor of
> an entire city, bearing the one exception of the miners, of which
> mention is made also, wherein he worked with the organizers
> mentioned above. And in speaking of every branch of labor,
> that takes in both skilled and unskilled, of which there is a large
> number. Thurber has a population of five thousand inhabitants,
> of which there are something like fourteen hundred on the pay
> roll. There are seven labor organizations in our little city at the
> present time. Clerk, Miners, Federal Labor, Meat Cutters, Car-
> penter, Bartender and Brickmakers.[56]

Before the conference began in Fort Worth, Marston sent Gordon the
following telegram:

> Official conference with union tomorrow. All surrounding
> states completely unionized. If their demands are unreasonable,
> I shall close down everything for men at Brick Plant and mines
> have all joined the union. If they are in reason everything will
> be done to give union opportunity to demonstrate and prove
> their representatives to men and company.[57]

It was no easy matter for the operators and miners to reach an agreement, but eventually they did so. There was to be an average increase of
35 percent in wages. This increase would cost the Texas & Pacific Coal

Company about $200,000 a year. Eight hours would constitute a day's work; the miners would be paid on a bi-monthly basis; the miners would pay the wages of a check-weigher, and all dues would be collected at the company pay office. For its part the union agreed to see that there was always a sufficient number of miners in Thurber to operate the mines.[58]

Edgar L. Marston signed this agreement on September 27, 1903, and when W. K. Gordon met a crowd of miners who were waiting in the lobby of the Worth Hotel, he said, "You boys now own the property."[59]

After Marston agreed to the unionization of the company employees, the Texas & Pacific Coal Company cooperated with the union leaders to the fullest extent until the mines were closed in 1921. Of the situation in Thurber, Woodman wrote:

> Thurber was said to be the only little city wherein every worker
> was a dues-paying member of his respective union. No addition
> to the employment could be without applicant first becoming a
> member of his union. So it continued for nearly twenty years,
> when oil came into general use and the demand for coal shrunk
> to practically nothing. . . .
>
> For several years it was my lot to be called to Thurber to
> adjust minor differences, not one giving any more trouble
> than a conference. No employers were ever more considerate
> of its [their] workers, of the system under which they worked,
> of their health, maintaining a hospital and a corps of the best
> physicians.[60]

On August 31, 1916, the 1915–1916 contract between the miners and operators of the Texas coal mines expired. For about three weeks before the expiration of the contract, representatives of both groups attempted to reach an agreement on a new contract. The miners demanded increased wages and the operators held "that they could not meet the miners' demands for higher wages without wrecking the coal industry of Texas by increasing prices to such an extent that railroads would eliminate soft coal and resort to the use of crude oil as a fuel."[61]

The miners presented the following demands to the operators:

We, of the United Mine Workers of America, members of the
Texas Scale Conference for Operators and Miners, herewith
respectfully submit the following terms upon which we are
desirous of entering into regarding a new wage agreement.

1st We demand 5¢ per T on all pick mined coal.

2nd We demand 3¢ per T on all machine mined coal.

3rd We demand that all day labor, dead work, yardage, and
room turning be advanced 5% over existing prices.

4th We demand that our contract be placed on a mine run
basis.

5th We demand that the conference make proper disposition
of all arbitrated decisions now in effect and the methods of
settling disputes.

6th We demand that this conference give consideration to
making changes on local inequalities now existing.

John Wilkinson, Res. Dist. No. 21[62]

In answer to those demands Gordon declared:

These increases, if granted, would add fully 15¢ to the T for pro-
ducing coal which increase at this time cannot be obtained by
the operators in the selling price of coal as your operators are
today and have been during the past 12 months placing the coal
mined by you on the market at a price not sufficient to equal
the cost of production. You should readily appreciate how impossible it is for us to continue operating our mines if the cost
of production is to be again increased 15¢ per T and the markets
remain stationary or go downward.[63]

The miners refused to believe that the demands could "either stop or
interfere with the operation of the Texas bituminous coal mines."[64] Af-

ter more than a month of idleness, the miners won and the 1916–1917 contract contained an increase in wages, but it was a victory with no future attached.

As Gordon and the other officials of the Texas & Pacific Coal Company had predicted, the demand for coal began to decline very rapidly. W. K. Gordon discovered the Ranger Oil Field in 1917, and with the discovery of this vast store of oil, the coal fields in that area were destined to become so unimportant that within a short time the majority of them would be shut down. The railroads were using more and more oil-burning locomotives, and their demands for coal decreased steadily.

In 1921, the Texas & Pacific Railroad Company used such a small amount of coal that the coal company was forced to abrogate its contract with the miners. The miners and the union leaders refused to accept a reduction in the wage scale, and the union ordered the miners to leave company property if they expected to secure union assistance. Hundreds of families once again left Thurber. They moved across the Erath County line into Grant Town in Palo Pinto County. Here they lived in tents and received some assistance from the union.

The majority of them hoped that once again the union could force the Texas Pacific Coal and Oil Company to meet the union demands, but this time they were indulging in wishful thinking. The development of the nearby oil fields had brought about a new economic situation in which coal did not play a major role. Since the Texas Pacific Coal and Oil Company controlled a large part of the Ranger oil field, it did not feel compelled to make ovations to the United Mine Workers of America. The company did make half-hearted attempts to mine coal with "scab" labor, but finally in 1923, all mining operations in Thurber were abandoned.

Thurber was born in the midst of a violent strike, and at no time during all the years of its existence was it ever to experience such serious labor difficulties. Strikes and disagreements did occur in the years between 1890 and 1921, but they are remembered for the influence they exerted on the life in Thurber rather than for any violent happenings. Labor troubles in Thurber were of a peculiar nature, and in all of the major difficulties, there was always the quality of uniqueness.

The first strike in 1888–1889 was not a strike in a true technical sense. Men who have never been hired by an employer cannot strike against him. However, the lawless element succeeded in proclaiming a strike against the Texas & Pacific Coal Company, and the situation had to be considered and dealt with as a strike regardless of the technical interpretations of the term "strike."

CHAPTER 4

Texas Pacific Mercantile
& Manufacturing Company

T he role of the T.P.M. & M. Company was an important one in the history of Thurber. The Texas & Pacific Coal Company gave the miners an opportunity to earn money, and the T.P.M. & M. Company gave the miners an opportunity to spend their earnings, and an excellent opportunity it was since company officials discouraged outside purchases and attempted to make the purchase of any article in Thurber as convenient as possible.

The T.P.M. & M. Company operated one store of each type and employees were encouraged to patronize these stores. Aware of the average miner's thirst, the T.P.M. & M. Company maintained saloons with well stocked shelves, and in order to make it more convenient for the Company employees to spend their earnings in Thurber, the T.P.M. & M. Company issued company check or scrip to those who wished to draw in advance part of their earnings.

Every effort was made to make Thurber self-reliant and comparatively speaking it came very close to being that type of community. The T.P.M. & M. Company was a major factor in helping Thurber achieve as much self-reliance as it did.

It was during the "so-called strike" in winter of 1888 and 1889, that the Texas & Pacific Coal Company, being unable to mine coal, turned

Food displayed inside the meat market in Thurber, one of the many enterprises of the Texas Pacific Mercantile & Manufacturing Company. Courtesy, AR 88, Special Collections, The University of Texas at Arlington Libraries, Arlington, Texas.

Panoramic view of the inside of the Thurber drug store, another of the enterprises of the Texas Pacific Mercantile & Manufacturing Company. Courtesy, 93-41, Thurber, Texas, Photograph Collection, Special Collections, The University of Texas at Arlington Libraries, Arlington, Texas.

The first hardware store in Thurber. Courtesy, 93-41, Thurber, Texas, Photograph Collection, Special Collections, The University of Texas at Arlington Libraries, Arlington, Texas.

its attention to merchandising. It began building quarters to house the business establishments essential in any town. A general store with a large warehouse attached, a drug store, and a hardware store were built. All three stores carried rather large stocks and after the first year's operation, it was evident that the company store could operate with a high degree of profit. At the end of the first year, December 1889, the inventory records showed a stock of goods on hand valued at fifty thousand dollars. The net profits from the stores for the first year averaged between sixteen and seventeen percent of the sales.[1]

In 1894, the officials of the Texas & Pacific Coal Company chartered a new company under the name of the Texas Pacific Mercantile & Manufacturing Company. The capital stock of this new company consisted of 2000 shares with a value of $10.00 each. Since the officers of both companies were the same, the president of the Texas & Pacific

Coal Company held these shares in trust for the Texas & Pacific Coal Company stockholders.[2] This new company managed the company stores, saloons, printing office, ice plant, livery stable, Opera House, dairy, slaughterhouse and bakery.

Just how much pressure was brought to bear on employees to patronize the company stores always will be questionable. Practically all persons who lived in Thurber during Hunter's period of presidency believed that one of the reasons for the wire fence and the guards who patrolled it was to prevent a "nickel's worth of merchandise being sold to residents of the 'Bull Pen' by the farmers or merchants."[3] The residents were convinced that the guard at each gate had instructions to report the names of all persons who made outside purchases. The following description by Daisy Varley Conn of how her mother smuggled in outside purchases is typical of many stories that still exist:

> My mother would wait until school was out and then she would
> hitch the horse to the buggy and slip away to Gordon to buy
> her groceries as she could get them much cheaper there. Often
> she would hide the groceries around her feet and let her long
> full skirt and lap robes cover them so they could not be seen as
> she came through town. She would run the buggy into the barn
> and after dark would slip the things she had bought in Gordon
> into the house.[4]

Of course Colonel Hunter defended the company in this matter, and in one instance commented on the company stores as follows:

> Gordon is the nearest town to Thurber. It is certainly a fact that
> all the people who live, by my permission, within the enclosure
> there at Thurber, traded at our stores, as a general rule; that our
> stores are more convenient to trade at than any other stores
> in that country. For the purpose of supplying our employees
> and such, these stores were all opened and operated by our
> company. It was placarded there publically on our stores and

all around that these stores were strictly for the benefit of our
employees. We did not necessarily expect all the people who
lived in that enclosure to deal with our stores and get supplies
from them. We did not know that they would do it. Many that
don't do it now. We do not compel them to trade there . . . A
great many of them, the majority do trade there . . . Of course
we expected the majority of our employees would trade there. It
is very true that all those stores were established there for profit
and gain, and that the company expected to sell to the people
who lived in there, so long as they would behave themselves
and pay the money, whether they were employees or not, if they
were not objectionable.[5]

The Company stores carried in stock almost every conceivable item from
coffins to birdcages. In fact as early as 1897, county officials "believed
the T.P.M. & M. Company of Thurber rendered the value of more goods
in stock for taxation than all the stores in Stephenville combined."[6] If
the desired item was not in stock, store managers were always willing
to order whatever the customer wanted.

Company officials were aware of outside competition and this alert-
ness is best illustrated in the following excerpts taken from annual reports for several years:

(1897) The percentage of profits did not come up to our monthly
estimates as owing to strong competition we were forced to
reduce prices on all articles, especially staples.[7]

(1900) There was a great decline in receipts of Grocery and
Saloon departments which was due to the competition of the
stores and saloons at Thurber Junction [Mingus] to which place
some of our trade has been diverted.[8]

(1902) During the past year we purchased two stores and a
saloon in Thurber Junction hoping to remove the competition
to which reference was made in annual report 1900. The invest-
ment should result in increased sales.[9]

Not only were the company officials aware of the outside competition, but they were also aware of the resentment which many of the miners felt toward the company stores and the total absence of "free competition." After the miners joined the union, there was much discussion as to whether employers could force employees to patronize company-owned stores. These discussions caused President Marston to make the following suggestion:

> The question of "company stores" having been discussed by the union miners in their union meetings and by members of the state legislature, it is best to have the Coal Co. and the Mercantile Co. more independent of each other than heretofore.[10]

Although the Texas & Pacific Coal Company and its subsidiary, the Texas Pacific Mercantile & Manufacturing Company, attempted to be more independent of one another, no great amount of independence was possible or practical. The entire population of Thurber was more or less dependent upon the T.P.M. & M. for supplies. Everyone became more aware of this dependence when in the early morning of February 25, 1902, fire destroyed the big department store. The following description of the fire was a front page story in the *Thurber Journal:*

> Vandy West discovered the "General Store" to be on fire. After firing his revolver Mr. West ran to the mine office yard and sounded the big triangle of the Thurber Fire Department.
>
> Mr. Farr ran to notify the firemen at the Ice Plant who soon turned loose the great fire alarm whistle whose multi-toned screech might awaken the Seven Sleepers. By this time the hardware and drug stores looked as if they were doomed. To the south a similar struggle was going on to save the mine office, and general office—while the big store and bakery buildings had fallen in.
>
> Mr. Gordon rounded up the printers and instructed them to print circulars announcing "that our citizens could get sup-

plies in the new warehouse by noon or a little after." So in the early morning while the only source of supplies yet burned the people read in different languages the announcement that business would be carried on.

Imagine the supplies of 5000 people as well as thousands in surrounding area cut off—gone up in smoke.

Wagons had been dispatched with competent buyers to neighborhood towns of Gordon and Strawn and soon began to arrive with loads.

Zeno Francis who saw service in the Civil War looked every inch a soldier as he paced his beat while on guard about the powder and dynamite even though sparks occasionally showered about the powerful explosives.

The fire in no way affected the mines. Across the blackened front of the Drug Store Supt. McLure wrote in huge letters "Mines will work today" and at 6:10 A.M. the "Black Diamond" left with her usual quota.

All the forenoon Tuesday from the smoking heaps of canned goods one could hear a smothered explosion, a can would mount high into the air and often fall far out of the burned district. Just about daylight a party of colored women were viewing the ruins. Suddenly there was an unusually heavy explosion and a large can of "Lunch Chicken" shot skyward describing a graceful circle and emptied its well-roasted contents into the flames. An old colored woman in the crowd was heard to exclaim with all the fervor of her race, "Good Lo'd! ain't dat too bad!" [11]

The following advertisement appeared in the *Thurber Journal*:

Still doing business—not exactly on the same old stand but exactly on the same old liberal plan close to the old stand where we are prepared to fill your every want in the Grocery Line. Our elegant stock destroyed in the recent fire has been fully duplicated both in quality and quantity. We are determined you shall not share our misfortune. We are grateful for your sympathy and patronage.[12]

Eventually the buildings were replaced, and in order to accommodate the miners who lived on Number 3 Hill, the company built a large combination Grocery and Market on that hill. Not only did this store lessen the distance a miner's wife had to go in order to purchase her groceries, but it also lessened the crowd at the main store. The "store on the hill" was manned by a group of clerks who had a fair understanding of the predominant languages, namely, Italian, Polish, and Mexican.

The clerks in all the company stores made most of their sales after four o'clock in the afternoon. This was owing to the fact that the miners' wives were inclined to let the children of the family or the miners themselves do the shopping. This failure to assume the task of shopping

The combined general offices (upstairs) and hardware store and meat market (ground level) in Thurber, 1914. Courtesy, AR 88, Special Collections, The University of Texas at Arlington Libraries, Arlington, Texas.

may be attributed to several reasons. Most families were fairly large and the mother rarely hired any one to "look after" the small children. Very few women had English vocabulary sufficient to enable them to execute the family business with ease. Then again many of them had just recently come to America from the "old countries" and they were not accustomed to the freedom allowed to women in this country.

One had to be willing to stand in line for an hour or more if it were necessary to do the shopping during the busy hours. This inability to prevent long hours of waiting was not because of an inadequate number of clerks, but because there was only one store of each type, and during the years when the population of Thurber varied from five thousand to ten thousand, overcrowding was unavoidable. Congestion was an every day occurrence in the grocery store and in the market since these two were frequented the most often by the greatest number of people.

To alleviate this situation, men in "order" wagons and later in trucks went about the town taking orders for supplies. They took these orders in the morning and made the deliveries in the afternoon. This service did much to ease the later afternoon rush.[13]

Each store had its own manager and these managers were always anxious to help encourage the company employees to patronize the company stores. Below is an example of how sales were encouraged. This material is from the Minutes of the Department Managers Meeting:

Through the medium of coupons in cases of Rolled Oats, the Grocery department had on hand a dinner set. Mr. Tennant decided to have a drawing for the set to see if it would stimulate trade. A numbered ticket was given with each 25¢ purchase of Rolled Oats, or each $1.00 purchase of other groceries. Each ticket was numbered in duplicate, original given to purchaser and duplicate deposited in box kept for that purpose.

The drawing was held this afternoon May 3d at 2 o'clock.

Mr. Tennant: I know that the drawing was a success and that it increased trade in all departments today. Mr. Creighton, having announced that all was ready for the drawing, I went to the Grocery department and found the building crowded with ladies. I made them a little talk, thanking them for their patronage, stating that it was fully appreciated by the company. Knowing that a great many tickets had been given out and that it was impossible for more than one lady to draw the dinner set, Mr. Creighton suggested that each lady be given a package of candy. This was found to be a good idea and all went away pleased.

Mr. Creighton: The idea of the drawing was a good one. It helped trade especially today. . . .

Mr. Reeves: These drawings are good trade stimulators. We had an exceptionally good trade today at Soda Fountain. . . .

Mr. Tennant: It has been my intention for some time to have a "Souvenir Day" at the Dry Goods Department. We can get good nice souvenirs at a minimal price, and we will have one at an early date.[14]

Trade Days were frequent as far back as 1905, but they really became important in the middle 1920s. The store managers held all sorts of indoor and outdoor contests, and the first Saturday of each month was usually the day set aside for these activities. Each store prepared special and elaborate displays of its wares. In the large show window of the dry goods store, there was always a "guessing" contest—such as beans in a fruit jar or buttons in a fish bowl. The winner was the person who could guess nearest the actual number of beans or buttons. One of the most attractive displays used by the market department was halves of watermelons or fruits frozen in large blocks of ice. This display always attracted attention, and there was an increased demand for goods displayed in this fashion.[15]

The main street was the field for the outdoor contests, and the younger generation monopolized such contests as the three-legged race, the pie eating contest, and the ever popular peanut pushing contest. The winners received cash awards, and these awards did not tarry long in the winners' pockets. The drug store was nearby and the winners usually felt the need for refreshments.

Fire of unknown origin destroyed the market, hardware, and general office on September 14, 1930.[16] This time the fire department was not a "bucket brigade," but a well-equipped modern department. The fire raged with such ferocity that the company officials asked the neighboring towns to rush in their fire departments in order to prevent the loss of the entire business district. After several hours of fighting, the firemen brought the flames under control without loss to the surrounding buildings.

The loss was estimated at $250,000[17] and included everything in the building except the company vaults. The company made no attempt to rebuild, but in order to provide space for the general office and market, it reshuffled other businesses. The largest remaining store, the dry goods, became the general office and remained as such until 1933. The market was combined with the grocery store and the building which housed the drug store became the dry goods and the drug store was placed in a smaller building which had been the barber shop.

In June 1933, the executive department in Fort Worth ordered that all existing stocks must be cleared from the store shelves. The printing department distributed circulars which announced a clearance sale of extraordinary proportions. This was not an exaggeration, because all clothing, accessories, shoes, millinery, piece goods and ready-to-wear sold at a fifty percent discount.

On the morning of the sale, great crowds of people thronged outside the doors, most of them from outside Thurber. They were people who had always taken a great delight in condemning Thurber as a company owned town, and as a general rule, they would buy nothing in Thurber. When the clerks opened the doors, they were almost trampled under foot by the crowd. People grabbed, pushed, and shoved. Women would seize bolts of cloth and share with no one.

Although a large group of clerks was on hand, it was all but impossible to wait on the customers. People gathered up what they wished and walked out without ever paying. Finally, it became necessary to station men at the door, and those men allowed no one to leave the store with unwrapped articles.[18]

At the end of the day, when the clerks were arranging the stock, it was not at all unusual to open a shoe box and find that the new shoes were gone, and in their place was a pair of worn out shoes. In the confusion, there had been ample opportunity for a dishonest person to sit down, try on a pair of shoes, and walk out with them. There were two or three instances when women waited on themselves and under the protection of a pushing, shoving crowd were able to leave the fitting rooms wearing new dresses that they had taken from the dress racks.[19]

Within a few days, the shelves were empty, and the Texas Pacific Mercantile & Manufacturing Company was no longer an active subsidiary of the Texas Pacific Coal & Oil Company. Mose M. Miller rented the grocery store building and purchased the stock on hand. He operated this store for several months, until the population of Thurber numbered less than one hundred people. From then on the people who remained in Thurber had to go to Strawn, Mingus, Gordon, or Ranger to buy supplies.[20]

The Texas Pacific Mercantile & Manufacturing Company was a profitable subsidiary of the Texas & Pacific Coal Company as indicated in the financial statement in the table.[21] Over the period of twenty-four years during the time of greatest prosperity in Thurber, the net profit of the T.P.M. & M. Company was $2,145,937.27 or approximately 13.9 percent. It is interesting to note that this was during the years in which the company employees called a strike and the company was forced to recognize the union. Complaints of high prices had been prevalent among the strikers, and although the company officials denied the charges that profits were excessive, the rate of net profit declined to 16.4 percent in 1904.

The discovery of the Ranger oil field and the company's participation in its development accounts for the large net profits from 1917–1920. These were the years when Thurber boomed on Ranger oil. The first net loss was in 1921, and although no figures later than 1923 are available, it is probable that the T.P.M. & M. Company continued to operate at a

TABLE 2

Texas Pacific Mercantile & Manufacturing Company
Statement of Cash and Check Receipts and Calculations and Net Profits for the
Years Ending December 31, 1900 to 1923 Inclusive

Year	Cash	Check	Total	Net Profits
1900	127,138.29	237,737.17	384,295.46	92,705.62
1901	162,625.77	266,658.89	429,284.66	94,031.62
1902	172,708.27	292,074.01	464,782.28	101,958.12
1903	183,184.06	288,633.57	471,817.63	115,010.50
1904	178,906.05	270,864.55	449,770.60	73,736.09
1905	193,315.91	281,168.01	474,483.92	74,302.09
1906	226,782.97	266,826.84	493,609.81	85,009.74
1907	249,679.30	267,261.27	516,940.57	69,958.22
1908	249,158.58	282,167.78	531,326.36	78,116.71
1909	298,601.50	394,332.86	692,934.36	110,995.04
1910	267,862.51	378,846.66	646,709.17	94,186.08
1911	266,982.16	418,532.60	685,514.76	108,330.26
1912	312,617.88	417,359.76	729,977.64	118,286.28
1913	357,481.55	423,473.65	780,955.20	108,597.65
1914	359,945.71	414,305.30	774,251.01	94,190.82
1915	333,143.25	396,651.55	729,794.81	94,844.25
1916	293,556.48	351,871.42	645,427.90	99,294.98
1917	337,966.82	468,520.65	806,487.47	125,633.06
1918	449,632.18	501,949.93	951,582.11	151,253.71
1919	621,432.82	401,915.70	1,023,350.52	197,600.63
1920	816,327.83	319,815.78	1,135,143.61	183,060.00
1921	411,141.27	152,248.95	563,390.22	64,796.40
1922	314,354.28	204,612.29	518,966.57	16,523.81
1923	303,508.60	161,267.96	464,776.56	43,884.26
	7,488,056.04	7,859,097.18	15,366,573.20	2,145,937.27[1]

[1] Since there were no totals on the financial statement, the writer computed a total for each column. There is an error of $19,420 in the total receipts column for the year 1900, causing the combined totals for cash and check receipts to be out of balance with the final total of the total receipts column.

loss. The last coal strike occurred in 1921, and the miners left Thurber by the hundreds. This accounts for the 50 percent reduction in total sales for 1921, as compared with the total sales of 1920.

In an attempt to operate the mines with scab labor, the company brought in non-union miners and allowed them credit to cover the cost of their tools, clothing, and food until they began working. The imported miners never received full-time employment, because there was little demand for coal. The company continued to extend credit to the miners and many of then later moved from the town without ever having paid their accounts. This fact and the 50 percent drop in cash and check sales while the overhead remained the same accounted for the subsequent losses.

Every Christmas for years, the T.P.M. & M. Company gave to each employee a package of oranges, apples, candy, and nuts. On Christmas Eve, or possibly on the day before, the company trucks would go up and down each street and boys would leave a Christmas package on each family's front porch. This was an exciting day for the children of the town. Even though they knew ahead of time just what would be included in the package, they could hardly wait for the truck to arrive. Usually they were hanging on the front fence long before the truck approached the end of the street, and they never failed to shout the news of its arrival. All up and down the street these children were as enthusiastic as if Santa Claus himself were driving his sled through the town. Usually they rushed out to get the Christmas packages when the truck stopped in front of their house, and their enthusiasm saved many steps for the boys delivering the packages.

These Christmas packages were as much a part of the traditional Christmas in Thurber as were the decorated Christmas trees and the usual Christmas dinner. An individual package did not have great monetary value, but it was the company's way of wishing each of its employees a "Merry Christmas and a Happy New Year." It was a pleasant custom that will always live in the memory of those who experienced it.[22]

In addition to the individual Christmas packages, the company gave fruit, candy, and nuts to each of the churches and this was to be distributed to the children who attended Sunday School. During the last few years of Thurber's existence when the population numbered only a few hundred, a community Christmas tree was provided and the company presented gifts to every child in Thurber.

No exact date is available as to when Colonel Hunter conceived the idea of issuing company check, but records show that the miners used company check several months prior to March 31, 1890.[23] So in all probability, the check system came into use about the time Colonel Hunter opened his stores. One book of checks, or scrip as it was often called, was similar to trade coupons used by some stores today. The value of the books varied from one to ten dollars and the coupons were accepted as money in the saloons and company stores.

The company held two weeks pay in trust for each employee to guarantee house rent and utilities, and any amount above this that the employees might have earned could be drawn in check. To a large degree, company check was the prevalent currency used by the employees from one payday until the next. This is evident from the figures on the financial statement mentioned earlier. For a period of twenty-one years, 51 percent of the T.P.M. & M. Company receipts was check.

Whenever an employee once began using check, it was almost impossible for him to be able to draw enough cash to take care of his needs for the coming month. The check system was an advantage to the company in that it was an assurance that the employee would have to spend practically every penny of his earnings in the company stores or saloon, the only places where check was good.

At one time, in about 1905, the company announced that each employee could draw check only once a day. The purpose of such a rule was to simplify bookkeeping and to prevent a person from drawing out more than was due him. The store managers objected to this rule on the ground that it interfered with sales. C. S. Campbell, Assistant General Manager of the Store, voiced the following criticism in a store meeting:

Mrs. Jess Mitchell whose husband is employed in the Ice Factory, while down town a few days ago, saw some furniture she wished to buy. The amount was $32.50. I asked a payment of $7.50. With plenty of money in the office, she had lost the right to same by drawing a small check, which she supposed would be plenty for her needs. . . . The inforcement of this rule is hurting our business every day.

I wish also to call attention to the fact that on the first of each month, and on Saturday night, the check office closes at 7 o'clock, while the stores keep open until 8:30 o'clock. I think that if the check office kept open until at least 8 o'clock on those nights it would result in large check revenue to the stores.[24]

The rule was amended and the people allowed to check out whatever amount was due them, and if they wished to draw check three times a day, they were permitted to do so. Often an employee would check out all of his earnings and on payday, his envelope would contain a statement of the amount withheld for his rent and utilities, and there would be no cash in the envelope. When this happened, the employee found it difficult to draw a large part of his earnings in cash for several months to come.[25]

At the end of each month, the cancelled check was hauled to the brick plant and burned in one of the kilns. While it was en route to be burned and while it was being dumped into the kiln, it was well guarded and every precaution was taken to prevent anyone from picking up any of the check for future use.[26]

When the Texas & Pacific Coal Company took over the Johnson Mines in November 1888, there was a saloon on the premises. The Johnsons had leased the saloon property to John L. Ward and this contract was in effect when Hunter took possession. Hunter was anxious to gain control of the saloon, because it was a meeting place for the former Johnson miners who were striking against him. In fact, after he fenced in the camp, the saloon was the only place within the enclosure that he did not control.

Hunter and Ward finally reached an agreement described by Hunter as follows:

> We were to pay John L. Ward $150 a month for the privilege he had there under a contract with Johnson when we bought the mines. He had a lease on the saloon property for a consider-able length of time, and our company was to buy him out and agreed to pay him twenty-seven hundred dollars and paid him that way, one hundred and fifty dollars a month by agreement with him.[27]

Colonel Hunter was not quite sure that the Texas & Pacific Coal Company could legally operate a saloon so he asked Thomas Lawson, a friend of his, to lease the saloon. Hunter gave Lawson an exclusive contract for the sale of liquors, wine, and beer. Lawson opened the saloon on May 20, 1889, and it probably had more business than any other establish-ment in the camp.[28]

Before many months had passed by, Hunter was determined to break the lease with Lawson so that the coal company could operate the saloon. On August 26, 1890, a distress warrant was levied on the saloon stock and Hunter entered the saloon and said, "I take possession of this property in the name of the Texas & Pacific Coal Company."[29] Hunter declared that Lawson had failed to carry out the terms of the lease and the coal company filed suit against Lawson, and the case finally reached the Supreme Court of Texas. This court held that Lawson's contract was void as being in restraint of trade.[30]

While the Texas & Pacific Coal Company vs Thomas Lawson case was going through the courts, the coal company began operat-ing a saloon. The building used by Lawson was not large enough to accommodate the saloon customers and the company built a red brick saloon in about 1897 or 1898. A second saloon on Polander Hill was pa-

---

tronized chiefly by the miners who lived on Polander and Italian Hills. The saloon in town was the "Snake" and the saloon on the hill came to be known as the "Lizard."

The whiskey, beer, and wine vaults contained vast stores of drinks, and one could purchase almost any kind of liquor in any quantity. A customer could order a glass, a bucket, or a keg of beer or wine, and many of them would order a bucket of beer to take home for the evening meal.

Company officials had been expecting Erath County to become dry by local option, and when this occurred in 1904, they built a large saloon just across the line in Palo Pinto County which was a wet county. The new saloon, known also as the "Snake," was one hundred and twenty feet long and about forty feet wide. Its horseshoe bar was spacious enough to accommodate several hundred men at one time and the saloon soon gained fame as the busiest saloon between Fort Worth and El Paso.[31]

Unless it was a holiday, four bartenders could wait upon the customers, but on a holiday, six or eight bartenders worked incessantly until closing time.[32] Literally thousands of dollars found their way across the horseshoe bar and into the cash registers. "When the day's receipts did not reach or exceed one thousand dollars, that day's business was described as slack and one wondered what had happened to the miners' thirst."[33]

In the yard around the saloon, there were many small sheds with benches under them. Most of the foreigners preferred to sit under these sheds and drink. A group of five or six men or even as many as twelve would buy a keg of beer and take it to one of these sheds. Often they had a barbecue feast along with their beer. Before the keg was emptied, they usually began to sing and as the night wore on, the air was filled with the native songs of almost every European country.

> Now and then if there were a few Irishmen present, and there usually were, we would have a few good clean fist fights. . . .

if some one had a grudge and wanted to demonstrate, there would be a space cleared and men stripped sometimes to their waist. . . . and they would fight until one said, "Enough," and then they would go back to the keg and drink together.[34]

Along with the fist fights, there were many "wind fights and more coal was mined in the saloon and under the sheds than ever was taken from the mines."[35] To most of the foreigners, the drinking sheds were probably reminiscent of the European beer and wine gardens and for that reason they preferred to drink under the sheds while the Americans preferred to put their feet on the brass rail and drink at the bar.

By the side of this retail saloon, there was a large warehouse, served by the railroad track. The kegs would be rolled with ease from the boxcars to the warehouse, and from the warehouse into the saloon. When hundreds of kegs were being rolled into the warehouse, or into the saloon, the noise sounded like the rumble of distant thunder. The company purchased most of the beer from the Fort Worth Brewing Company and during the year 1914, the company purchased 11,935 barrels of beer from this company alone, more than thirty barrels a day. This amount represented one hundred and sixty carloads and the purchase price and freight charges amounted to $82,100.58.[36]

A saloon of such magnitude could not escape notice and visitors were always aware of its presence. It is not remembered as an "evil place," and neither is it remembered as a typical western saloon. In fact, it portrayed no western characteristics such as are common in the descriptions of southwestern saloons.

National prohibition closed the doors of the "Snake" in 1918 and stilled forever the rumble of kegs rolling down the incline. It silenced the impromptu concerts and obliterated from reality, but not from memory, the greatest and most colorful saloon west of Fort Worth.

The closing of the mines and the national law against the sale of liquor curtailed the activities of the T.P.M. & M. to such an extent that after 1920 the profits were negligible. In 1933, the company officials ordered the liquidation of the subsidiary that had once provided enormous profits. The T.P.M. & M. served its purpose for nearly forty years, and during that time, its business establishments grew from crude shed-like buildings to modern department stores. Its sales in 1920 reached a peak of $1,136,143.61,[37] and in 1933, the company recorded a loss of $20,341.72[38] on the final liquidation of the merchandise inventory.

CHAPTER 5

Living Conditions

Officials of the Texas & Pacific Coal Company planned to build what they hoped would be a permanent camp around their new coal mines. Within a few years, hundreds of houses were constructed, and water and light plants were installed. Schools and churches received immediate attention, and doctors were brought in to give care to the company employees and their families. A great deal was done to provide satisfactory living conditions so as to keep the employees content to remain in the employ of the company.

When the Texas & Pacific Coal Company bought the Johnson Mines in November, 1888, there were a few privately owned shacks on the property. The company bought these shacks from the owners, and in this way all buildings became the property of the Texas & Pacific Coal Company. At no time thereafter was an individual allowed to erect any building on the company's property in Thurber.

During the winter of 1888 and 1889 the company, under the leadership of Colonel R. D. Hunter, began building homes for the miners. In the beginning the houses were simple and rather small, and the majority of them were little more than roofs over the occupants. Many of them were T or L shaped. Later larger houses were built, some more or less in the manner of bungalows, and eventually a number of brick cottages were constructed.

In the older parts of Thurber, there was an obvious lack of planning as far as the location of houses was concerned. Front doorways often opened into someone else's back door, and the houses were placed at various angles to one another. It has been told that since the carpenters were allowed to use their own judgment about selecting the site for a house, they were inclined to choose any level open space that presented itself even if it meant constructing the house "out of line" with the neighboring houses.[1]

With the exception of a few streets near the business district, the Thurber residential areas were far from attractive. Many of the old houses were painted red, green, or a dull yellow. Occasionally there would be a house painted grey. It was not customary to re-paint the outside of the houses when the original paint wore off, and after several years, most of the structures acquired a definite weather beaten and drab appearance.

Many of the yards were rocky and not suitable for grass and, with the exception of the downtown areas, lawns were not in evidence to any extent. The characteristic red picket fence certainly did nothing to enhance the appearance of a weather beaten house and a bare, rocky yard. Not all yards had a fence, however, because the company increased the rent whenever a fence was added to the premises. Hundreds of houses lacked modern sewage and bath facilities. At the same time, there were scores of houses that were very attractive in appearance. Many were equipped with every modern convenience in contrast to houses occupied by the greater part of the population.

W. K. Gordon was correct when he made the following appraisal of living conditions in Thurber: "In the beginning housing and living conditions were extremely poor, but as time passed conditions improved until the town became a model village with all the conveniences found in other progressive towns of Texas."[2]

Visitors usually came to Thurber expecting to see an insignificant mining camp, but their reaction was much like that of Ranger Captain McDonald when he reported to Adjutant General Mabry: "I was greatly surprised at the magnitude of these mines and it would pay you well to visit them. The Mining Co. owns and manages all stores and everything in the town is very systematically managed."[3]

Governor Sayers' reaction was similar to that of McDonald's when he visited Thurber in May, 1902, and commented: "That is the greatest thing in Texas. Why I expected to find only a little coal mining town, but it far surpassed all my expectations."[4]

If in 1920[5] one stood on Graveyard Hill which commanded the town from the north, it would have been possible to look down upon the quadrangle and across to each of the hills which surrounded Thurber, and if the visibility was good, an observer would be able to pick out the distinguishing features of each section. It would only be natural that the observer would focus his attention on the hills first, since from Graveyard Hill, he had an excellent view of the three other hills which were residential areas. These hills were New York Hill to the southeast, Stump Hill to the southwest, and No. 3 Hill to the west.

After scanning the surrounding hills, attention would be drawn to the area within the circle, and the first structure that would be noted would be the giant red brick smokestack which towered above the northeastern section of the quadrangle. This quadrangle was formed by company owned buildings—some of wood and others of red brick. Scattered across the quadrangle were stepping stones for the pedestrians, because in spite of the fact that Thurber had the largest brick plant west of the Mississippi River, there were few sidewalks and no paved streets.

The Opera House and the Dormitory were on the north side of the "Square;" on the west side were the grocery store, dry goods store, store office, mining office, and two or three residences. The hotel was west of the mining office. The public school playground and one or two residences bounded the southern side, while on the east there were the drug store, barber shop, post office, hardware, market, and fire station. Just slightly out of line with the eastern side of the quadrangle was the combination ice factory and water and light plant, and in the center of the southern half of the quadrangle was the band stand.

Several roads and streets radiated from this quadrangle. Beginning on the northeast corner, there was a roadway to Graveyard Hill.

Immediately east of this road was Park Row. South of Park Row and at the extreme southern end of the eastern side was the road to Stephenville. Almost due west of the Stephenville road was a road to Stump Hill. North of this road and practically in the center of the west side of the quadrangle was the road to Ranger, Strawn, and Number 3 Hill. North of the grocery store on the west side was the road to Mingus and due north of this road was Hunter's Avenue which today (1946) is the highway to Mingus and Strawn.

An observer on Graveyard Hill would note that there were other roadways scattered about the populated areas, but with the exception of two there was nothing impressive about these roads. The exceptions were Marston Street and Church Street, parallel streets which ran north and south. They radiated from the Stephenville Road a short distance from the quadrangle.

Marston Street, or Silk Stocking Row, as it was often called, was named for Edgar L. Marston, one time president of the company.[6] Most of the houses on this street were built of Thurber brick. The houses, larger than most Thurber houses, were surrounded by well-kept lawns, neatly trimmed hedges, and shade trees. Company officials and office employees, Thurber's aristocracy, occupied these houses.

Church Street just east of Marston Street was given this particular name because it led to the Baptist, Negro, and Episcopal churches. With one or two exceptions, every house on this street was made of red brick, but unlike those on Marston Street, these houses had no individuality. They were exact replicas of one another, and they reminded one of small general stores. The houses were square with flat roofs, and the front wall extended about three feet higher than the other walls.

Southeast of Church Street was Nigger Town. The negro population of Thurber was never very large and certainly not of a migratory nature. Many of the negroes worked in the mines, and when the mines closed, they continued to live in Thurber by doing odd jobs, particularly yard work. A few old negroes still live in their old company shacks, and the company has never insisted that they move elsewhere.[7]

Many of the men who worked at the brick plant lived on Park Row which began at the northeast corner of the quadrangle. This street was so named because the baseball park was at its eastern end. It was not an attractive street, because the houses were weather-beaten in appearance; the yards were bare and rocky, and during the baseball season, the heavy traffic made the street extremely dusty.

Hunter's Avenue, named for R. D. Hunter, began on the opposite side of the quadrangle from Park Row and extended west to the Palo Pinto County line. During Hunter's active years in Thurber, his official residence was on this street. The Methodist Church, Catholic Church, and Catholic School were located on Hunter's Avenue.

Just below Stump Hill and extending west and north along the base of Number 3 Hill was an area known as the Flat. This area, being one of the older residential sections, was crowded with scores of red and green houses and was occupied principally by the Irish.[8] There was nothing really outstanding about the Flat unless it was the Thurber jail which was located in the northernmost part of the section.

This jail, built of red brick, measured sixteen feet by twenty feet and it had two cells.[9] The size of the Thurber jail was a fair indication of the scarcity of lawlessness in the town. Occasionally some drunkard would be put in jail until he sobered up, or some hot headed Irishman might engage in too many fist fights and would be put in jail until he could control his temper.

Number 3 Hill, the most western of the hills which encircled the town, was known as Number 3 because Mine #3 was opened there. From a great distance, one could see the almost triangular shaped mine dump, and near this bluish-gray shale dump, there was a tall, slender mine smoke stack that towered above everything else. As the distance decreased, one could distinguish the single-track railroad which climbed the steep incline to the top of the hill. This railroad led to the mines and during most of the day, engines puffed up and down the grade—sometimes pulling empty cars and at other times a long string of cars heaped with coal.

Upon reaching the top, the railroad bisected Number 3 Hill. Of all the residential areas in Thurber, Hill Number 3 was by far the most colorful and the most interesting. To go to this part of Thurber was like stepping into the native lands of Poles, Italians, and many other nationalities. In many of the yards, there was a rock or brick oven and the smell of fresh bread filled the air most of the day. Grape arbors were quite common, and there was always a comfortable bench or two in the shade of the arbor. Entrances to these quaint transplanted European homes usually were at the side or rear and not at the front as is common in American homes.

When the last strike occurred in 1921, most of the miners and their families moved into the tents set up just across the Erath County line in Palo Pinto County. As the houses were vacated, the company removed all windows and doors and stored them away.[10] With the exception of just a few families who remained, Number 3 Hill was deserted by 1923. In the daylight, the people of Thurber did not think so much of the rows of houses standing without windows and doors, but as darkness began to fall and the last rays of light streaked through the gaps, the remaining population became conscious of the ghost-like appearance of the forsaken homes.

There was about the place such a look of desolation and neglect that one could not help but feel the impending doom that overshadowed the entire town. Number 3 Hill was as vital to Thurber as is the heart to the human body. Those who lived on this hill were the producers of Thurber's prosperity, and their departure was the beginning of the end of Thurber. Those who remained behind were wise enough to sense the ultimate abandonment of the town, but they continued to live in the hopes that some new and unexpected force would intervene and save Thurber from the fate that was to be.

Those who continued to live in Thurber after the miners from a dozen nations had left missed the songs of the "old countries"; the friendliness and cheerfulness of the people on the hill; they missed the smell of the fresh baked bread, and they missed the blasts of the Number 3 Mine whistle.

Stump Hill, so called because of the great number of stumps in evidence when houses were first constructed there, was southeast of Number 3 Hill. There were fewer houses on this hill than on Number 3. At the extreme northern end of Stump Hill, there was a small white building, the Christian Church. Leading up the side of the hill to this church was a brick pathway. This pathway was not the usual set of steps, but was a brick incline about three or four feet wide, and about every eighteen inches a row of bricks protruded about three-quarters of an inch and thus served to give the pedestrian a foothold as he mounted or descended the hill stairway with slight incline.

Immediately after the mines closed, there was a decline in the population not only among the miners, but among workers in other trades and occupations. From 1921 to 1926, the houses on Stump Hill were vacated, torn down, and sold as second-hand lumber.[11]

This demolition continued until Stump Hill was just a bare hill overlooking the town. Newcomers to Thurber never thought of it as ever having been a residential section of the town, especially after the company constructed a first class nine hole golf course on the southern end. The name Stump Hill gradually fell into disuse except when the "old timers" referred to that particular site. In the later years of Thurber's existence, people spoke of the former Stump Hill as "up on the golf course."

New York Hill was southeast of Stump Hill and between the two hills was a body of water known as Little Lake. Work was begun on the New York Hill addition in 1918 when houses were needed for company executives who were moving from the East to Thurber after the Ranger oil boom. Since so many of the persons for whom these houses were built were from the East, the hill was named New York Hill.[12] The homes on this hill were by far the most attractive in Thurber. Many of them were two-story houses with beautiful hardwood floors, and spacious living rooms. The outside of each house was painted a soft grey and trimmed in white. The yards were inclosed with low, grey fences, rather than the ugly red picket fence, and the people who occupied the homes had a commanding view of the town and the surrounding countryside. A single roadway and a set of brick steps led to New York

Hill. In 1933, the order came to abandon Thurber and the houses on New York Hill, like the houses on Number 3 Hill and Stump Hill, were sold to anyone who wished to buy them, provided they would be moved from company lands.[13]

Graveyard Hill overlooked the town from the north. The location of the cemetery here accounted for the name. The company began building houses on this hill in 1909.[14] Long before this section became a residential area, two large wooden water towers were built on the hill. Water from these towers supplied the people who lived near the quadrangle.[15] Sometime prior to the 1920s a large steel standpipe replaced the wooden towers.

The cemetery was on the western end of the hill. At one time, an effort was made to maintain a well-kept cemetery, but the lack of

A Mexican grave in the Thurber Cemetery, with an iron bedstead used as a fence. Photograph by Mary Jane Gentry, 4 July 1941. Courtesy, 93-41, Thurber, Texas, Photograph Collection, Special Collections, The University of Texas at Arlington Libraries, Arlington, Texas.

Graveyard scene in the Thurber Cemetery. Photograph by Mary Jane Gentry, 4 July 1941. Courtesy, 93-41, Thurber, Texas, Photograph Collection, Special Collections, The University of Texas at Arlington Libraries, Arlington, Texas.

systematic planning and landscaping made this impossible. People were allowed to dig a grave wherever they wished, and in consequence of this policy, graves were located in all directions and at every possible angle. Fences of all descriptions surrounded the graves and every type of decoration was in evidence.

As a person looked across the cemetery, he could see here a child's grave fenced in by the iron frame of the child's own bed, and nearby one covered with pieces of colored bottles and broken dishes. Many of the graves were decorated with photographs of the deceased person and members of his family, and although these photographs were under glass to protect them from the rain, the sunlight faded them until only scraps of discolored paper remained. Once a year, the company sent men to burn the grass and cut back the brush. Other than this annual service, dozens of graves received no care whatsoever. The reason for such neglect was that people moved away from Thurber without making arrangements for the upkeep of the family graves.[16]

There is one grave in this almost forgotten cemetery that has an interesting story attached to it. Anton Bercilli, a Pole, was a bachelor who presumably had no relatives or very close friends in this country. He feared that when he died no one would want to be responsible for his burial. Along with the dread of being neglected, the fear that dirt might touch his body became an obsession.

Several years before he died, he went to the cemetery, selected the location for his grave and began to dig it. People laughed about him, and the more curious ones would visit him while he was preparing his last resting place. When he finished digging the grave, he lined it with sheet iron. He made two sets of iron doors—one set just above the casket, and the second set near the top of the grave. He planned that when he was buried, the doors just above the casket would be locked and the key was to be slipped through a crack in the doors and allowed to fall onto the casket. The second set of doors would be locked in the same manner and then dirt would be piled into the remaining opening.

The old man died in 1925 and his wishes were fulfilled. To this day, one can see the fairly large cross which he erected at the head of his grave, to which he fastened a framed picture of Christ and several pictures of himself.

Today the Thurber cemetery is almost hidden from view. Bushes, briars, and grass have grown higher than the markers. Many of the picket fences have fallen over, or like many of the taller monuments, seem to be hanging in mid-air. Dozens of graves can never be accurately located again, and within a few years few traces of this cemetery will be visible. It is only with great difficulty that the cemetery can be reached.

There are no houses on any of the hills today, and little evidence remains to remind one of the hundreds of homes that were once there. Possibly ten houses remain in Thurber at the present, and they are near the quadrangle.

Provision had to be made for those company employees who were not married and who had no place to live. As early as 1890, the company maintained boarding and rooming houses for the convenience of these employees.[17] Later it was the policy of the company to operate a hotel and allow individuals to maintain private rooming and boarding houses if they were interested in such enterprises.[18]

Many of the unmarried men stayed at the Knox Hotel, one of the famous buildings in Thurber. This hotel was also the headquarters for all travelers passing through Thurber. The local paper advertised the Knox Hotel as follows:

Best Hotel West of Fort Worth. This Hotel is first-class in every respect; Lighted throughout by Electricity; Hot, Cold and Mineral Water Baths at all hours, free; a home for the Traveling Man; Rates $2.00 per day, with Special Rates to opera troupes.

First-Class Livery Stable in Connection. Where Good Teams can be Hired at Reasonable rates. This Concord Stage Meets all trains at Thurber Junction.

Flowing Mineral Water in Hotel Knox Yard.[19]

On April 25, 1907, fire destroyed the Knox Hotel.[20] The company built a new hotel to replace the Knox. This new building, later known as the Plummer Hotel, surpassed the Knox in a material way, but those who had lived at the Knox felt that the fire had destroyed something that could never be replaced.[21]

During the Ranger oil boom, there was a great increase in the office personnel of the Texas Pacific Coal and Oil Company. In order to accommodate the single men and women who came in at that time, the company built a large two story dormitory just west of the Opera House.[22] When the company moved its offices to Fort Worth in 1933, there was no longer any need for the Dormitory; so like many other buildings in Thurber, it was torn down and sold as second-hand lumber.[23]

Along with the problem of providing for adequate housing facilities, for both married and single employees, the company had to provide for a satisfactory water system. In the early years of Thurber's existence, the problem of securing safe drinking water was not easy to solve. Colonel Hunter described the situation as follows:

> When I reached there they [Johnson miners] were getting water from the ponds or tanks as they called them, but I did not think the water was good enough. I made arrangements then with the T&P Railway Company to haul water from the railroad tank. We had water hauled in iron railway tanks; hauled from near Strawn; from what there is termed the Strawn tank. That must be about five or six miles from our camp at Thurber. Our nearest supply of water suitable for drinking and things of that sort was at Strawn—according to my estimate of those things. . . .[24]

Later, in an *Annual Report,* Hunter explained why this means of securing water was unsatisfactory and the steps which the company took to improve the situation.

> The Company since its organization has had to depend on the T&P Railway Co. for its water supply for the use of the camp and which entailed a very great outlay on the part of the Co. say from $400 to $500 per month. Not only this but during the drought last summer and fall we were threatened with a famine of the necessary supplies, the wells along the line of the road becoming dry and at this juncture I became somewhat alarmed about the supply for our mines and concluded that the best and only feasible plan was to construct tanks and a reservoir capable of holding sufficient water to supply our village for such a length of time as would remove all doubt as to our wants in this respect. I have therefore gone to considerable expense in carrying out the plan and now have a large reservoir about complete which covers an area of about 20 acres and capable of containing 30,000,000 gallons of good water which will not only sup-

ply our camp for a number of years but also will be valuable in
case of fire—the fall being great enough to throw water 40 feet
above the top of the highest building in our village.[25]

Work on this reservoir which was to be known as the Little Lake was
begun in 1891 and completed in 1892. W. K. Gordon did the actual planning of this lake and he made the dam three times the strength required
to hold back the water. As a result of this forethought, the people whose
homes were just below the dam always felt secure.[26]

The water from the Little Lake was piped to a central water station
down in town and then stored in wooden tanks on Graveyard Hill. The
water was distributed about the town by wagons equipped with wooden
tanks capable of holding five or six barrels. The price of this water varied from ten cents to twenty-five cents a barrel during the various years
in which the water wagons were used.[27] The water was muddy and had
to be settled before it could be used. Although the "water barrels" did
not solve the problem as far as sanitation was concerned, they did provide each family with an adequate supply of water.

By 1896, the company officials decided that a greater supply of water
was needed.[28] W. K. Gordon began the construction of a new reservoir
which was to be known as the Big Lake. This new lake was southeast of
Thurber and its capacity was many times that of the Little Lake.

A great dam was thrown up just southeast of Thurber and a
lake impounded on the Company property. The whole water-
shed was fenced off and no cattle permitted to graze on the
ground that drained into the lake.[29]

Also in 1896, the company officials ordered the construction of a new
water plant. The cost of the Big Lake and the improved plant was
$21,138.45.[30] The company began to pipe water into the houses, but as late
as 1920, there were still some families in Thurber who depended upon a
water barrel.[31] A large steel stand pipe replaced the old wooden tanks on
Graveyard Hill, and in 1919, the company installed a modern filtering

plant. From then on, the Thurber water system was very satisfactory.[32] "The city water system kept pace with all modern improvements and the company officials spent thousands of dollars keeping the water supply pure. People in Thurber used all the water they wished and paid a flat rate of one dollar and fifty cents each month—this included all water used in the house, on the lawns and on the gardens."[33]

A small electric light plant was built in 1895,[34] making Thurber one of the first places in West Texas to have electric service. The first generator was made from a wooden armature and was constructed in the Thurber machine shop. In 1901 a big direct current dynamo was installed,[35] and years later (the date is not available) the company installed an alternating current dynamo which generated 23,000 volts. After the installation of this dynamo, people in Thurber used both direct and alternating currents. Everyone spoke of "day" and "night" current—the AC being used at night and the DC being used during the day. Every house was wired with two circuits. Changes in the type of current were not made by the clock but by the sun. The AC came on when the sun set and turned off when the sun began to rise regardless of the season of the year. It was necessary to use the two currents because motors, fans, and other mechanical equipment were on direct current, and it would have entailed too much expense to get new AC equipment. Company employees used all the electricity they wished and the only charge was 25¢ a month for each drop in the house.[36]

From 1889 to June 1890, Thomas Lawson, who operated the saloon, supplied the camp with ice. After June of 1890 the coal company supplied the camp with ice.[37] After the company took over the saloon and the population of the town increased, Colonel Hunter decided to build an ice plant. A seventeen ton ice plant was installed and put into operation in 1896.[38] This plant manufactured all the ice used in Thurber and also provided ice for much of the surrounding country. During its first year of operation, the company received an order for ice from the T&P Railroad and the company carried this item regarding the order: "The Thurber Ice Plant for the next sixty days will run day and night. The contract has been secured to furnish the Texas and Pacific Railway

Company 600 tons of ice, to be delivered at Big Springs for storage as fast as made. It is stored there for use next summer."[39]

Towering above the combination water plant and ice plant was a giant red brick smokestack bearing tall metal numerals 1908. The daughter of one of the men who helped build the stack often tells the story of how her father climbed to the top of the smokestack, swung one leg over the rim, gulped down the whiskey in his flask, christened the stack by smashing the empty flask on its side, and then hurried down the ladder before the "altitude" could make him dizzy.[40]

When the Texas & Pacific Coal Company began the development of Thurber, it was mindful of the health of its employees. The company maintained a small hospital and employed a staff of doctors, whose duty it was to maintain a healthful condition. In the early days a family made known its need for a doctor, and one of the company doctors would report to the home and prescribe for the sick.

The plan for medical care of company employees up until 1899 is adequately described by R. H. Ward, assistant general manager of the company:

> We collect or deduct from the wages of all our employees fifty
> cents per month, which goes to the hospital fund. We charge
> fifty cents a month for hospital funds. For that fifty cents per
> month we give the miner his medical attendance, hospital
> service, and everything the officers think proper in connection
> with the health and efficiency and maintaining of the people
> there. Every man is supposed to agree to the fifty cents deduc-
> tion when we hire him. Most who come there understand it.
> It might have to be explained to him. We would explain it to
> him of course,—tell him we would keep that for the purpose
> of employing a physician to attend him when sick or hurt. We
> never make any exception in the management of the mines on
> account of one man. . . . The Company makes contract with
> all the physicians, and the miners have nothing to do with
> employing the physicians, nor with the dispensation of this

fund. . . . There are no physicians living there [in Thurber] except the two employed by the Company.[41]

Many people distrusted the company doctors, because they felt that the doctors acted as "spies" for the company officials. No doubt they did make more than the usual routine reports; in fact the following extracts from the minutes of the store managers meetings prove that they did their bit toward furthering the sales of the T.P.M. & M. Company:

> I think perhaps the doctors employed by the Company could do some missionary work for the Mercantile Co. They cover the entire camp several times each day and when they see a peddler at the miners door, if they would find out why they preferred to patronize the peddler in preference to the company, letting the General Manager of the Mercantile Co. know the results of their questioning, it would give us something to work on.[42]

Two weeks later Tom Tennant, general manager, and C. S. Campbell, an employee in the store office, reported, "That they had called on the company physicians, and that they had all promised to use every effort possible to advance the company's best interests."[43]

At stated periods these company doctors attended eastern schools of medicine, and the company paid all their expenses. In this way the company attempted to keep its doctors aware of the advances being made in the fields of medicine and sanitation. Epidemics were rare in Thurber and precaution was taken to keep the water supply pure, and to dispose of all sewage, garbage, and trash in such a way that they would not contaminate living conditions in Thurber.

In later years, the company deducted a dollar each month from the pay of all employees and the employee was allowed to choose whichever company physician he preferred. By the middle of the 1920s, employees paid the medical fee only if they wished. In almost all cases this was more desirable because the people felt that the doctors were more efficient when they engaged in private practice than when they made "sick calls" in the capacity of a company employee.

The Texas & Pacific Coal Company provided for schools and churches almost from the beginning of Thurber. In his *Annual Report, 1889,* Hunter listed churches and schools in his list of buildings erected during that year.[44] Along with his desire to provide schools, Colonel Hunter was anxious to establish a public library. The *Stephenville Empire* carried this item regarding his efforts: "The mines will soon have the only public library in the County as Colonel Thurber has just donated 500 volumes and Mr. Hunter, the president, donated $15 per month for its support. An old miner and a most excellent citizen of Thurber has been selected as librarian." [45]

The first school, established in 1889, was little more than a shack, but in 1906, the company erected a new building just south of the quadrangle.[46] Since no school taxes were paid in Thurber, the company supplemented the per capita appropriation so that salaries would be comparable to those paid in larger school systems.

In 1933, the company transferred the few remaining high school students to Strawn, providing bus and driver. In the same year, the elementary faculty was reduced to four instead of the usual seven or eight teachers. In 1935, the school was closed and all students rode the company bus to Strawn. By the end of 1937, all school equipment was either sold or distributed among the neighboring schools, and the school buildings were torn down.

In addition to the pubic school, there was a Catholic Academy which was built in 1894. It was under the supervision of the Sisters of Incarnate Word from San Antonio. This academy was closed in 1923.[47]

All major religious denominations were represented in Thurber. Whenever the demand rose for a particular church, the company built the church and the parsonage. Regardless of the many criticisms which might be made with regard to the Texas & Pacific Coal Company, no one can rightfully criticize the attitude of its officials toward the Thurber churches. The company furnished water, lights, coal, and later gas to all churches and parsonages free of charge. All ministers were given free house rent, and since the church buildings belonged to the company, the company paid for all painting, roofing, and other repair work.

The Presbyterian and Catholic churches were built in 1892; the Baptist and Methodist churches in 1901, and the Negro Church in 1909.[48] Exact dates are not available for the years in which the First Christian and Episcopal churches were built.

The First Christian Church burned when lightning struck it in about 1922 and it was never rebuilt. The Episcopal Church was disbanded in the late 1920s and the Methodist Church ceased to function in the early 1930s. The Baptist Church burned in 1933,[49] and in 1937, the Catholic Church was moved to Mingus where the building is still used as a church.

CHAPTER 6

Recreation

Recreational activities in Thurber were more colorful than those of any nearby town. Why shouldn't they be? Thurber's population was drawn from at least twenty different countries, and each group of people carried on its entertainment in its own way. During Thurber's heyday, a person might attend an Irish wake, a Polish wedding dance, an Italian baptism ceremony, and a real west Texas badger fight all in one night.

There were many people outside Thurber who disapproved of some of its activities, and it is a well established fact that Thurber was considered to be a "tough town." It was "wet" when all the rest of Erath County was "dry"; public dances were numerous in Thurber at a time when the staid populace of the county frowned upon dancing, and badger fighting and free beer that followed the fight were questioned by the disapproving rural population. In many ways Thurber shocked its neighbors, and no doubt the activities within the town provided a juicy morsel for those bent on gossip. But in spite of all outside criticism, life in Thurber went on. It was as impossible for the people of Thurber to settle down to a set of cut-and-dried social activities as it would have been for them to converse in any one language.

In many ways the Opera House was the "heart" of Thurber's social life. On its stage appeared the most popular shows of the day. It was there that the cowardly badger was forced to come out and meet the vicious bull dog, and it was also there that one attended the most brilliant balls of the season.

The Opera House was a large frame building which the company built in 1896,[1] on the north side of the quadrangle. The building measured 50 x 100 feet and the stage was 30 x 50 feet. The outside of the building was too bare and flat looking to be attractive, but upon entering the Opera House, one was favorably impressed. Within the spacious lobby was the ticket office, and on the right as one entered was the stairway leading to the "family circle" and the balcony.

The dress circle accommodated 158 persons, and the seating capacity of the parquet was 288. The family circle was equipped to seat 185 and on either side there were a few private boxes. The overall seating capacity for the Opera House was 655.[2] The Opera House was further described in the *Texas Mining and Trade Journal:*

> There are three large dressing rooms in the rear of the stage and the entire building is lighted with 136 incandescent lights, with a large and beautiful cluster in the center. In the parquet as in other portions of the house, it is arranged to give the seats sufficient symmetrical elevation to give an unobstructed view of the stage, but the parquet was built with the view of utilizing for balls, and can be cleared of the seats with but little inconvenience. The building is heated by steam, large bronze mains encircling and crossing the entire structure.[3]

Many balls were held in the Opera House and they were said to be brilliant affairs. The first Grand Ball was held on October 19, 1896, and was the first attraction held in the Opera House. The following excerpt from the local paper may be a bit on the gushing side of journalism, but it gives a good description of the first Grand Ball:

> Of the ball, we can give but a faint idea of its brilliancy. It was a grand success, over thirty-five couples participating among

them many visitors from other towns. The scene presented in the ballroom was a lovely one—beautiful ladies, handsomely attired, and gallant men, and one could not see depicted in their countenances any thought of yesterday or tomorrow, all living in the present, and getting from these few hours all of life. . . . The music was furnished by Prof. Mueller's orchestra of Fort Worth, and was pronounced superb. Handsomely-gotten up souvenir programmes were given out as the guests entered. These programmes contained twenty-one numbers, consisting of grand march, waltz, two-step, schottische, polka and minuet dances to which were added four extra—making twenty-five numbers in all. After the eleventh number a light lunch was served, consisting of coffee, cake, and dainty sandwiches, after which the programme was taken up again, and 'twas 3 A.M. when the orchestra struck up the "Home Sweet Home" waltz. . . . [4]

The chief reason for the construction of the Opera House was to bring traveling show companies to Thurber. All dramatic and operatic companies touring the Southwest stopped at Thurber[5] where there was always a great deal of money. Such performances as "Kentucky Colonel," "Pawn Ticket 210," "Plunger," "A Brother's Crime," and "Race for the Widow" were well attended.[6] The company spent vast sums of money for stage settings and almost any type of setting could be found there.

Each year the junior and senior classes of the Thurber High School presented their annual plays in the Opera House and this was always a gala occasion for the high school students. The Opera House was not well suited to high school plays because the acoustics were poor and few students were able to speak loudly enough to be heard in all parts of the building.[7]

The Opera House changed with the times, and it eventually became a movie house, though road shows and vaudeville troupes occasionally made Thurber during these later years. With the advent of sound films, the Opera House was abandoned as a movie house. Remodeling would have been too expensive and the remaining population did not need so large a place. Sound films were shown in the former Presbyterian Church until 1936, after which time there was no movie house in Thurber.

The Thurber Opera House made its debut with a Grand Ball, but its last performance was a Baptist revival. In 1933, the Baptist Church burned during a revival and the services were continued in the Opera House. Like all other buildings in Thurber, the Opera House was torn down and sold as second-hand lumber.

"The Fourth of July and Labor Days were Holy Days in Thurber."[8] Both celebrations were all day affairs. The opening event would be a parade led by the Queen of the day and her attendants. The parade began in the vicinity of the quadrangle and ended at the pavilion. This pavilion was an open structure about 120 feet long and 40 feet wide, and it

Labor Day Parade on the quadrangle in Thurber. Courtesy, 93-41, Thurber, Texas, Photograph Collection, Special Collections, The University of Texas at Arlington Libraries, Arlington, Texas.

The Labor Day Queen in Thurber with her court. Courtesy, 93-41, Thurber, Texas, Photograph Collection, Special Collections, The University of Texas at Arlington Libraries, Arlington, Texas.

was located just north of Park Row. Around the pavilion, there was a great open space which was used as picnic grounds.

To end the day's festivities, there was a dance. An imported orchestra might furnish the music, but often one or more of the Thurber bands would be used. Dances were held frequently at the pavilion, particularly during the summer months. An invitation to a Calico Ball at the pavilion read as follows:

> For the giddy whirl
> You will find the girl
> Whose dress will compare
> With the tie you'll find there.
>
> A dollar bill
> Dropped in the till
> Will quite suffice
> For music and ice.[9]

Carnivals or medicine shows which stopped in Thurber used the pavilion and the surrounding grounds. In later years it served as a skating
rink and was used for the weekly dances.

There were always several bands in Thurber. The Mexicans had
their own band, the Italians theirs, and the third one was the so-called
American band. All these bands were rated as good, but the Italian
band was rated the best.[10] The band stand was located in the center of
the quadrangle near the Knox Hotel.

The Sunday night concerts were the most popular, and people came
to Thurber from miles around to hear the music. These bands participated in many types of celebrations and often played for conventions
and public gatherings in the nearby towns. The Italian band often
played at the Dallas Fair.[11]

Costume balls were popular in Thurber, and whenever such a ball
was scheduled, costumers would come to Thurber, set up headquarters
in the Knox Hotel and outfitted those who were to attend the ball. These
costumes were rented for a nominal fee and saved one the trouble and
expense of making costumes.[12]

Apron and necktie parties were in evidence in the early 1900s. At this
type of party, each lady was requested to bring an unhemmed apron and
a tie to match. A cake would be given to the gentleman who did the neat-
est job of hemming his lady's apron. During the remainder of the evening
the lady wore the apron and the gentleman wore the matching tie.[13]

Another mode of entertainment was to go sightseeing to the mines.
This was often reserved for out-of-town guests, and on a Sunday afternoon, it was not uncommon to see the engine pulling two or three car
loads of young men and women up the hill and out to the mines. The
local paper described one of these sightseeing trips as follows:

Last Tuesday night a jolly crowd of young people accepted an
invitation from Mr. J. R. Williams to visit and explore No. 7,
or Queen Bess shaft, he having arranged the trip in honor of
several young lady friends, guests at the Hotel Knox, and at

9 o'clock a special coach on the "Calamity Central" pulled by engine No. 142 . . . was boarded and the run made.

Arriving at the shaft, the party was met and welcomed by Pit Boss Heatherington, who . . . landed the guests safely on the pit's bottom . . . and continued their acts of courtesy by showing them through the mine and explaining to the young ladies everything of interest, and finally . . . gave them a ride over the incline to the "face" of coal. The cars, a dozen in number, in which the excursionists took this ride, are manipulated by the "rope haulage" system, and went skimming through the weird and craggy roadways at a fearfully rapid rage of speed, but with the utmost safety, for perhaps a half mile.

The "face" inspected and the modus operandi of mining explained, the electric signal was given to the "rope haulage" engineer, and the crowd of sightseers were landed again in the brilliantly-lighted terra firma. Experiences were exchanged, and an all-round jolly good time indulged in, and then the ascent to the top was made, and the special coach boarded for Thurber, everyone indulging in merry-making.[14]

Volunteer firemen always managed to celebrate at least once a month after fire practice. They would have a barbecue which was often preceded by a Kangaroo Kort Session. During the Kort Session, the men indulged in a great deal of hilarity as the copy of the following court summons indicates. The summons is reproduced verbatim.[15]

THURBER FIRE DEPT.
State of Thurber
vs
Mr. E. Buchanan
Asst. Cheese
YE HONORABLE SUMMONS
Mr. Mose Miller

Dear Sir:-

KNOW YE THIS:

The Honorable Kangaroo Kort at Thurber Fire department will convene Wednesday Night at Seven O'clock for the purpose of spreading it's stuff.

It is alleged that the defendant in the case to be tried has failed to live up to the high ideals of a Brave Fireman.

He is furthermore charged with tardiness and Truancy in attending fires. Also, in the case of a feed or banquet he is ALWAYS on time and is alleged to have been on the spot on two or three different occasions before time and generally starves himself from three to five days before a feed.

In plain United States he is charged with being a "BELLY FIREMAN."

Therefore, you (whose names appear above), are hereby summoned to appear in this Honorable Kangaroo Kort of Jury Service.

The Kort requests that you state your price to the Attorneys thus saving time by eliminating competitive bidding.

Given this day January 30, 1923 under seal my hand.

T.A. PARKER
Judge Kangaroo Kort, Thurber
Fire Dept. State of Thurber
ATTEST: J. IRVINE & M. L. ODOM
Prosecuting Attorneys

There was a social and athletic club to which a large number of the employees belonged. This club was open every night and members could go there to read, listen to the radio, bowl, play pool, or visit with other members. Dances were held frequently and invitations were sent out to non-members. Dances were well attended and people came from as far as Fort Worth and Dallas. The dance of the year was the "Annual." In addition to all these social activities, there were always social activities in progress on Number 3 Hill. These activities are described in the chapter, "Foreign Population."

In the field of sports, baseball, golf, tennis, boating, fishing, swimming, and badger fighting were the town's most popular activities. Next to badger fighting, the men of Thurber were most interested in baseball. Men engaged in various trades would organize their own teams and these teams played against one another for practice or an individual team would challenge a baseball team from a nearby town.

The first baseball park was on Graveyard Hill, but sometime about 1906 or 1907, a new park was made at the east end of Park Row. The park was surrounded by a high board fence which was erected in 1907.[16] Games with out-of-town teams were played on Sunday afternoon and in most instances the schedule would provide for a double header. In 1896, the Thurber Colts were the amateur baseball champions of Texas. *The Texas Mining and Trade Journal* commented on the championship game as follows:

The colts "tuk it outen 'em." The Colts are now the champion amateurs of the State.

The Colts claim this, because the Riddle Wonders of Fort Worth held that title, and declared the team that bested them was entitled to it.

So on last Sunday, the game arranged two weeks ago between the Colts and the Wonders was played here in the Thurber park, said to be the fastest in the State, and the Wonders were defeated by a score of 9 to 5 . . . The Wonders team is composed of the best amateur talent to be had from numerous clubs in Fort Worth, with two professionals to strengthen them . . . The Colts is composed of three professionals . . .

They came here as the "Riddle Wonders."

They departed "The Wonders riddled." [17]

Throughout the years of Thurber's baseball activities, its teams were considered "fast teams" in the state baseball.

Boating and fishing were allowed on the Big Lake as well as on the Little Lake, but bathing was prohibited in the Big Lake since it was the source of the town's water supply. The Little Lake was open to anyone, but in order to hunt or fish in the Big Lake one had to belong to the Thurber Club. Originally this Club was the "R. D. Hunter Fishing and Boating Club."[18]

The Little Lake was a popular place to swim, attracting people from neighboring towns. The company constructed a pier and a diving tower, and a set of wooden steps led up the steep incline of the dam. During the 1920s on the fourth of July, a water carnival was held and contestants from outside the town were allowed to enter the many races and contests.

Just above the Little Lake and to the west and south of it on the former Stump Hill was a nine hole golf course maintained by company employees. Golf was a popular game in Thurber, and annual tournaments were well attended. This was one of the last places in the town to be abandoned because even when the order to abandon the town came, men and women played golf until the very end.

Since Thurber was best known for its badger fighting, and since this was the most spectacular sport, more emphasis will be placed on it than any of the others. The *Dallas News* commented on badger fighting in Thurber as follows:

> ... the San Antonio badger fighter is a novice when compared to the Thurber badger fighter. Thurber is the Bayreuth of the sport. There, it is said, the whole population takes part in the sport, and it is carried on with artistic detail that astonishes those who attend the festivals. When the business men of New York came to Texas a few years ago they went home convinced that Thurber stood first in the knowledge of how to construct a badger fight in an artistic way.[19]

Another writer declared that, "More distinguished personages have yanked the ferocious badger right here in Thurber than in any other town in the badger-fighting state."[20] In addition to this boast, it might have been added that more Yankees pulled the badger in Thurber than in any other place in America. Edgar L. Marston, the company president, was an ardent badger fan, and his enthusiasm for the sport did much toward bringing many uninformed Yankees to Thurber to tangle with the badger.[21] Rarely did Marston come to Thurber from New York without at least one "innocent northerner." During the trip, he told the guest of the rare sport of badger fighting, and he never failed to emphasize with much regret that since badgers were getting so scarce, badger fighting would soon be a thing of the past.

It was hard for Marston's guest to keep from wondering about his chances of at least attending a badger fight. He might even get a chance to tussle with this rare Texas fighter. Soon his enthusiasm would be aroused to such a point by Marston's colorful stories that he would ask if it would be at all possible for him to witness such a rare event.

Marston, always the gracious host, would agree to wire his friends in Thurber and ask them to search high and low until they found a badger for his friend. He never failed to ask his confederates in Thurber to wire him as soon as the badger was captured. It was important that his guest have several hours in which to exercise his imagination regarding the terrific struggle he was soon to behold.

Marston's telegram was always answered and in effect read: "Have just captured an unusually fierce badger. Old Dewey is straining to be at him." Marston then explained that Old Dewey was a white, squatty bull dog and a real badger-trimming dog. Even though Old Dewey has been "ripped open" by the vicious claws of badgers so many times that his body was covered with scars, he was still tough and there was plenty of fight left in him.[22]

As Marston's private car neared Texas, his stories increased in color and scope. By the time the car reached Thurber, the Yankee guest was steeped in the traditions of the Old West, and his feeling of adventure increased when he heard Marston's friends assuring him that he would see a first class badger fight that night. The natives told him that he was indeed lucky to see this particular badger fight, because if one wishes to rely upon the opinion of the old timers, this was the most vicious looking badger ever seen in Thurber. In fact, they went on to say that probably there was not another one like it, even in the remote hills beyond the town. Yes, indeed, the Yankee was a lucky man. Never again would he experience quite the same gamut of emotions that he was to experience that night in the Thurber Opera House.

As nine o'clock, the usual starting time, approached, men began to make their way toward the Opera House. Throughout the crowd ran a wave of genuine excitement and enthusiasm. The people thrilled to a good badger fight and every effort was made to make each fight better than the last one. The entire population was in on the conspiracy and the guest never had a chance to suspect the deception.

As the stranger entered the well lighted Opera House, his attention was drawn immediately to the stage. There was Old Dewey, snarling, growling and tugging at his rope. All of his attention seemed to be centered upon a barrel which had been placed on its side in a not too obscure section of the stage. It was very likely that Marston's friend was quick to surmise that the "fiercest badger ever brought to Thurber" crouched within that barrel.

Since a gunny sack hung over the opening of the barrel, he could not see the badger, but he noticed a long rope which trailed out of the barrel and on across the stage. No doubt the badger would have to be pulled out in order to get the fracas started. Near the barrel stood a bald-headed man of stern and sweaty aspect; armed with a brick, and he threatened murder in every degree to anyone who came near and unduly agitated the excitable badger.[23]

"A large crowd assembled . . . and everyone was anxious to get a few dollars up on the result. The bulldog was fierce and had many backers, but the badger was not without friends who had the money to back their judgment and many large bets were made."[24]

Since the newcomer knew nothing of the badger's size, and since he had only other people's word that the dog could really fight, he decided to place no bets, and as a matter of fact, he was not encouraged to do so. He was content to listen to the excited men around him and to wonder just what would happen when the badger was pulled out upon the stage.

Once or twice he wondered if Old Dewey might not snap his rope and ruin his hopes of seeing a good, fair fight.

What struck him with the most force was the amount of money in evidence. It seemed that every man had a handful of paper money, and many of the bills were of larger denominations, tens, twenties, and fifties. Men argued, gesticulated, and often seemed on the point of exchanging blows. The action was so fast that the stranger found no time to think or make a cool analysis. In fact, he was completely ignored as a sort of interloper who could observe but not participate.

When it was almost time to start the fight, a search was made for some one to pull the badger out of the barrel. *The Thurber Journal* reported that "quite a contest came up as to who should pull the badger from his hiding place and several strove for the honor, but were disqualified on account of having money on the result. Several minutes were consumed in finding some one who did not have anything wagered on the result." [25]

The fundamental law of fair badger fighting was that no undue advantage should be given to either the dog or the badger. It always so happened that the Yankee would be the only man in the Opera House who had not placed a bet and someone would suggest that he pull the badger. "An effort would be made to disqualify him for the honor, but he could prove to the satisfaction of all that he was fully qualified and did not have a cent to bet on the result." [26] Upon the establishment of the necessary proof, he was permitted to pull out the badger.

This was more than he had ever dared to dream. Here was a real thrill and it was with much pride and even more excitement that the newcomer made his way to the stage. Already he was visualizing the astonishment of his eastern friends when he would tell them of his tussle with the most ferocious animal to be found in Texas.

Time was called, the crowd became tense; Old Dewey tugged and yelped for action. Just as the Yankee rather timidly picked up the end of the rope, some one yelled, "Jerk the blamed thing's head off. I'm a-bettin' on the dog." [27]

"A NEW MEMBER"

A "badger fighter" in Thurber. Courtesy, 93-41, Thurber, Texas, Photograph Collection, Special Collections, The University of Texas at Arlington Libraries, Arlington, Texas.

Suddenly, as if a surge of confidence had rushed upon him, he "rared back" his shoulders and got all set for a terrific pull whenever the signal was given. Finally, the signal was given and the rope was pulled with all the might the newcomer could muster. Out of the barrel and onto the stage rolled the "badger."

The force of the pull had been such that the badger rolled to the feet of the Yankee. The nearness of this unexpected type of badger was certainly awe-inspiring. Like those who had "pulled" before him, he stood "amazed, speechless, gazing intently at the object of his pull." [28] Should he drop the rope and run or should he just stand there amid the yelling and hurrahing of the crowd and gaze at this badger which was no animal at all? Instead of pulling out a badger, he had exposed a very ordinary household article whose usefulness was to pass with the installation of bathrooms.

If the Yankee was a good sport, he stood and laughed with the hundreds of roaring men all around him, and claiming his property, he had all sign on the shiny enameled surface. No joke was ever quite so thoroughly enjoyed as a Thurber badger fight, and no beer ever tasted quite so good as the drinks which the victim of the joke set up to the crowd. To show how much he enjoyed the joke played on his friends, Marston would invite the men to the Snake and order many kegs of beer needed to "set them up" to the men. "The visitor then became a life member of the famous 'Badger Club' whose members are scattered all over the world, but whose initiations took place in Thurber." [29]

CHAPTER 7

Foreign Population

Thurber depended primarily on foreign population to mine its coal; there were some negro miners and a few Mexican miners, but Europeans exceeded any other group in numbers. Some of these came to Thurber from other mines in the United States, but many of them came direct from Europe. Those who came directly from Europe usually did so upon the advice of friends or relatives who lived in Thurber. Often a man would come to Thurber and work for many months before sending to his native land for his family.

In order to accommodate those immigrants in Thurber who wished to become American citizens, the District Court for Erath County was allowed to grant citizenship to those who could qualify. Hundreds of Thurber miners took advantage of this arrangement and between 1892 and 1917, many of them received their citizenship papers in Stephenville. While the naturalization records in Stephenville show that men from sixteen European nations applied for and secured their citizenship papers, the records also show that Italians and Poles predominated.[1]

Each applicant was required to file with the District Clerk a (1) Certificate of Arrival, (2) Declaration of Intention, and (3) Petition for Naturalization. The certificate of arrival named the vessel on which the immigrant made his journey to the United States, the port of entry, and the date of arrival. In the declaration of intention, the immigrant announced his intention to become an American citizen and renounced allegiance to his former sovereign. The final paper, the petition for naturalization, contained much of the material included in the declaration of intention and also contained the name of the immigrant's wife and his children if he had any, and his occupation.

When the petition for naturalization was duly signed by the immigrant, his witnesses, and the district clerk, the applicant received his citizenship papers. S. P. Williams who was district clerk during many of the years when immigrants could be naturalized in Stephenville relates this incident:

> An immigrant who signed his name as Novit applied for his citizenship papers. He did not present a certificate of arrival, and I wrote to Galveston, the port of entry, and asked if a man whose last name was Novit, had entered the port on a specified date.
>
> Within a few days, word came from Galveston that no one by that name had entered the port of Galveston. I contacted Novit and explained to him that the immigration authorities had no record that anyone by the name of Novit had entered the port of Galveston.
>
> Novit seemed quite surprised as he listened to my story, and then he hastened to explain that his name had been Astronovitsky when he entered the port, but because it was too long and too hard to pronounce, he had "cut it off at both ends and now his name was Novit."[2]

The records show that there were few refusals to grant citizenship, and only a few of the applicants signed with an X. These naturalization records are very active today, and there is a constant stream of requests for information regarding these naturalized citizens. Most of the information is sought for the purpose of completing old age assistance records.[3]

It was natural for each group of immigrants to bring to Thurber its native customs and practices. Just as the names of the Italians and Poles were more numerous in the naturalization records so were the customs and practices of these two groups more outstanding than those of any other group. People of other nationalities which were in a minority joined the Italians or Poles and accepted their way of life. If they did not ally themselves with one of the two large groups, they made little impression on life in Thurber.

Almost all Italians and Poles lived on Number 3 Hill which was bisected by the railroad that went out to the mines. The Polish people lived on the south side of the track, that is, on the southern end of the hill, and their section of the hill was known as Polander Hill. The Italians lived north of the railroad and their section became known as Italian Hill.

Within each of these sections, there were smaller settlements of Polish or Italian people who came from a particular part of the "old country." For example, the people from around Padua would live near one another, while those from another part of Italy would form a separate, inner group. The natives of southern Italy, particularly the Sicilians, were less apt to mix with the other groups. Northern and southern Italians are much like the Highlanders and Lowlanders of Scotland in that they each think the other inferior and barbaric.

These foreign peoples retained much of their old ways, and visitors in Thurber were amazed to find such European civilizations in a West Texas setting. Because these peoples were newcomers in a strange land, they developed more clannish characteristics than would have existed in their own country. This was evident in their social life. The Poles had their own Dance Hall and the Italians had theirs, and each hall was in use most of the time. Other than the usual Saturday night dances, celebrations were customary after weddings and baptisms, and any national holiday of either the United States or the "old country" called for a dance.

In the early days whenever a Polish couple married, they rode to church in an open buggy. Behind them came the numerous attendants of the bride, and the other friends of both the bride and groom, all laughing and singing. An accordion player sat in the back of the buggy and played the traditional Polish wedding songs. The ride to and from the church offered an opportunity for the bride to display her wedding finery, and she made an attractive picture as she sat high in the seat of the shiniest buggy. Her dress was usually of the traditional white, but regardless of the color of the dress, she always wore a very full white veil. The groom was dressed in his best, and it was with much pride and joy that he drove the bride-to-be to the church.

Most of the weddings were performed in the Catholic Church, but it often happened that the couple was married by a Protestant minister. Whichever church was chosen, that building was decorated with a profusion of flowers. The pews were all occupied, because the Polish people, like the Italians, wanted to be present when their friends were married.[4]

After the ceremony, the newly married couple, the attendants, and all the friends and relatives returned to the bride's home, and the three-day celebration began. There was an endless supply of food and drink and hundreds of people would be served three meals a day. The food was highly seasoned and was prepared by old Polish recipes. Pastries were abundant and varied. Beer, several kinds of wine, and whiskey were within easy reach of anyone who wanted to drink.

When night came the bridal party prepared for the wedding dance. The dance was held either in the bride's home or in the Polish Dance Hall. The orchestra consisted of Polish musicians who were familiar with the fashionable tunes of the day as well as the native folk dances.

In one corner of the Dance Hall there was a very large stack of cheap dinner plates. Before any man could dance with the bride or any of her attendants, he had to throw a silver coin with enough force to break one of these plates. The most effective coin was the silver dollar. Should the man attempt to use a smaller coin, he might find the dance more expensive than he planned for it to be. No matter how many times the man missed the mark, he could never regain any of the coins. They became the property of the bride and he either had to keep on trying or give up his plan to dance.

Before the wedding celebration was over, hundreds of these cheap plates were broken and hundreds of half dollars and silver dollars had been thrown across the room. The bride received all this money, and she could use it to help pay the expense of the celebration, or if her family wished to pay the initial cost, the bride used the money to furnish her new home. It was not uncommon for the newly married couple to receive three or four hundred dollars by the time the celebration was over. If the bride was pretty and popular, and if she chose her attendants with care, the "plate breaking" income would often be more.[5]

Most of the Italian families kept roomers and boarders. These lodgers were usually men the family had known in Italy or men who came from the family's former home town. "As many as six men would share a room, each sleeping on a cot. In these Italian homes, the boarders paid about twenty-eight dollars per month for room, board and laundry."[6]

Two things were essential to every Italian home—an outside oven and a cellar, the first for bread and the second for wine. The oven was made of bricks and clay and resembled an Eskimo igloo in shape. From fifteen to eighteen large loaves of bread could be baked at one baking. Everywhere on the hill and during all the daylight hours, one could smell the delightful yeasty odor of the new-baked bread.[7]

This bread was crusty and the loaves were much larger than the usual baker's loaf. Few Italians purchased their bread from the store, because to them, our bread did not have enough body and toughness. Many Americans liked the Italian bread and would buy a loaf of "pang" whenever there was an extra loaf. The Italian and Polish housewives who kept boarders baked every day, because they firmly believed that "new bread and old wine are best."[8]

The cellar was near the house, and it was in this cellar that the wine, cheese, and meats were stored. As a rule, these cellars were much more than just holes in the ground. Many were well built and had concrete steps and floor. Some of the more elaborate ones had niches in the walls for the wine casks and coolers for the cheese and meats. The wine press and all the other equipment needed to make the wine were in the cellar also.[9] At least one table and a chair or two were in the larger cellars, and it was a cool and inviting spot for a glass of wine on a hot summer afternoon.

Most Italians preferred the Californian grapes for their wines. They ordered carloads of grapes, and the Italian children would be envied by all others, because they had luscious grapes in their lunch boxes when there were none on the retail market for miles around. Even if there had been grapes available in the company stores, they would not have been as tasty as the grapes ordered for the wine. At least that is what the children of the town thought. There was something fascinating and romantic about the truck loads of grapes that went up to the hill, and this was especially true when prohibition was the law of the land. Many children who were not of Italian extraction, wished they were Italians so a car load of grapes would be brought to their home.

Although wine was an essential part of Italian home life, there was little drunkenness among the members of the household. Wine was served with the meals for those who wished it. Each boarder kept his own quart of wine and he placed it upon a special "wine shelf" in the dining room. Whenever he wanted a drink with his meals or between meals, he could pour it from his own supply.[10]

> The children were allowed to have a bit of wine with their meals
> if they wished, but they were absolutely forbidden to drink at
> a public gathering. Each child was taught that he could drink
> in public places only when he was grown. Should his parents
> find him drinking at a wedding dance, or at any other public
> gathering, they sent him home immediately. Italian boys and
> girls were accustomed to having wines in their home, and they
> never felt the need to slip off and drink in secret just because it
> was the smart thing to do.[11]

A favorite Italian meat was salami. Lean hog meat was used to make the salami. In the winter when the family killed the hogs, everyone, including the boarders, helped with the cutting and grinding. The wife prepared many other types of sausages, and she used these meats for breakfast and cold lunches. The greater part of the meat was set aside for the miners' lunches.

In the Italian homes in which there were boarders, there was a huge ice box built on the side of the house. This was the "beer icebox." Each night the men tapped and drank a keg of beer, and Saturday nights they emptied two or more kegs. Sometimes men from the nearby houses would come over and drink, and when they emptied a keg, each man would contribute his part toward the cost of it. On Sunday afternoon when the weather was warm, the men would empty many kegs of beer.[12]

While the men drank their Sunday beer, they engaged in their favorite sport—boccie (bōchi) ball, a game similar to English bowls.

> In this game any number of players could play so long as the sides were equally divided. Solid wooden balls about the size of coconuts were used. One side used balls which were marked with two small grooves cut into the ball and encircling it. The opposing side used balls which were not marked. The game score was usually twelve, but it could be increased if the players desired. A small ball, called a "balline" was thrown to the end of the alley used for playing. Then the players tried to hit the balline with the big balls. Each hit on the balline counted as a score. Should none of the players hit the balline, the large ball nearest to the balline won the score. If the balls of several players were equally spaced from the balline, each was allowed to score. Each player attempted to knock the opponents' balls away from the balline, and he also attempted to move his partners' balls nearer to the balline.
>
> After each game, the losers bought a round of beer for the winning side. And so it went on—playing boccie ball and drinking beer until darkness made it impossible to see.[13]

Most families on the hill had an arbor in the yard. Although most of these arbors were covered with grapevines, many of them were built of oak and mesquite limbs. The men sat under these arbors, drank their beer, sang their native songs, and played games.

The Italians loved music, and they always sang selections from the operas. Since many of the Italians who lived in Thurber were really artists and had beautiful voices, they frequently gave operatic performances. "Il Trovatore" was quite a favorite. On almost any evening one could hear the accordion player as he sat in his doorway and played the music of his native land. Rarely did he have to enjoy his music alone, because there was always someone who was anxious to sing or play along with him. The neighbors would come out into their yards or sit on their doorsteps and listen as long as he would play. Not only would they listen, but they would join him in song.

Each month the Italian miners put away money, and when the savings amounted to a few hundred dollars, they sent the money to banks in Italy.[14] The more skeptical ones refused to trust the banks or postal savings, and they put their money in jars and buried it until they had enough to send overseas. From time to time individuals left Thurber for Italy.

The following story is rather interesting and it shows how much the Italians trusted those whom they liked: An Italian woman who spoke very little English came to my mother who was not an Italian and asked her to come into the garden. When they reached the garden, the Italian woman stepped over the various plants, and finally she found the spot for which she was searching. She pushed aside some of the plants and began digging. In a few seconds, she withdrew a quart jar which was filled with greenbacks. My mother was startled to think that so much money should be buried in the garden. While she was stricken with amazement, her Italian friend quickly replaced the jar and carefully covered it with dirt and plants.

She told her American friend that she and her family had to leave town for a few weeks and would she watch to see that no one came to dig in the garden while they were gone. My mother agreed to keep a watchful eye on the garden, but as the days passed by, she suffered mental agony. Every time she looked out across the garden, it seemed to her as though the "money spot" was so obvious that no one could miss seeing it. Anxiously she awaited the return of the Italian family. What if some one had seen them that day in the garden and had come back at night and had carried away the jar of money. Thoughts like this were constantly in her mind. It was a day of relief when the family returned. To quiet all fears, the Italian woman went out into the garden and proved that the jar of money was still there. Within a few days, the money was sent to Italy.

Like the Polish wedding, an Italian wedding called for several days of feasting and dancing. Rita Buffo Studdard describes her older sister's wedding celebration as follows:

> At my sister's wedding, the feast lasted several days. The band was hired to play for dancing for the first day, and from then on, an accordion player was hired to play for the singing and dancing. It was customary among these northern Italians to have rice as their special dish for weddings or other large dinners. This rice was called rizzotto, and it was special indeed for the rice at most large weddings was cooked in a large wash tub. Into this rice, they poured gallons of chicken broth, chicken giblets, tomato sauce and pounds of Italian grated cheese. A salad, a great variety of meats, and a very special barrel of wine would be served along with the rizzotto.
>
> Although wine was available, beer was always a favorite drink. As the kegs were emptied during the wedding celebration, they were stacked on top of each other, and by the time the celebration ended, the stack of empty kegs reminded one of a pyramid.[15]

On the eve before the Lenten Season began, some of the Italian families had what might be called a miniature Mardi Gras. Some of the men would dress in costumes and wear grotesque or comical masks, and they would go from house to house and entertain the children with their antics and pranks. Each housewife in whose home they visited would serve them wine and "crostoli."

"Crostoli" was a special pastry that required a great deal of work to prepare. In fact, the Italian woman spent almost an entire day preparing it. She mixed dough from flour, eggs, and brandy. She then rolled the dough into an extremely thin layer, and cut it into strips. She tied these strips of dough into bowknots and fried them in deep grease. When the bowknots were removed from the grease, she rolled them in sugar and set them aside to cool. The "crostoli" or bowknots were delicious and literally melted in one's mouth.[16]

During prohibition days there were few Italians left in Thurber. Those who remained continued to make their own beer and wine in spite of the laws. Eventually they found themselves in the bootlegging business, and a very profitable business it was, too. "These Italians made a brandy from the hulls of grapes. They called this drink 'graspa.' Other nationalities liked this drink, and it became quite popular. Many of those who enjoyed 'graspa' never learned to pronounce the name correctly, and they began to speak of the drink as 'grappo.'"[17] To this day, Thurber and "grappo" are closely associated with one another in the minds of the people who lived in and around Thurber during the pro-hibition days.

Frequently the federal officers would raid these houses on the hill. As a general rule, some one would warn the persons concerned and most of the wine, beer, and grappo would be moved to secret hiding places. Occasionally, the Italians would pour the beer, wine, and grappo down the hillside if they did not have a safe hiding place in which to put it. By the time the federal officers arrived, there would be no liquor of any kind in the house and no one knew anything about the liquor running down the hillside.[18]

After the mines closed in 1921, many of these Italian families re-turned to Italy. It is rather interesting to note that so many of the chil-dren of these families later came back to America to live. The Buffo fam-ily is a typical example of this return. After the mines closed, Antonio Buffo, his wife, and three children returned to Italy. By 1930, the three children, no longer minors, returned to America and are still living in the United States. These children had been old enough to remember life in America, and the opportunities offered to them in this country. America had been the place of their birth; they had left it because they were dependent upon their parents, but when they were old enough, they returned to the land of their choice. Today in America, they do not sit and dream of a bit of land in Italy as their parents did, and they will probably never return to Italy even for a visit.[19]

Much of Thurber's color and uniqueness may be attributed to this strange, but interesting development of European culture in a West Texas setting. The Europeans retained many of their native customs and assumed many western ways, and while the Americans did not actually assume the European customs, they accepted them as part of their surroundings and learned to enjoy the strange ways of their fellow citizens. The foreign population was vital to Thurber, not only from an economic standpoint but for its cultural influence as well.

CHAPTER 8

Abandonment

The gradual abandonment of Thurber began immediately after the coal mines were closed in 1921. From then until 1937, the process of dismantling and abandoning Thurber continued, and by the end of 1937, few traces of its existence remained. The first section to be abandoned was Number 3 Hill. When the mines closed, most of the miners moved their families from Thurber and Number 3 Hill was literally covered with hundreds of empty houses.[1] As the houses were vacated, the company removed the windows and doors and stored them in warehouses. The lack of windows and doors, the effect of wind, sand, and rain blowing into and through the houses created an air of desolation. The houses appeared more weather-beaten than before, and with the loss of all elements that make a house a home, these former homes rapidly assumed the appearance of mining camp shacks.

By 1926, the company had sold most of the houses on Number 3 Hill, and within a few years, one would have had difficulty in finding even traces of the foundations. Stump Hill was abandoned in much the same manner, and by 1926, all houses were torn down and sold as second-hand lumber or moved away intact. As houses were vacated in the Flat or on Graveyard Hill, they were sold to anyone who would move them from the company property.

REMOVAL NOTICE

On July 1, 1933, the Thurber General Office
of

TEXAS PACIFIC COAL AND OIL COMPANY

will be combined with its Executive Offices
and will occupy the 23rd and 24th floors
of the

Fort Worth National Bank Building, Fort Worth, Texas

Beginning July 1st, all communications should be addressed to the Company at Fort Worth, Texas.

Notice of the removal of the offices of the Texas Pacific Coal and Oil Company from Thurber to Fort Worth on 1 July 1933. Courtesy, 95-13, Thurber, Texas, Collection, Special Collections, The University of Texas at Arlington Libraries, Arlington, Texas.

When the brick plant closed in 1930, a few of the houses on Park Row were sold. The brick plant closed during the beginning of the depression, and its former employees were unable to secure work elsewhere. The company allowed them to continue to live in the houses, even though the people were unable to pay rent or for utilities, and during the months they were unemployed, each family was allowed about thirty dollars credit in the company stores.[2] This condition made it impossible to sell the houses on Park Row with the same speed that had been used with Number 3 Hill and Stump Hill had been abandoned.

In June, 1933, the announcement came that the T.P.M. & M. Company was to be liquidated, and the general office was to be moved to Fort Worth and combined with the executive office. Dozens of moving vans entered the town and carried away the household effects of the office employees. Scores of houses on Church Street, Marston Street, and New York Hill were vacated and sold.

Between 1933 and 1937, entire streets of houses were wrecked or moved out simultaneously, and it was not at all uncommon to look out some morning and see several houses being moved about the town in various directions. A few two story structures from New York Hill were moved intact (with the exception of the porches) as far as Stephenville. Many of the Thurber houses were destined for the West Texas oil fields, particularly Odessa; however, these houses were town down and rebuilt upon reaching the new location. In order to get rid of the houses as quickly as possible, the company sold them at reasonable prices ranging from $300 to $800, the average price being about $500.[3]

In about 1935, the public school buildings were sold, and one of the smaller buildings was moved to Bluff Dale where it was used as a home economics building. The company gave the school equipment to other schools in the county. The following from the *Stephenville Empire* accounts for the disposal of the Thurber High School library: "The entire Huckabay community is exceedingly appreciative of what the Thurber High School did upon its dissolution. The act referred to was the donation of the library to the Huckabay school, making it possible for the latter institution to boast of one of the largest and most complete libraries of any rural school in the county."[4]

Whenever a street or section of the town was closed, all gas and water mains, and electric wires were removed and sold to any interested person or salvage company. By the end of 1937, the brick buildings which lined the quadrangle, four houses north of the quadrangle, two or three houses on Marston Street and Church Street, and a few negro shacks were the only buildings which remained in Thurber.

The red brick buildings, with boards over their windows, still line the east and west sides of the quadrangle. One building is used as a combination café and service station and is leased to Bill Boyd, a former postmaster. The company maintains a large vault in the old general office building, and several times a year, a few company employees from Fort Worth come to Thurber to work in the vault. While they are in Thurber, they live in the spacious house which was formerly the W. K. Gordon home.[5]

Mary Jane Gentry inscribed the back of this photograph, "The former 'Main Street' in Thurber. Water reservoir on Graveyard Hill may be seen in the background." Photograph by Mary Jane Gentry ca. 1946. Courtesy, 93-41, Thurber, Texas, Photograph Collection, Special Collections, The University of Texas at Arlington Libraries, Arlington, Texas.

The 1908 smokestack still towers above the quadrangle and the tall steel standpipe on Graveyard Hill maintains its lonely vigil. Both structures will eventually be torn down, and in all probability, most of the brick buildings along the quadrangle will be sold. Roadways and streets are fenced in; grass has grown over the sites of former residential areas; and herds of cattle graze upon the hills that once were covered with hundreds of homes.

For nearly fifty years, Thurber existed as the only industrial town in the midst of an agricultural area. Its entire economy was built around the need for coal by the Texas railroads. The Johnsons made the first attempt to supply the demand, but they were unable to cope with the difficult problems that arose in connection with the field's development.

Hunter, determined to "run his business or run it to Hell," took over the Johnson interests and defied all who opposed him. His determination, defiance, and vigorous if not ruthless methods, made it possible for him to open up mine after mine. Hundreds of immigrants flocked into the area, and Thurber's foreign population was looked upon with distrust by Anglo-Americans who held sole possession of the surrounding communities.

To keep his miners satisfied, Hunter opened up saloons and this met with the disapproval of the rural population. Their disapproval meant nothing to Hunter. He was not interested in pleasing them or trying to secure their trade. His only interest was the development of his mines and the profits that might be realized therefrom.

Hunter continued to build up his camp, and by the time he resigned in 1899, Thurber was one of the largest settlements in Erath County. After Hunter's resignation, the presidency of the Texas & Pacific Coal Company went to Hunter's son-in-law, Edgar L. Marston, who was more tactful and less antagonistic toward criticism than Colonel Hunter. Marston, who never took up permanent residence in Thurber, turned the management of the town and the mines over to W. K. Gordon.

Gordon was a kind and understanding person who knew the value of gaining the confidence of his employees, and he also succeeded in alleviating some of the feeling of ill will which the people in neighboring areas felt toward Thurber and the Texas Pacific Coal and Oil Company. Through his influence, the company employees became more appreciative of the company and they developed a strong personal interest in the welfare and appearance of Thurber.

Under Gordon's guidance, Thurber reached the peak of its prosperity and the peak in its population. It was never incorporated, and although there are no accurate population figures available,[6] most persons who lived there during the 1918–1920 period agree that the population was between eight and ten thousand.[7]

Thurber had all the conveniences of a modern town—churches, schools, clubs, stores, ice factory, up to date water and light plants, a golf course, tennis courts, baseball diamonds, and two lakes—yet technically speaking, it was a company owned camp. The company owned every building and every inch of ground and was financially responsible for the upkeep of the entire town.

There are those who contend that civic pride could never develop in such a camp and that the lack of privately owned homes kept the people of Thurber from being interested in the welfare of the town. If this is the general rule, then Thurber was the exception, because the majority of the people who lived in Thurber did have a feeling of civic pride and were loyal to Thurber.

When Texas railroads found it more convenient and cheaper to burn oil instead of coal, Thurber ceased to be Texas' most productive mining town, and Thurber was doomed to extinction. Slowly it was reduced in size to the vanishing point until today a stranger motoring along the highway which passes through Thurber would find it hard to believe that ten thousand persons once lived there.

Today, the population of Thurber is scattered to the four corners of the earth, but each year some of them return on the fourth of July for a reunion. Some have come back from as far as California, and many persons arrange their summer vacations so that they can spend the fourth of July in Thurber.[8]

The former residents come back and spend hours wandering about the area that was Thurber, searching for some indication of their former residences. Much time is spent reminiscing about the days when Thurber was the biggest town between Fort Worth and El Paso. E. Buchanan, a former resident of Thurber now living in Strawn, has made a hobby of filming these reunions each year, and during each reunion, he shows the pictures of the previous gathering. Needless to say, he never lacks an audience.

Thurber lived a unique and interesting life—one filled with gaiety and color; its death was dramatic, and its memory is still preserved in the hearts and minds of all its people.

In the following paragraphs, the writer gives a few of her impressions and remembrances of Thurber during the years she lived there:

My family moved to Thurber in the fall of 1919, and evidently my mother's first impression of the town was an unfavorable one, because her first remark upon arriving was, "We'll stay and put the children in school, but as soon as the school term is over, we are leaving." No one left Thurber with more regrets than my mother did seventeen years later.

School began for me the next morning, and since school was a new experience, I was unable to make a comparison with other schools. Children have few inhibitions, and before the school day was over, I had quite a list of new friends. They made no objection to my Yankee ancestry, and I certainly did not object to such surnames as Bida, Galik, Biondi, Maletski, Marchoni, Vietti, Zinnani, Buffo, or Chyz. So far as I could detect, they were no different to the Jones, Smith, or Carr children I had known elsewhere.

In a few days, I was sent to town to get the mail and to buy groceries. This trip to the business section was my first real impression of Thurber. The Post Office had been described to me as a red brick building, but upon entering the quadrangle, I saw several red brick buildings. I decided to enter the one in which there seemed to be the greatest number of people standing in line. After taking my place in the line, I began to notice the others who were lined up before the windows. Many of them were miners still dressed in their working clothes. My interest in the carbide lamps which they wore on their caps, and the strange languages in which they were talking made the waiting seem very short.

When it came my turn to do to the window, I asked for our mail, and the clerk at the window explained that I was in the Check Office and not the Post Office. Of course, never having heard of company check, I had no idea what he was talking about. The miner directly behind me offered to take me to the Post Office if I would wait until he had drawn his check. Glad to have some one to direct me to the proper building, I waited, and from the Post Office, we went to the market and then across the street to the grocery store.

In each store, there were long lines of people waiting to place their orders and needless to say, it was almost dark before I reached home.

My mother had not been aware of the long lines at the stores, or she probably would not have sent me to town alone. She was still a bit skeptical about the large foreign groups within the town, but within a few weeks, she discovered that there was no basis for her fears. She was soon to learn what I had learned on my first trip to the quadrangle—that the miners and their families were friendly, kind, and sincere in their friendships.

In 1921 the mines closed and hundreds of families moved to Grant Town in Palo Pinto County. Rows and rows of tents were set up and these tents served as living quarters for the miners' families. The miners were confident that the company would re-open the mines, and they wanted to be as near Thurber as possible while they waited for the company and the union to reach an agreement. The company made a few feeble attempts to operate with "scab" labor, but full scale production was impossible. The use of "scab" labor caused a slight wave of excitement, but there was no organized attempt on the part of the union members to keep the "scabs" out of the mines.

The loss of the miners' children made a noticeable decrease in the class rooms, at church gatherings, and in the picture show. The lines in the grocery store and market were not nearly so long, but the most noticeable decrease was in the line at the pay windows on the first and fifteenth of each month.

As the years passed, Thurber continued to decline. Its population was reduced from several thousand to a few hundred. Houses were torn down as fast as they were vacated, and one rarely ever had to stand in line while shopping. The store on Number 3 Hill was closed, and the train service to and from the mines was discontinued.

Most people in Thurber realized that Thurber was marked for extinction, but somehow they always had hopes that Thurber would regain its former prosperity. Many of these hopes were shattered in 1930 when fire destroyed the market, hardware, and general office building, and when the company made no attempt to replace the loss. Later the order for the removal of the general office to Fort Worth and the liquidation of the Texas Pacific Mercantile & Manufacturing Company astounded the entire population.

For months people could talk of nothing else. To them it was unbelievable that a town could be erased as if it had never existed. The old timers gathered in small groups and talked of the days when Thurber was in its heyday, and they spent many hours remembering the pleasant experiences they had had in Thurber. Even while they talked, entire sections of the town were being torn away; moving vans were leaving in all directions, and scores of people were rushing about the town paying bills, turning in their house keys, and leaving forwarding addresses at the Post Office.

Less than two years ago, I went back to Thurber and spent a few hours wandering over the area. I climbed the brick stairway which led to the top of New York Hill, and from the hill top, I had an excellent view of the entire valley. With the exception of the few buildings along the former quadrangle, grass, brush, and mesquites have quickly reclaimed the entire townsite, and no doubt the valley appears today much as it did when the Johnsons opened the first coal mine in 1886.

As I looked down upon the scene, I remembered the colorful stories of the Lizard, the Snake, the badger fights, and the Thurber Opera House. I remembered with pleasure the smell of fresh baked bread as it baked in the rock ovens, the music of the Italian accordion player as he sat on the doorstep and sang his native songs, and the roar of the mine train as it moved to and from the mines. Everything is gone except the memories, and I, like so many others who lived in Thurber, wish that Thurber could live again.

Appendix

Fort Worth, Texas, July 5th, 1890
General W. H. King
Austin, Texas

Dear General

As I have always called upon Gov. Ross and yourself in my troubles at these mines as your Rangers has been my only Protection as against the unlawfull element has prevailed against our enterprise in the county with the Presence of your Rangers. We have saved bloodshed, and Peace and Prosperity has reigned, and we have built up a flourishing village of some fifteen hundred souls. And our Payroll now amounts to over $20,000 Dollars Per Month, but a new trouble is now threatening us the Knight of Labor element finding that they were defeated as an organization are now secretly trying to get up a race war. We have about 800 negroes in camp men, women and children and the rest are white, and they have all been very Peaceable and orderly untill very lately.—when this new movement has been inaugurated, and I cannot tell what moment the flame may burst forth. I ask you again for a little assistance if you can consistantly give it. Please send me Capt. McMurray and a few men. He as I before said has saved plenty of blood shed and his Presence here with a squad of men in my opinion will do it again. I am not an alarmist but I do not think there is any time to lose. There is a lot of bad men hanging around here with there arms on their saddles. Some of them are well-known Horse thieves, and exconvicts, who are friends of the old strikers, who are ready to commit any crime at a moments notice. Platt arrested one of them yesterday for drawing a pistol on a negro and he gave bail. He has just been arrested today again for the like offense. Would you also Please send John L. Sullivan a Permit to carry arms. He is one of the Captains old men now in the employ of this company in trying to preserve the Peace but not having the right to carry side arms. He is in great danger. Please wire me at Coal Mines Junction, Tex my expense your conclusion as I shall await it anxiously.

> *Thanking you and Gov. Ross for all past Courtesys*
> *I am sincerely yours,*
> (Signed) R. D. Hunter

Thurber, Texas, 8/30/03.
Honorable S. W. T. Lanham,
Governor
Austin, Texas.

Dear Sir:—
The employees of the Texas & Pacific Coal Company are not organized and a large majority of them (Perhaps ninety-eight per cent.) do not want the union to get a foothold here. For years past, we have quietly operated here, without a strike or misunderstanding, or trouble of any kind.

The United Mine Workers of America, whose local headquarters are at Mineral City, a small mining town near Strawn, have for some time past been endeavoring to create discontent amongst our people They are now advertising a three-days picnic for September 7th, 8th & 9th, for the avowed purpose of organizing the Thurber Mines. They may then succeed in creating such disturbance as may lead to serious consequences.

I am writing to ask Your Excellency to send us three or four of your Ranger Boys, to be here from September fifth to tenth.

This will have a most quieting effect on the agitators and the mere presence of the Rangers will be worth a great deal to us. If you can send them, they need not bring their horses as we can furnish them mounts and as they will be the company's guests, the State need not be put to any expense.

Kindly advise at your earliest convenience if we may expect them.

Yours very respectfully,
(SIGNED) W. K. GORDON
General Manager

Poteau, Oklahoma
Aug. 14, 1944

Dear Miss Gentry:
Attached is installment of my version of Labor Difficulties to appear in your history of Thurber.

With the coming of Mr. Gordon into the General Managership of the company, notwithstanding his very liberal management, he, like the hostile Colonel, had that nightmare every present, man-shortage, to disturb his slumbers right up to the very last. My next contribution will concern the causes for this condition.

Did you receive the two packages of pictures? Some of them will fit nicely into your sports and social chapters.

Judging from my experience in composing and typing these poorly written contributions, I realize what a huge task you have on your hands. Stay with it and you will succeed.

Sincerely yours
(SIGNED) GOMER GOWER

P.S.
As I have been selected as a delegate to attend the convention of the United Mine Workers of America, which convenes

at Cincinnati, Ohio, September 12 to 21st, I will be away from home the greater part of next month. I plan to visit my son, now on sick-leave in New York, either before or after the convention. However, if it will not be too late, I will make other contributions after my return.

G.G.

Labor Difficulties

Mine #1, sunk to the coal by the Johnson Brothers, Will and Harvey, in December, 1886, had a short and hectic existence, barely over five years. Several factors entered into the cause of its early demise, but two very important factors, one being unfavorable mining conditions, the other, a somewhat exacting body of miners.

Sunk, as it was, near the cropping, being but fifty-two feet in depth, the roof conditions were bad, causing costly squeezes especially to the north and east of the shaft site, while to the west and south, the nearby hills were found to be underlaid by extremely thin coal resting upon hard rock with no mining clay between the coal and the rock. The working force during the first two years of its existence, was composed principally of men who had worked at "Coalville" where the Gould system had operated two mines for the purpose of augmenting its locomotive fuel. The coal at Coalville proved to be so charged with impurities, sulphur, boney and slate, causing innumerable engine failures, that the mines at that point, approximately eight miles to the north-east of the Johnson Brothers mine, were closed and abandoned in January 1886. These miners, who were not "MOLLY MCGUIRES AND FUGITIVES FROM JUSTICE," as charged by Colonel R. D. Hunter, when submitting his first annual report to the Texas Pacific Coal Company, successors to the Johnson Brothers, in December 1889, they were, at the same time, men who, above all else, required they be paid wages which would enable them to support themselves and families in a fairly decent manner. At any rate, the wages they had been paid at Coalville and at the Johnson Brothers mines. The "narrow work," that is driving the narrow entries through and around the pillars of the shaft was paid for at the rate of $2.50 per day of ten hours, the same rate per day as was the rate at the Coalville mines. However, when the time came to fix the mining rate, which was $1.75 per ton at the Coalville mines, to $1.50 per ton. This thwarted effort on the part of the Johnson Brothers resulted in the first LABOR DIFFICULTY occurring at what later came to be known as Thurber and a strike became necessary, or so the miners viewed it, to retain the standard of wages paid at the Coalville mines.

After two months of idleness, the Johnson Brothers gave way and withdrew their effort to lower the mining rate which had been paid at the Coalville mines, and the mine operated with amicable relations existing between the miners and the Johnson Brothers until September 1889, when the Johnson Brothers announced they were unable to meet the payroll for the month of August. Obviously, there were more than seven weeks of the miners earnings involved by the latter part of September, some miners having as much as two-hundred dollars earned. In the face of this, the miners gave the Johnson Brothers five days grace and continued work until September twenty-fifth with the hope that the Johnson Brothers would find some way out of the difficulty. At the expiration of the five days grace, in the absence of the much looked for pay, there was nothing for the miners to do but stop until they did receive their hard-earned wages.

This failure to meet the payroll was not, necessarily, caused by unprofitable operation of Mine #1, but more likely was caused by a lot of the profit being invested in the sinking and equipment of Mine #2, which was just ready to produce coal when the financial difficulties mentioned were revealed. That occurrence, whatever the cause, resulted in the sale of the property to the Texas & Pacific Coal Company, a company organized and financed by New York capitalists in October 1888, with Colonel R. D. Hunter named as its general manager. The Colonel being inherently averse to any semblance of unionism among the miners, let it be known to the former employees of the Johnson Brothers that they would be employed by his company only on condition that they would accept a reduction in the mining rate from $1.75 per ton, to $1.15 per ton, and a reduction in the day wage rate from $2.50 to $2.25 per day and, to top it off, demand that the miners renounce their allegiance to the Knights of Labor and promise to refrain from joining or otherwise assisting in the formation of a union of any sort. This latter condition had the same effect on the miners as the shaking of a red shawl in the face of a bull. A committee of miners was selected to confer with the Colonel who received the committee cordially, yet with an ill concealed belligerency and finally dismissed it with the admonition: "I will make a dollar look as big as a wagon wheel to you s-o-bs before I get through with you." He very decidedly made his word as good in this respect. But it is the opinion of this writer that had he assumed a more conciliatory attitude toward the skilled and needy miners who proffered a hand of peace and good will, he would have been spared the humility of reporting to his company that he had spent more than ten thousand dollars of the company's money, in an effort to secure miners who would accept his terms of employment, during the first year's operation of the mines.

Another condition submitted by the Colonel to the idle miners was that the mining rate—piece work—$1.15 per ton, be on the screened coal basis. This meant that only such coal as passed over a screen, six feet wide, twelve feet in length, with one and one-quarter inch spaces between the screen bars would be credited to the miner and paid for. The former mining rate, under the regime of the Johnson Brothers, $1.75 per ton, was on a mine run basis, which is to say that all coal, large and small lumps, loaded into the mine car by the miners, was weighed before being passed over a screen and the miner was paid for the full weight. This proposition, if accepted by the miners, would have had the effect of further reducing the earnings of the miners another twelve to thirteen per cent, as that percentage of the coal loaded by the miner passed through the screen for which he received no remuneration. So iniquitous is the practice of paying the miners on a screened coal basis that now practically all of the states in which there are coal mines have enacted laws providing that the mining of coal, when done on a tonnage basis, be paid for on the mine-run basis.

The miners very promptly and emphatically rejected all the conditions proposed by the Colonel and more particularly the condition that they forever renounce the union and make a YELLOW DOG pledge and they forthwith declared a strike against the company. Here the LABOR DIFFICULTIES of the company began, as the Colonel's report to his stock-holders discloses. The miners stood firm against relinquishing the protection afforded them by the Knights of Labor, a branch of which, District #135, they were a part. Contributions of money and food were sent on to the Texas miners by, not only the parent organization, but also by Local Assemblies from all parts of the country. The official journal of the Knights of Labor, the Labor Tribune, published items concerning the strike and warned miners in other mining regions to stay away from Johnson's Mines that being the name at that time.

The underground also put in some effective though perfectly legitimate work, just as the underground is doing today in the occupied countries of Europe. The writer, then a boy of barely nineteen years of age, took occasion to visit a sister and her family near Belleville, Illinois. Holding membership in the Local Assembly at Johnson's Mines gave him access to the many Local Assemblies in southern Illinois and he lost no opportunity to visit them, solicit contributions and state to the membership the iniquitous conditions the company was seeking to impose on the miners in Texas. Others, like myself, took occasion to visit other parts of the country where, they too, performed valiant services in the interest of the striking miners. Then, too, when it was noised around that one of the Colonel's trains was on tour through the mining regions in the east seeking miners to man his mines, the home boys would be notified of the approximate date of arrival of the train at Fort Worth, when the train would be met by a delegation of the striking miners who would persuade, or mayhap intimidate, the would-be strikebreakers to return to their homes in the east.

Many a dollar was paid by the strikers and their sympathizers for return transportation back to the homes of these deluded men, all to the aggravation of the belligerent Colonel. In February 1889, however, a shipment of around one hundred negroes, men women and children, picked up in Clay County, Indiana, arrived safely within the BULL-PEN, that being the name given the enclosure of one section of land surrounding the mines around which the Colonel had, for obvious reasons, placed a four wire barbed wire fence. Access to this group while en route at Fort Worth was made impossible by the simple expedient of passing the station, then a comparatively insignificant edifice, at full speed. This ruse was the result of previous arrangement with the railway officials. This group of negroes were habitual and confirmed strikebreakers, having participated in the breaking of mine strikes first, in Iowa, then in Colorado and from there they were shipped to Indian[a] from which state they were inveigled by the Colonel's agents to continue their nefarious practice in Texas. With the arrival of this group of negroes the Colonel's hopes for a complete victory over the striking miners were bolstered considerable and the strikers' dream of unionizing the mines of the company began to wane. These negroes were all practical miners and, as indicated, had worked in the low-coal fields in Iowa, which fact made them the more desirable as workers in the low coal mined at Johnson's Mines, because to mine low coal is an art which can only be acquired after months of painful effort accompanied by sore knees and strained muscles.

Still another contributing factor which favored the company was the replacement of President Grover Cleveland on March 4, 1889, by President Harrison. This change in national administration brought with it a general let-down in the coal industry throughout the nation. Mines were closed, miners were thrown out of work in many mining centers, making it easier for the Colonel's agents to secure miners, strike or no strike. In January 1890, at Columbus, Ohio, the United Mine Workers of America was founded and jurisdiction over the coal miners was bequeathed by the Knights of Labor to that organization. So, first, with a change in national administration and then shortly thereafter being taken over by a new miners union, the United Mine Workers of America, still in its swaddling clothes, and with meager, if any fund, the struggling miners were forced, in a measure, though not in principle, to give up the fight, and to secure work elsewhere.

Yet, the Colonel's difficulties were not surmounted. The low wages paid; the arduous task of mining coal in such a low vein of coal, together with the many restrictions with which he surrounded his enslaved employees, such as compelling them to deal at the company stores, shops and saloon and, indeed voting in county, state and national elections the way he would have them vote; and perhaps, the vilest of them all, the espionage of stooges to report on any movement having the appearance of an effort to unionize the miners, taken altogether, were obviously not conducive to the procurement and the retention of a satisfied group of workmen as he was, over the years, compelled to spend many other thousands of dollars of the company's money recruiting his constantly disappearing working force. His dream of a strictly monopolistic empire, over which he dreamed to reign as a feudalist of old, was gradually being shattered and he finally acquiesced in the employment of members of the union, (Robert Brown, present State Mine Inspector for the State of Oklahoma) and many others so long as they did not agitate. As he relaxed his dictatorial attitude, conditions grew to be much better and still better as old age advanced on him and he went to his grave a much more tolerant man than when he first crossed swords with the "men from the old railroad mines, Molly McGuires and fugitives from justice."

By 1894, a goodly number of English-speaking miners from the north and east were in the employ of the company, together with a number of Italians, Poles and Mexicans. The wily Colonel again, seemingly, became alarmed with fear that this conglomerate group would unionize his camp. He surreptitiously brought in a spy—whose name should not be disclosed at this late day—. He, like the detective mentioned, appeared among the miners after nightfall, wearing white ducking pit-pants, and represented to them he had come for the purpose of organizing them into a miners union, under the jurisdiction of the Knights of Labor. Some of the better informed English-speaking miners knew that the jurisdiction over the coal miners by the Knights of Labor was relinquished and turned over to the United Mine Workers of America, and became suspicious of the intentions of the spy. Others, however, promised to consider the matter. The names of these were promptly reported to the Colonel who summoned them to appear at a hearing to be held each evening at the old Opera House, where a great array of legal lights from Dallas and Fort Worth quizzed suspected employees for almost a week, at the end of which, all the accused proved to the satisfaction of the Colonel that they were not interested in the formation of a union.

The whole affair was perfectly staged, with the Colonel, as always, dressed in his pleated white, spotless shirt plus trousers and coatless, presiding. Although the legal lights had been selected because of their high standing in their profession, and the spy selected because of his past performances in railway labor difficulties, the untutored miners, being well versed in the art of dealing with spies and evading the hypothetical questions of the inquisitors, baffled the Colonel and his aides at every turn and the whole inquisition died a-borning. One wag was heard to exclaim: "Let them bring on their high class lawyers, the higher they are the more they will show their posterior." (Though that wasn't the word he used.)

Apparently, the adroit Colonel staged this highly dramatized inquisition for the purpose of intimidating the miners into quiet submissiveness in preparation for a reduction in wages which he had in mind and which he announced shortly afterward. If that was his purpose, he succeeded beyond his wildest dream, because his announcement, properly printed and posted at various places, that the wages of *All* employees would be reduced ten per cent went over without an audible murmur. The Colonel, being a keen student of human nature, knew that in the make-up of most men, that feeling "well, he got it too" would go far in reconciling the miners in their universal grief over the reduction, and that a burden imposed upon all the employees at the mines, from the lowly trapper boy who had been paid seventy-five cents per day, to the lordly pit-boss, who had been paid one hundred dollars per month, in the same proportion would greatly assuage any ill feeling stemming from their loss in earnings. At least, these were the reactions of this writer to this reduction. He had been paid sixty dollars per month as weigh-man and his wages were reduced to fifty-four dollars per month;

exactly ten per cent. The mining rate was reduced at that time from $1.15 per ton to $1.00 per ton, slightly more than ten percent. This discrepancy, or rather, discrimination against the coal miner, was explained away with the comparative ease with which he could calculate his earnings—one ton, one dollar—as compared with the more difficult task of calculating them if the tonnage rate was one dollar, one and one-half cents. So it was swallowed.

The wages of the employees were maintained at that standard until September 5, 1903, at which time the BIG WALKOUT occurred and the United Mine Workers of America took over, organized the miners and secured an advance in the tonnage rate from $1.00 to $1.32 per ton. Day-men who had been receiving $1.80 were advanced to $2.25 per day and the poor little trapper boy who had been paid fifty-seven cents per day was advanced to $1.00 per day, and, to his greater delight, his working day reduced from ten to eight hours. This accomplishment was brought about only after a strike which was launched on September 5th. and ended September 30th. In the meantime, scores of miners moved, or had been shipped by the union, to other coal fields and the company again found itself facing another LABOR DIFFICULTY: a serious man shortage. A standing advertisement for miners was placed in the United Mine Workers Journal. This advertisement was carried over a period of several years, with more or less successful results. Under the contractual relations entered into between the company and the union, matters moved along smoothly until May 1905, when a two days stoppage of work occurred because of unsatisfactory train service. This difficulty was settled by Mr. W. K. Gordon, then General Manager of the company, who succeeded Colonel Hunter, who, as well may be imagined, had passed on to his reward some two or three years before Mr. Edgar L. Marston, the president of the company, capitulated and recognized the union in September 1903. Here, it is quite safe to say, that the company prospered far more under the kindly, able and wise management of Mr. Gordon that it ever had under the prejudicial and hostile management of the Colonel. But more about Mr. Gordon later.

Poteau, Oklahoma
Jan. 18, 1945
Miss M. J. Gentry
527 Pulliam St.
San Angelo, Tex.

Dear Miss Gentry:

Your letter of the 8th. inst. is at hand and belatedly I am un-dertaking to answer it. The holidays left me rather tired and perhaps over-fed. At any rate this is the first real opportunity I have had to devote a little time to the task.

The fence to which you refer was one of the first creations of Colonel Hunter's resourceful mind, and was built during the winter of 1888–1889 to enclose a square mile of land immedi-ately surrounding the two mines then in operation—Numbers 1 & 2—The primary purpose being the exclusion of the Johnson Brothers employees from the property of the new company.

Its location:

The South-West corner was located a short distance S.W. of, what later was known as Stump Hill, thence eastward across Marston and Brickyard Hills to a point near what is now known as the Big Lake. Thence North to a point East of Cemetery Hill. Thence West across Cemetery Hill and the valley and railroad spur to a point on top of the hill immediately north of Mine New # Three, Thence South to the railroad trestle near the Lizard and thence in a general direction southward to the point of origin.

A gate was placed near the corner next [to] the Big Lake. Another, was placed on the East side of the Cemetery Hill. An-other immediately on the West side of the same hill at a point about three hundred yards north of the Catholic Church, and still another gate about two hundred yards south of the "Liz-ard." At first, all these gates were kept securely locked. It was this feature particularly that caused the Colonel to be hailed into court at Stephenville, on the charge of creating a condition which deprived patrons of the Post Office from its use. In a former letter to Mr. Owens, I recited that a large number of people had been moved off the company property by the Colonel and were domiciled at Strikertown near Gibson Branch where the Knights of Labor had purchased ten acres of land adjoining the company property near the South-East corner of the inclosure. Another group had purchased one-acre blocks of property adjoining the North line of the inclosure. Obviously both these groups were cut off from access to the post office which was located inside the company property and was designated as Johnson Mines. It was presided over as Post Master by a Mr. Ward who also operated a drug store in the same building which stood quite near what was afterward known as "The Snake." As I now remember, the action against the Colonel was lodged for the purpose of compelling him to remove the locks from the gates. This he did without further prosecution of the case. At about the same time, the name of the Post Office was changed to "Thurber," after a prominent stockholder of the company. While as stated, the locks were removed from the gates, the Rangers kept watch over them to see that anyone entering the inclosure for the purpose of going to the post office did not have an opportunity to mingle with non-union employees and also to prevent a nickel's worth of merchandise being sold to residents of the "Bull Pen" by farmers or merchants. However, public opinion became so outspoken against the arbitrary rule of the Colonel that he finally removed the gates and provided lanes inside the inclosure to and from the Post Office. This arrangement precluded the possibility of an enterprising farmer who had produce to sell to a thrifty housewife, such as eggs, butter, chickens, meats and vegetables, driving with his load of produce among the company houses to dispose of his wares. That humiliating condition was tolerated for a time by the nonunion blacks who constituted a majority of the inhabitants but as the whites slowly gained supremacy, a necessarily silent but effective sentiment grew apace and the monopoly enjoyed by the company for several years of all business activities came to its final ending in 1903, with the removal of all fences and other restrictions, from the premises.

Those of us who lived through that hectic period in the history of Thurber it seems to me, can the better understand mention of underground activities in Europe today because of our experiences in Thurber. We know what it means to be run over by a ruthless element whose only purpose was to exploit us. We, too, had our underground forces, yes, in supposedly free America at that time. Brave men and women bore unbelievable hardships rather than submit to an Americanized Hitler who sought to control our every movement to his own gain. It was due to the silent and patient activity of this band of underground patriots that Thurber was transformed from a "Bull-Pen" in its early history, into one of the most desirable and pleasant mining communities in the entire country. Yes, I am proud that I played a part in the transformation, and left "footprints in the sands of time."

Do you have access to the files of the "Thurber Miner?" If so, you will likely find contributions, in verse, by a Mr. J. R. Williams. Mr. Williams was manager of the livery stable and, of course, was one of the members of the "Gestapo" maintained by the Colonel. However, "Big Jim" as he was called, was quite a decent fellow. For a time, he was associated with Dr. Charles Binney in a horse and mule ranch on Ioni Creek in Palo Pinto County. He then married and moved to Mineral Wells. I feel sure that he left some papers at his death which should cast some interesting sidelights on the early history of Thurber. It will be, at least well worth your while to make inquiry in the matter.

How pleasantly duty and inclination have clung together throughout my life as a miner. My loyalty to the miners in all their struggles for betterment of their condition is now rewarded by signal trust and emoluments showered upon me by the United Mine-Workers of America. On February 23, I leave for

Washington, D.C. to represent the miners in Oklahoma in the forthcoming negotiations of a new working agreement to be effective on and after April 1, 1945. In short, a member of a two hundred man policy committee. Should the press and radio, as they did two years ago, vilify that committee as being traitors, saboteurs and lacking in patriotism, I trust you will withhold adverse criticism and remember that one of the earliest workers in the mines at Thurber, is a member of that committee and is one who has always opposed unAmerican practices wherever imposed.

Sincerely yours
(Signed) Gomer Gower

Notes

EDITOR'S INTRODUCTION:
MARY JANE GENTRY AND HER HISTORY OF THURBER

1. Church of St. William, Dorchester, Massachusetts, Certificate of Baptism for Mary Jane Catherine Gentry, 3 April 1912, manuscript certificate, photocopy in Mary Jane Gentry Collection, W. K. Gordon Center for Industrial History of Texas, Tarleton State University, Thurber, Tex.; City of Boston, Mass., Registry Department, Birth Certificate for Mary Jane Catherine Gentry, no. 2850, 24 March 1912, manuscript certificate, photocopy in Mary Jane Gentry Collection; Dan R. Gentry, "Mary Jane Catherine Gentry (Always Known as Mary Jane Gentry)," manuscript, 10 August 2003, p. 1, Mary Jane Gentry Collection; Dan R. Gentry, interview by T. Lindsay Baker, Thurber, Tex., 17 December 2003, typescript, W. K. Gordon Center; United States, Census of 1900, Population Schedules, Erath County, Tex., p. 20, National Archives, Washington, D.C.; United States, Census of 1910, Population Schedules, Military and Naval, U.S.S. *Missouri* at Navy Yard, Boston, Mass., p. 141, National Archives.

2. Dan R. Gentry interview by Baker, 17 December 2003; United States, Census of 1920, Population Schedules, Erath County, Tex., p. 248, National Archives.

3. Dan R. Gentry interview by Baker, 17 December 2003; Mary Jane Gentry, "Thurber: The Life and Death of a Texas Town," master's thesis, University of Texas, 1946, pp. 208, 210 (quotation); United States, Census of 1920, Population Schedules, Erath County, Tex., p. 248; United States, Census of 1930, Population Schedules, Erath County, Tex., p. 232.

4. Mary Jane Gentry, "Thurber," pp. 208, 210.

5. Dan R. Gentry interview by Baker, 17 December 2003; Dan R. Gentry, telephone interview by T. Lindsay Baker, 26 September 2006, typewritten notes in Mary Jane Gentry Collection; Dan R. Gentry, "Mary Jane Catherine Gentry," p. 1; "It Won't Be Long Now," *Thurber Tiny Journal* (Thurber, Tex.), May 1930, p. 1; Junior College of Ranger, Ranger, Tex., Diploma for Mary Jane Gentry as Graduate with Associate in Arts Degree, 23 May 1932, manuscript diploma, photocopy in Mary Jane Gentry Collection; Junior College of Ranger, Ranger, Tex.; *Junior College of* Ranger[,] *Ranger,*

Texas[,] *Commencement*[,] *Monday Evening, May 23, 1932*[,] *8:15 o'Clock*[,] *High School Auditorium* (Ranger, Tex.: Junior College of Ranger, 1932), program for commencement ceremonies, photocopy in Mary Jane Gentry Collection; Junior College of Ranger, Transcript of Coursework for Mary Jane Gentry, 1930–32, typescript, photocopy in Mary Jane Gentry Collection; Odessa College, Odessa, Tex., "Instructor Record of Work Completed for Rank," typescript, [ca. 1977], 1 lf., photocopy in Mary Jane Gentry Collection; Texas, Department of Education, First Class High School State Certificate Issued to Mary Jane Gentry, 28 April 1933, manuscript, 28 April 1933, photocopy in Mary Jane Gentry Collection; Thurber Grammar School, Thurber, Tex., Diploma for Mary Jane Gentry as Graduate of Thurber Grammar School, Thurber, Tex., 13 May 1926, manuscript, photocopy in Mary Jane Gentry Collection; Thurber High School, Thurber, Tex., *Class of 1930*[,] *Thurber High School*[,] *Thurber, Texas*[,] *Class Flower Lilac*[,] *Class Colors Orchid and White*[,] *Class Motto Take the World as You Find It, but Leave It Better* (Thurber, Tex.: Thurber High School, 1930), program for commencement ceremonies, photocopy in Mary Jane Gentry Collection; Thurber High School, Thurber, Tex., Diploma for Mary Jane Gentry as Graduate of Thurber High School, 19 May 1930, manuscript, photocopy in Mary Jane Gentry Collection.

6. Dan R. Gentry interview by Baker, 17 December 2003; Dan R. Gentry telephone interview by Baker, 26 September 2006; Dan R. Gentry, "Mary Jane Catherine Gentry," pp. 1–2; Odessa College, "Instructor Record of Work," 1 lf.; San Angelo Independent School District, San Angelo, Tex., Verification of Service for Mary Jane Gentry, Certified Personnel Prior to 1968, reel 6, microfilm, unpaged, San Angelo Independent School District Offices, San Angelo, Tex.; Texas, Department of Education, First Class High School State Certificate issued to Mary Jane Gentry, 28 April 1933, manuscript, photocopy in Mary Jane Gentry Collection; Texas, Department of Education, Permanent Elementary Certificate of the First Class issued to Mary Jane Gentry, 25 August 1939, manuscript, photocopy in Mary Jane Gentry Collection; [Texas Education Agency], "Teacher Service Record for Foundation School Program Act" (typescript and manuscript form for 1934–35 teaching service by Mary Jane Gentry), 23 February 1959, 1 lf., photocopy in Mary Jane Gentry Collection; Thurber, Tex., School Board, Minutes (2 May 1924 to 6 September 1934), p. 85, Thurber, Tex., Collection (S 1076.1), Southwest Collection, Texas Tech University Libraries, Texas Tech University, Lubbock, Tex. (quotation); University of Texas, Austin, Tex., Diploma for Mary Jane Gentry as Graduate with Bachelor of Science Degree in Education, 5 June 1939, manuscript, photocopy in Mary Jane Gentry Collection; University of Texas, Austin, Tex., Transcript of Coursework for Mary Jane Gentry, 1935–46, typescript, photocopy in Mary Jane Gentry Collection.

7. Dan R. Gentry interview by Baker, 17 December 2003; Dan R. Gentry telephone interview by Baker, 26 September 2006; Dan [R.] Gentry, [Dallas, Tex.], to

Dr. [T. Lindsay] Baker, [Thurber, Tex.], 3 October 2006, manuscript letter in Mary Jane Gentry Collection; San Angelo Independent School District, Minutes, vol. 5 (20 September 1938 to 31 August 1942), typescript in loose-leaf binder, pp. 101, 138, 149, 156, 172, 179, 190, 203, 210, 224, 232, 243, 250, 258, 268, 275, 285, 291, 303, 312, 320, 330, 338, 347, 354, 364, 374, 382, 395, 406, 411, 422, San Angelo Independent School District Offices; San Angelo Independent School District, Verification of Service for Mary Jane Gentry, microfilm, unpaged; Tom Green County, Tex., School Records, Teacher's Certificate Record (1929 to 1956), p. 26, Regional Historic Records Depository, West Texas Collection, Angelo State University, San Angelo, Tex.; *Worley's San Angelo (Tom Green County, Tex.) City Directory 1941* (Dallas: John F. Worley Directory Co., Publishers, 1941), pp. 162, 333.

8. "Affairs of the Association," *Southwestern Historical Quarterly* 44, no. 1 (July 1940): 136; Boyce House, Austin, Tex., to W. K. Gordon, Fort Worth, Tex., 20 May 1940, typescript letter with enclosed newspaper clipping, W. K. Gordon, Jr., Scrapbook, Oversize Box 386, Special Collections, University Library, University of Texas at Arlington, Arlington, Tex.; *The New Handbook of Texas,* 6 vols. (Austin: Texas State Historical Association, 1996), 3:710; 6:862–63; Walter Prescott Webb, "Texas Collection," *Southwestern Historical Quarterly* 43, no. 1 (July 1939): 93–94.

9. San Angelo Independent School District, Minutes, vol. 5, pp. 374, 382, 395, 406, 411, 422, 431, 447, 451, 460, 469, 474, [489]; San Angelo Independent School District, Minutes, vol. 6 (15 September 1942 to 31 August 1946), typescript in loose-leaf binder, pp. 6, 14, 32, 42, 51, 61, 69, 74, 83, 91, 99, 115, 126, 133, 140, 150, 156, 166, 174, 182, 185, 193, 202, 211, 223, 234, 239, 250, 258, 267, 274, 283, 296, 298, 307, 317, 326, 345, 354, 363, 374, 382, 392, 402, 430, 460, 468, 433, 473, 501, 512.

10. *Worley's San Angelo (Tom Green County, Tex.) City Directory 1941,* pp. 162, 333; *Worley's San Angelo (Tom Green County, Tex.) City Directory 1942* (Dallas: John F. Worley Directory Co., Publishers, 1942), pp. 146, 292; *Worley's San Angelo (Tom Green County, Tex.) City Directory 1944* (Dallas: John F. Worley Directory Co., Publishers, 1944), p. 156; *Worley's San Angelo (Tom Green County, Tex.) City Directory 1946* (Dallas: John F. Worley Directory Co., Publishers, 1946), p. 163.

11. San Angelo Independent School District, Minutes, vol. 5, p. 422; San Angelo Independent School District, Minutes, vol. 6, pp. 6, 99, 126, 234, 354.

12. "Armored Force Officer Promoted," *Fort Worth Star-Telegram* (Fort Worth, Tex.), 10 January 1945, evening edition, clipping in Fort Worth Star-Telegram Collection (AR 406-7-66-4 "Gentry A–Z"), Special Collections, University of Texas at Arlington Libraries, Arlington, Tex.; "Bomber Hits Gas Tank, 12 Fliers Killed," *Dallas Morning News* (Dallas, Tex.), 21 May 1943, sec. I, p. 1; Dan R. Gentry interview by Baker, 17 December 2003; Dan R. Gentry, telephone interview by Baker,

19 September 2006; "Last Two Identified in Plane-gas Tank Blast," *Dallas Morning News,* 12 June 1943, sec. I, p. 4.

13. Mary Jane Gentry, "Thurber," p. 215; Mary Jane Gentry, San Angelo, Tex., to [Walter Prescott] Webb, [Austin, Tex.], 15 May 1944 (second and third quotations); Mary J[ane] Gentry, McCamey, Tex., to Walter P[rescott] Webb, Austin, Tex., 18 June 1944; Mary Jane Gentry, San Angelo, Tex[as] to Dr. Webb [Walter Prescott Webb, Austin, Tex.], 11 Sept[ember] 1945 (fourth quotation); [Walter Prescott Webb, Austin, Tex.], to Mary J[ane] Gentry, McCamey, Tex., 31 August 1943 (first quotation); [Walter Prescott Webb, Austin, Tex.], to Mary Jane Gentry, San Angelo, Tex., 18 May 1944; [Walter Prescott Webb, Austin, Tex.], to Mary J[ane] Gentry, McCamey, Tex., 15 June 1944; [Walter Prescott Webb, Austin, Tex.], to Mary J[ane] Gentry, McCamey, Tex., 28 June 1944; W[alter] P[rescott] Webb, Austin, Tex., to Mary Jane Gentry, McCamey, Tex., 17 June 1946 (fifth and sixth quotations), all of the above typescript and manuscript letters in Boxes 2M263 and 2M264, Walter Prescott Webb Papers, Center for American History, University of Texas at Austin, Austin, Tex.; W[alter] P[rescott] Webb, Austin, Tex., to Mary [Jane] Gentry, San Angelo, Tex., 17 February 1946, typescript letter, Mary Jane Gentry Collection; Odessa College, "Instructor Record of Work," 1 lf.; University of Texas, Austin, Tex., Diploma for Mary Jane Gentry as Graduate with Master of Arts Degree, manuscript, 29 August 1946, photocopy in Mary Jane Gentry Collection; University of Texas, Transcript of Coursework for Mary Jane Gentry.

Walter Prescott Webb chaired Mary Jane Gentry's master's thesis committee. Born in Panola County, Texas, in 1888, Webb grew up in several places, including Eastland and Stephens Counties, and attended the Ranger, Texas, high school. After teaching in several country schools, he attended the University of Texas, graduating in 1915. In 1918 he joined the faculty of the University of Texas. He received his doctorate in history in 1932 on the basis of his book, *The Great Plains* (1931). Remaining a faculty member in the history department at the University of Texas, Webb lectured for a year at the University of London and in 1939 became the director of the Texas State Historical Association. In the latter position he began the project to compile and publish the *Handbook of Texas* and joined with H. Bailey Carroll in creating the Junior Historian organization to help train public school pupils to research and write on local history topics under the supervision of their teachers. Webb remained at the University of Texas, writing additional scholarly books, until his death in an automobile accident in 1963 (*The New Handbook of Texas,* 6: 862–63).

The second reader on Gentry's thesis was Rudolph Leopold Biesele, a Texas German best remembered for *The History of the German Settlements in Texas, 1831–1861* (1931) and for his devotion to his students. Biesele, who was from Guadalupe County, attended Southwest Texas State Normal School and then the University of Texas, became a high school teacher in Corsicana and then Waco, and then earned a doctorate in history from the University of Texas. He subsequently taught at the University of Alabama and the Louisiana Polytechnic Institute and served as a visiting instructor at the University of Texas before becoming a regular faculty member at the university in Austin for the remainder of his career, until his death in 1960 (*The New Handbook of Texas*, 1:524–25).

Mary Jane Gentry's third reader was William N. Peach, who was a sociologist rather than a historian. Born in 1912, Peach was teaching as an instructor at the University of Texas in 1942 when he and three other economics teachers were dismissed by its board of regents for making a statement to correct what they viewed as false claims made at an anti-labor "patriotic" rally held in Dallas. Their dismissal became a cause célèbre among proponents of freedom of speech. After Gov. Coke Stevenson appointed six new members to the board of regents of the University of Texas, the body offered the dismissed instructors their former positions, and Peach in early 1946 accepted the reappointment with promotion to assistant professor. This meant that he had just returned to the university when he served on Mary Jane Gentry's master's thesis committee. Peach remained in Austin for a time, but he accepted appointment as a faculty member at the University of Oklahoma, where he authored more twenty books and monographs and was honored in 1965 with a George Lynn Cross Research Professorship. He died in 1984. ("Regents Oust Detractors of Dallas Meeting," *Dallas Morning News*, 29 June 1942, sec. 1, p. 2; Jack Krueger, "Regents Asked to Reinstate Ousted Economics Teachers," *Dallas Morning News*, 28 October 1944, sec. I, p. 1; Ray Osborn, "Capitol News—A Summary," *Dallas Morning News*, 24 February 1946, sec. I, p. 4; Susana Richardson, "Reds, Race, and Research: The Grand Tradition of Political Interference," pp. 125–72 in *Perspectives on the History of Higher Education*, edited by Roger L. Geiger, History of Higher Education Annual 24 [New Brunswick, N.J.: Transaction Publishers, 2005], pp. 148, 153).

14. At least as early as 1952, Gentry's work was identified to other scholars in H. Bailey Carroll and Milton R. Gutsch's checklist of theses and dissertations on Texas history (H. Bailey Carroll and Milton R. Gutsch, "A Check List of Theses and Dissertations in Texas History Produced in the Department of History of the University of Texas," *Southwestern Historical Quarterly* 56, no. 2 [October 1952]: 272). Among the subsequent historians of Thurber who have built on Gentry's pioneering work are Marilyn D. Rhinehart, Leo S. Bielinski, and Don Woodard (Marilyn D. Rhinehart, *A Way of Work and a Way of Life: Coal Mining in Thurber, Texas, 1888–1926* [College Station: Texas A&M University Press, 1992], pp. 120–22, 124, 126–38, 143–49; Leo S. Bielinski, *The Thurber Connection* [n.p.: privately printed, 1999], pp. 189–95, 198–200; Don Woodard, *Black Diamonds! Black Gold!* [Lubbock: Texas Tech University Press, 1998], pp. 269–71, 275–76).

In 1993 Mary Jane Gentry deposited her personal files of the Thurber newspapers, portions of her Thurber research materials, and a substantial collection of historic Thurber photographs in the Special Collections Division of the University of Texas at Arlington Libraries. Then in 2006 her surviving brother, Dan R. Gentry, donated a collection of letters she had received from former Thurber residents between 1939 and 1946 to the W. K. Gordon Center for Industrial History, Tarleton State University, at Thurber, Texas.

15. "Bombardiers Get Battle Training in West Texas 'Finishing School,'" *Fort Worth Star-Telegram,* 24 October 1943, clipping; "City Has Doubled since 1940 Census," *Fort Worth Star-Telegram,* 11 October 1953, clipping; Vance Gilmore, "San Angelo's Growth Sound," *Fort Worth Star-Telegram,* 29 December 1940, morning edition, clipping; "Growth since 1923 Session Is Seen Easily," *Fort Worth Star-Telegram,* 13 May 1934, clipping; "'Pilot Factory' Two Years Old," *Fort Worth Star-Telegram,* 12 February 1943, clipping, all in Fort Worth Star-Telegram Collection (AR406-7-141-181 "San Angelo, Texas, Prior to 1950").

16. "Classrooms Crumble," *San Angelo Standard-Times* (San Angelo, Tex.), 12 June 1979, morning edition, sec. A, p. 1; "School Demolition Set for Next Week," *San Angelo Standard-Times,* 6 June 1979, morning edition, sec. A, p. 3; Nancy Sullivan, "The Story of a Schoolhouse," typescript, [1946], 4 lvs., "Schools (S.A.)" Vertical File, Tom Green County Library, San Angelo, Tex.; Nancy Sullivan, "The Story of a Schoolhouse," *The Junior Historian* 6, no. 6 (May 1946): 5–6; Thomas Wright, "County History Ever-present in Sturdy Reminders of Past," *San Angelo Standard-Times,* 22 January 1967, sec. C, p. 1. For documentation of Gentry's service teaching at San Angelo Junior High School, see San Angelo Independent School District, Minutes, vol. 5, pp. 431, 447, 451, 460, 469, 474, [489]; San Angelo Independent School District, Minutes, vol. 6, pp. 6, 14, 32, 42, 51, 61, 69, 74, 83, 91, 99, 115, 126, 133, 140, 150, 156, 166, 174, 182, 185, 193, 202, 211, 223, 234, 239, 296, 350, 258, 267, 274, 283, 398, 307, 317, 326, 345, 354, 363, 374, 382, 392, 402, 430, 433, 460, 468, 473, 501, 512; San Angelo Independent School District, Minutes, vol. 7 (17 September 1946 to 30 July 1949), typescript in loose-leaf binder, p. 36, San Angelo Independent School District Offices; San Angelo Independent School District, Payroll Records, vol. I (30 September 1946 to 31 December 1951), typescript in loose-leaf binder, unpaged, San Angelo Independent School District Offices.

17. H. Bailey Carroll, *The Junior Historian Movement in Texas: A Guidebook and a History* (Austin: Texas State Historical Association, 1961), pp. 1–9.

18. Ibid., p. 10.

19. Grace Bitner, San Angelo, Tex., to Gentlemen [H. Bailey Carroll and Walter Prescott Webb, Austin, Tex.], 7 April 1941, typescript letter, Texas State Historical Association Records, Box 3J192, Center for American History, University of Texas at

Austin; Grace Bitner, San Angelo, Tex., to H. Bailey Carroll, Austin, Tex., 13 May 1944, manuscript letter, TSHA Records, Box 3J174; Grace Bitner, San Angelo, Tex., to H. Bailey Carroll, Austin, Tex., 11 December 1945, typescript letter, TSHA Records, Box 3J175; [H. Bailey Carroll], Austin, Tex., to Mr. Anderson, Assistant Principal, San Angelo, Tex., 16 September 1941, typescript letter, TSHA Records, Box 3J172; H. Bailey Carroll, [Austin, Tex.], to Mary Jane Gentry, San Angelo, Tex., 2 April 1945, typescript letter, TSHA Records, Box 3J174; H. Bailey Carroll, [Austin, Tex.], to Mary Jane Gentry, San Angelo, Tex., 21 November 1945, typescript letter, TSHA Records, Box 3J175; Mary Jane Gentry, San Angelo, Tex., to [H. Bailey] Carroll, Austin, Tex., 27 March 1945, typescript letter, TSHA Records, Box 3J174 (quotation); Mary J[ane] Gentry, San Angelo, Tex., to H. Bailey Carroll, Austin, Tex., 19 November 1945, typescript letter, TSHA Records, Box 3J175.

20. "Affairs of the Association," *Southwestern Historical Quarterly* 51, no. 1 (July 1947): 76; H. Bailey Carroll, [Austin, Tex.], to Mary J[ane] Gentry, San Angelo, Tex., 10 March 1947, typescript letter; H. Bailey Carroll, [Austin, Tex.], to Mary Jane Gentry, San Angelo, Tex., 27 April 1948, typescript letter; Mary Jane Gentry, San Angelo, Tex., to [H.] Bailey Carroll, Austin, Tex., 7 March 1947, typescript letter; Mary Jane Gentry, San Angelo, Tex[as], to H. Bailey Carroll, Austin, Tex[as], 28 April 1947, telegram; Mary Jane Gentry, San Angelo, Tex., to H. Bailey Carroll, Austin, Tex., 22 May 1948, typescript letter, all in TSHA Records, Box 3J176; H. Bailey Carroll, [Austin, Tex.], to Llerena Friend, Wichita Falls, Tex., 21 October 1940, typescript letter, TSHA Records, Box 3J172.

21. H. Bailey Carroll, "Texas Collection," *Southwestern Historical Quarterly* 52, no. 2 (October 1948): 241; Gentry to Carroll, 22 May 1948, TSHA Records, Box 3J176; "Local Teacher to Wales on Exchange Basis," *San Angelo Evening Standard* (San Angelo, Tex.), 10 May 1948, clipping in Grace Bitner, [San Angelo, Tex.], to [Dorman Winfrey, Austin, Tex.], 11 May 1948, typescript letter, TSHA Records, Box 3J178; San Angelo Independent School District, Minutes, vol. 7, p. 94; San Angelo Independent School District, Payroll Records, vol. I, unpaged; "Texans in London," *Fort Worth Star-Telegram,* 1 November 1948, p. 2; "Welsh Teacher Coming: Mary Jane Gentry to Sail July 24 for Wales Post," *San Angelo Evening Standard,* 23 June 1948, p. 10; Jacquelin Worden, "Queen, Pope, Europe: Exchange Teacher in Wales Makes the Holidays Count," *San Angelo Standard-Times,* 11 September 1949, sec. B, p. 14 (quotations).

22. H. Bailey Carroll, [Austin, Tex.], to Mary [Jane] Gentry, San Angelo, Tex., 5 April 1950, typescript letter; H. Bailey Carroll, [Austin, Tex.], to Mary Jane Gentry, San Angelo, Tex., 21 April 1950, typescript letter; H. Bailey Carroll, [Austin, Tex.], to Mary Jane Gentry, San Angelo, Texas, 18 May 1950, typescript letter, all in TSHA Records, Box 3J178; Carroll, *Junior Historian Movement,* p. 11; Bryan Dickson, San Angelo, Tex., to "Dear Miss Gentry" [Mary Jane Gentry, San Angelo, Tex.], 24 April 1950, typescript

letter, San Angelo Independent School District, Certified Personnel Prior to 1968, reel 6, microfilm, unpaged; Mary Jane Gentry, San Angelo, Tex., to H. Bailey Carroll, Austin, Tex., 17 April 1950, typescript letter; Mary Jane Gentry, San Angelo, Tex., to [H. Bailey] Carroll, [Austin, Tex.], 25 April 1950, manuscript letter, both in TSHA Records, Box 3J178; "Pupils Report Today: Faculty Meeting Monday Opens City School Year," *San Angelo Standard-Times,* 4 September 1949, sec. A, p. 4; Sally Rau, San Angelo, Tex., to H. Bailey Carroll, Austin, Tex., typescript letter, TSHA Records, Box 3J178; San Angelo Independent School District, Minutes, vol. 6, p. 44; San Angelo Independent School District, Minutes, vol. 7, p. 184; San Angelo Independent School District, Payroll Records, vol. I, unpaged; Robert Wear, "San Angelo in Midst of a Postwar Business Boom," *Fort Worth Star-Telegram,* 3 March 1946, clipping, Fort Worth Star-Telegram Collection (AR 406-7-141-181 "San Angelo, Texas, Prior to 1950"); *Worley's San Angelo (Tom Green County, Tex.) City Directory 1950* (Dallas: John F. Worley Directory Co., Publishers, 1950), pp. 187, 282.

23. "Affairs of the Association," *Southwestern Historical Quarterly* 54, no. 1 (July 1951), 101; Bryan Dickson, San Angelo, Tex., to Dear Miss Gentry [Mary Jane Gentry, San Angelo, Tex.], 20 April 1951, typescript letter, San Angelo Independent School District, Certified Personnel Prior to 1968, reel 6, microfilm, unpaged; H. Bailey Carroll, [Austin, Tex.], to Mary Jane Gentry, San Angelo, Tex., 8 March 1951, typescript letter; Mary Jane Gentry, San Angelo, Tex., to H. Bailey Carroll, Austin, Tex., 5 March 1951, typescript letter; Mary Jane Gentry, San Angelo, Tex[as] to H. Bailey Carroll, Austin, Tex[as], 22 April 1951, telegram, plus other Carroll-Gentry letters, all in TSHA Records, Box 3J178; *The 1951 Westerner* (San Angelo, Tex.: San Angelo High School, 1951), unpaged; *The 1952 Westerner* (San Angelo, Tex.: San Angelo High School, 1952), unpaged; *1953 Westerner* (San Angelo, Tex.: San Angelo High School, 1953), unpaged front matter; San Angelo Independent School District, Minutes, vol. 8 (20 September 1949 to 31 March 1951), typescript in loose-leaf binder, p. 178; San Angelo Independent School District, Minutes, vol. 9 (5 April 1952 to 17 June 1953), typescript in loose-leaf binder, pp. 265, 276; San Angelo Independent School District, Payroll Records, vol. I, unpaged; San Angelo Independent School District, Payroll Records, vol. II (31 January 1952 to 31 August 1953), typescript in loose-leaf binder, unpaged; Loretta Stewart, San Angelo, Tex., to H. Bailey Carroll, Austin, Tex., 24 March 1951, typescript letter; Loretta Stewart, [San Angelo, Tex.], to H. Bailey Carroll, Austin, Tex., 7 May 1951, typescript letter, both in TSHA Records, Box 3J178; *Worley's San Angelo (Tom Green County, Tex.) City Directory 1952* (Dallas: John F. Worley Directory Co., 1952), pp. 205, 780.

24. Joe Connally, interview by T. Lindsay Baker, Odessa, Tex., 10 July 2006, manuscript notes (first quotation); Cheri Dalton, interview by T. Lindsay Baker, Odessa,

Tex., 11 July 2006, manuscript notes (third quotation); Larry Gatlin, telephone interview by T. Lindsay Baker, 8 February 2007, manuscript notes (fifth quotation); Dr. Paul Johnson, interview by T. Lindsay Baker, Odessa, Tex., 10 July 2006, manuscript notes (sixth quotation); Debbie Morris, telephone interview by T. Lindsay Baker, 16 July 2006, typescript notes (fourth quotation); Kay Thomas, telephone interview by T. Lindsay Baker, 16 July 2006 (second quotation), typescript notes, all in Mary Jane Gentry Collection.

25. Irby B. Carruth, Austin, Tex., to Mary Jane Gentry, [Austin, Tex.], 16 July 1953, typescript teacher contract, photocopy in Mary Jane Gentry Collection; Connally interview by Baker, 10 July 2006 (second quotation); Dalton interview by Baker, 11 July 2006 (third quotation); Morris interview by Baker, 16 July 2006 (first quotation); *1953 Westerner,* unpaged front matter.

26. W. T. Barrett, Odessa, Tex., to Mary Jane Gentry, Ranger, Tex., 5 August 1955, typescript letter, photocopy in Mary Jane Gentry Collection; Irby B. Carruth, Austin, Tex., to Mary Jane Gentry, [Austin, Tex.], 22 June 1954, typescript teacher contract, photocopy in Mary Jane Gentry Collection; Irby B. Carruth, Austin, Tex., to Mary Jane Gentry, [Austin, Tex.], 11 May 1955, typescript teacher contract, photocopy in Mary Jane Gentry Collection; *The Comet* (Austin: Students of Stephen F. Austin High School, 1955), pp. 16 (second quotation), 109; Mary Jane Gentry, Austin, Tex., to [J. Carl] Hertzog, [El Paso, Tex.], 31 Oct[ober] 1953, manuscript letter, J. Carl Hertzog Papers, Box 32, C. L. Sonnichsen Special Collections Department, University Library, University of Texas at El Paso, El Paso, Tex. (first quotation); *Morrison & Fourmy's Austin (Travis County, Tex.) City Directory 1954* (Dallas: Morrison & Fourmy Directory Co., 1954), pp. 237, 84; *The 1954 Comet* (Austin: [Students of Stephen F. Austin High School], 1954), p. 14. It should be noted that Mary Jane Gentry did not serve as a faculty sponsor for the Junior Historians chapter at Stephen F. Austin High School but deferred this role to fellow teacher Samuel B. Hamlett ("Questionnaire for Junior Historian Chapters[,] Spring, 1954[,] Chapter Number 123," manuscript on printed form, and "Questionnaire for Junior Historian Chapters[,] Spring, 1955[,] Chapter Number 123," manuscript on printed form, both questionnaires in TSHA Records, Box 3J193).

27. E. D. Alexander, "Boomtown Odessa Still That; 'Roughneck' Tag Fading," *Fort Worth Star-Telegram,* 2 November 1958, sec. 1, p. 20; H. Bailey Carroll, "Texas Collection," *Southwestern Historical Quarterly* 63, no. 4 (April 1960): 615; 64, no. 1 (July 1960): 143; *Corral* (Odessa, Tex.: Odessa High School, 1956), p. 18; *Corral* (Odessa, Tex.: Odessa High School, 1958), pp. 238, 251; *Corral 1959* (Odessa, Tex.: Odessa High School, 1959), pp. 22, 272; *The Corral 1960* (Odessa, Tex.: Odessa High School, 1960), pp. 16, 223, 231; *Corral '64* (Odessa, Tex.: Odessa High School, 1964), p. 30; *Corral '65* (Odessa, Tex.: Odessa High School, 1965), p. 147; *Corral '66* (Odessa, Tex.: Odessa High School, 1966),

p. 146; *Corral '67* (Odessa, Tex.: Odessa High School, 1967), p. 180; *Corral '68* (Odessa, Tex.: Odessa High School, 1968), p. 194; Mary Jane Gentry, Odessa, Tex., to Carl Hertzog, [El Paso, Tex.], 20 Sept[ember] 1965, manuscript letter, J. Carl Hertzog Papers, Box 32 (third quotation); Mary Jane Gentry, Odessa, Tex., to Carl Hertzog [El Paso, Tex.], 3 Sept[ember] 1966, manuscript letter, J. Carl Hertzog Papers, Box 32 (first and second quotations); Carol L. Horton, interview by T. Lindsay Baker, 11 July 2006, tape recording and typed transcript, Mary Jane Gentry Collection; *1961 Corral* (Odessa, Tex.: Odessa High School, 1961), pp. 17, 272; *1962 Corral* (Odessa, Tex.: Odessa High School, 1962), pp. 17, 269; *Odessa, Texas[,] City Directory 1956* (Oklahoma City: Lloyds Directory Service, 1956), unpaged; *Odessa, Texas[,] City Directory 1957* (Oklahoma City: Lloyds Directory Service, 1957), unpaged; *Odessa, Texas[,] City Directory 1958* (Oklahoma City: Lloyds National Directory Co., 1958), p. 123A; *Odessa, Texas[,] City Directory 1959* (Oklahoma City: Lloyds National Directory Co., 1959), p. 132A; *Odessa, Texas[,] City Directory 1960* (Oklahoma City: Lloyds National Directory Co., 1960), p. 125A; *Odessa, Texas[,] City Directory 1961–62* (Odessa, Tex.: Lloyds Directory Service, [1961]), p. 132A; *Odessa, Texas[,] City Directory 1962–63* (Odessa, Tex.: Lloyds Directory Service, 1962), p. 127A; *Odessa, Texas[,] City Directory 1964* (Odessa, Tex.: Lloyds Directory Service, [1964]), p. 127A; *Odessa, Texas[,] City Directory 1965* (Odessa, Tex.: Lloyds Directory Service, Inc., [1965]), p. 233; *Odessa, Texas[,] City Directory 1966* (Odessa, Tex.: Lloyds Directory Service, Inc., [1966]), p. 199; *Odessa, Texas[,] City Directory 1966–67* (Odessa, Tex.: Lloyds Directory Service, Inc., [1966]), p. 277; *Odessa, Texas[,] City Directory 1967–68* (Odessa, Tex.: Lloyds Directory Service, Inc., [1967]), p. 292.

28. H. Bailey Carroll, Frances Nesmith, and Mary Jane Gentry, *The Story of Texas* (New York: Noble & Noble, 1963); Dan R. Gentry interview by Baker, 17 December 2003; Frances J. Nesmith, "Biographical Information for the Texas State Historical Association Files," 27 October 1952, manuscript on printed form, TSHA Records, Box 3J209; "Name Mary Jane Gentry," manuscript on printed form, [ca. 1972–73], "Gentry, Mary Jane" File, Office of Media Relations and Publications, Odessa College, Odessa, Tex.; Odessa College, Odessa, Tex., *Hunting a Speaker? Odessa College Can Help* (Odessa, Tex.: Odessa College, Public Information Office, [ca. 1970]), unpaged, in "Odessa—College—Faculty" Vertical File, Southwest History and Genealogy Department, Ector County Library, Odessa, Tex.; Bill Warren, "Books," *Austin American-Statesman* (Austin, Tex.), 28 January 1973, Show World supplement, pp. 28, 30. All ephemeral items issued by Odessa College cited in this work are located in Odessa College Historical Files, Learning Resources Center, Odessa College, Odessa, Tex., unless otherwise noted.

Gentry seemingly felt no personal animosity toward H. Bailey Carroll, though she must have felt slighted by the lack of recognition for her contributions to *The Story of*

Texas. Several years after his death in 1966, she wrote to an associate, "Dr. Carroll was a friend of mine. In fact about twelve years [ago] he, a teacher from Austin and I co-authored a Texas history for seventh grade pupils. During that time so many tragedies descended upon him—first his serious illnesses, his home burned and almost all of his entire library was lost or damaged by smoke and water damage. It was a heart-breaking time" (Mary Jane Gentry, [Odessa, Tex.], to Carl Hertzog, [El Paso, Tex.], 6 September 1975, manuscript letter, J. Carl Hertzog Papers, Box 32).

29. Dr. Judy Cornes, interview by T. Lindsay Baker, Odessa, Tex., 10 July 2006, manuscript notes, Mary Jane Gentry Collection; Dalton interview by Baker, 11 July 2006 (first and second quotations); Horton interview by Baker, 11 July 2006; Paul Johnson interview by Baker, 10 July 2006 (fifth quotation); Mary Nell Johnson, telephone interview by T. Lindsay Baker, 28 July 2006, typescript notes in Mary Jane Gentry Collection; Mary Manitzas, telephone interview by T. Lindsay Baker, 25 July 2006, typescript notes in Mary Jane Gentry Collection (third and fourth quotations).

30. Cornes interview by Baker, 10 July 2006 (third and fourth quotations); Dan R. Gentry, "Mary Jane Catherine Gentry," p. 3; Truett L. Hilliard interview by T. Lindsay Baker, Odessa, Tex., 10 July 2006 (sixth quotation); Paul Johnson interview by Baker, 10 July 2006 (first, second, and fifth quotations); Odessa College, Odessa, Tex., *Hunting a Speaker?*, unpaged; Odessa College, Odessa, Tex., "Name Gentry, Mary Jane," manuscript on printed form, [ca. 1972–73], 1 lf., "Gentry, Mary Jane" File, Office of Media Relations and Publications, Odessa College.

31. *Branding Iron '69* (Odessa, Tex.: Odessa College, 1969), p. 196; *Branding Iron '70* (Odessa, Tex.: Odessa College, 1970), pp. 136, 179; *Branding Iron '71* (Odessa, Tex.: Odessa College, 1971), p. 156; "By Academic Senate: Committees Chosen," *Pulse* (Odessa College, Odessa, Tex.) 2, no. 4 (December 1972): [2]; *Corral '68*, p. 194; "Instructors Added to College Faculty," *The Roundup* (Odessa College, Odessa, Tex.), 4 October 1968, p. 6; "OC Enrollment Reaches 2,756," *Odessa American* (Odessa, Tex.), 17 September 1968, sec. A, p. 11; Odessa College, Odessa, Tex., *Faculty Meetings Fall 1969* (Odessa, Tex.: Odessa College, 1969), pp. 20, 24, 31; Odessa College, Odessa, Tex., "Instructor Record of Work," 1 lf.; Odessa College, Odessa, Tex., *Odessa College Class Schedule Spring—1971[,] Bulletin[,] Spring Semester 1971* (Odessa, Tex.: Odessa College, 1971), 1 lf.; Odessa College, Odessa, Tex., *Odessa College Faculty Meetings Fall 1968* (Odessa, Tex.: Odessa College, 1968), pp. 9, 14, 20; Odessa College, Odessa, Tex., *Odessa College[,] Fall Semester[,] 1968* (Odessa, Tex.: Odessa College, 1968), lf. 5; Odessa College, Odessa, Tex., *Odessa College[,] Spring Semester[,] 1969* (Odessa, Tex.: Odessa College, 1969), lf. 5; Odessa College, Odessa, Tex., *Report of the Odessa College Faculty Self-evaluation Study Prepared for Examination by the Southern Association of Colleges and Schools 1969–1970* (Odessa, Tex.: Odessa College, 1970),

pp. iv, 58, 251–54; Odessa College, Odessa, Tex., *25th Faculty (Announcements)* (Odessa, Tex.: Odessa College, 1971), p. 297; *Odessa,* Texas[,] *City Directory 1967-68,* p. 292; Southwestern Bell Telephone Company, Odessa, Tex., *Southwestern Bell Telephone Directory for Odessa*[,] *Area Code* 915[,] *June 1967* (Odessa, Tex.: Southwestern Bell Telephone Company, 1967), p. 50; Thomas telephone interview by Baker, 16 July 2006 (quotation).

32. Arizona State University, Tempe, Ariz., Transcript for Mary Jane Gentry, 6 September 1974, photocopy in Mary Jane Gentry Collection; Cornes interview by Baker, 10 July 2006 (second quotation); Mary Jane Gentry, [Istanbul, Turkey], to Carl Hertzog, [El Paso, Tex.], 31 July 1978, manuscript letter, J. Carl Hertzog Papers, Box 32; Fred Giffin, [Tempe, Ariz.], to Mary Jane Gentry, Odessa, Tex., 12 August 1974, postcard, photocopy in Mary Jane Gentry Collection (first quotation); Hilliard interview by Baker, 10 July 2006 (third quotation); University of Oregon, Eugene, Oreg., Transcript for Mary Jane Gentry, [ca. 1969], photocopy in Mary Jane Gentry Collection; University of Virginia, Charlottesville, Va., Student Grade Report for Mary Jane Gentry, Summer 1970, photocopy in Mary Jane Gentry Collection.

33. Mary Jane Gentry, [Odessa, Tex.], to Carl Hertzog, [El Paso, Tex.], 14 January 1975, manuscript letter; Mary Jane Gentry, [Odessa, Tex.], to Carl Hertzog, [El Paso, Tex.], 18 January 1978, manuscript letter(first quotation); Mary Jane Gentry, [Odessa, Tex.], to Carl Hertzog, 10 January 1980, manuscript letter (second quotation), all in J. Carl Hertzog Papers, Box 32; "OC Teachers Seek Tenure," *Odessa American,* 26 March 1974, sec. A, p. 2; "OC Trustees Approve Tenure Status for 20," *Odessa American,* 24 April 1974, sec. A, p. 2; Odessa College, Odessa, Tex., "Instructor Record of Work," 1 lf.; Odessa College, Odessa, Tex., *Odessa College Faculty Office Hours*[,] *Fall, 1977* (Odessa, Tex.: Odessa College, 1977), photocopy publication, lf. 4; Odessa College, Odessa, Tex., *Odessa College (Odessa Junior College District)*[,] *Odessa, Texas*[,] *Fall Semester 1977* (Odessa, Tex.: Odessa College, 1977), lf. 4; Odessa College, Odessa, Tex., *Odessa College*[,] *P.O. Box 3752*[,] *Odessa, Texas 79760*[,] *Campus Telephone Extension and Office Numbers*[,] *Fall 1977* (Odessa, Tex.: Odessa College, 1977), photocopy publication, lf. 1; "Retired Teachers Meeting Slated," *Odessa American,* 3 October 1976, sec. A, p. 10; "Service Awards to OC Staffers," *Odessa American,* 9 April 1979, sec. D, p. 8; Phil Speegle, Odessa, Tex., to Mary Jane Gentry, Odessa, Tex., 29 June 1978, typescript letter, photocopy in Mary Jane Gentry Collection.

More than a decade before Mary Jane Gentry retired, she expressed to Carl Hertzog her fantasy of moving to Florence, Italy, after leaving teaching: "Florence intrigues me to the degree that I frequently announce that I would like to spend my retirement years there. Twice I have had the good fortune to linger there and marvel at the 'cultural treasures' and wonder how it would be to live, browse, and meditate in such surroundings" (Mary Jane Gentry, [Odessa, Tex.], to Carl Hertzog, [El Paso, Tex.], 5 Sept[ember] 1966, manuscript letter, J. Carl Hertzog Papers, Box 32).

34. Cornes interview by Baker, 10 July 2006, interview (fourth quotation); Gatlin interview by Baker, 8 February 2007 (sixth quotation); Larry Gatlin and Jeff Lenburg, *All the Gold in California and Other People, Places & Things* (Nashville, Tenn.: Thomas Nelson Publishers, 1998), p. 300; "Gatlin Performs Nov. 7," *The Roundup*, 7 November 1975, p. 1; "Gatlins to Appear in Special Concert Nov. 19," *The Roundup*, 16 November 1973, p. 1; Dan R. Gentry interview by Baker, 17 December 2003; Paul Johnson interview by Baker, 10 July 2006 (first, second, and third quotations); Thomas interview by Baker, 16 July 2006 (fifth quotation).

35. "Death Notices: Mary Gentry," *Odessa American*, 6 December 1993, sec. B, p. 3; Dan R. Gentry interview by Baker, 17 December 2003; Dan [R.] Gentry to Baker, 3 October 2006, manuscript letter; Dan R. Gentry, "Mary Jane Catherine Gentry," p. 3; Mary Jane Gentry to Special Collections Division, University of Texas at Arlington, 16 August 1993 and 1 September 1993, typescript gift agreements, photocopies in Mary Jane Gentry Collection; *Polk 1993 Odessa[,] Texas[,] City Directory* (Dallas: R. L. Polk & Co., [1993]), p. 105; Thomas interview by Baker, 16 July 2006.

CHAPTER 1

1. Gomer Gower to M.J. Gentry, July 17, 1944.

2. E. T. Dumble, "Report of Progress," *Second Annual Report of the Geological Survey of Texas, 1890*, p. 436.

3. W. F. Cummins, "Report on Geology of Northwestern Texas," *Second Annual Report of the Geological Survey of Texas, 1890*, p. 437.

4. E. T. Dumble, "First Report of Progress," *Texas: Geological and Mineralogical Survey*, p. 47. The report on the coal mines around Gordon, Strawn and Thurber was made to Dumble by W. F. Cummins. Dumble, the state geologist, included Cummins's Report in his "First Report of Progress."

5. Dumble, "First Report of Progress," pp. 47–48.

6. Cummins, "Report on Geology of Northwestern Texas," p. 441.

7. C. S. Wilkins, "Thurber: A Sociological Study of a Company Owned Town," M.A. thesis, University of Texas, Austin, 1929, pp. 2–3.

8. Details of this labor dispute are included in Chapter 3.

9. Mrs. John S. Graham to M.J.G., January 31, 1940.

10. Dumble, "First Report of Progress," p. 48.

11. Vallie Eoff, "A History of Erath County, Texas," Master's thesis, University of Texas, Austin, 1937, p. 134, states that "in 1885 Captain Johnson sold this mine to Colonel Hunter and Edgar Lewis Marston, who organized the Texas & Pacific Coal

Company with Colonel Hunter as president." Colonel Hunter states in his *Annual Report, 1889* that the Texas & Pacific Coal Company was organized in October, 1888, and took possession of the Johnson coal mines in November, 1888.

12. *Dallas Morning News,* September 19, 1903.

13. *Annual Report of the Texas & Pacific Coal Company, 1889,* p. 2.

14. *Farm and Ranch,* January 22, 1898.

15. Wilkins, "Thurber: A Sociological Study of a Company Owned Town," p. 6.

16. *Annual Report of Texas & Pacific Coal Company, 1889,* p. 2.

17. Mack Creswell to M.J.G., interview, December 30, 1944.

18. T&P Coal Company vs. Thomas Lawson, p. 293, Office of the Clerk, Supreme Court of Texas, Austin.

19. Ibid., p. 268.

20. Criminal Court Docket, Vol. D, p. 70, Office of the County Clerk, Stephenville, Texas.

21. Criminal Court Docket, Vol. D, p. 70, Office of the County Clerk, Stephenville, Texas.

22. Minutes of the County Court, Vol. C, p. 183, Office of the County Clerk, Stephenville.

23. Gomer Gower to M.J.G., January 18, 1945.

24. *Dallas Morning News,* November 8, 1902. Wilkins states on p. 5, "Thurber: A Sociological Study of a Company Owned Town," that Colonel Hunter died in 1899. Hunter died November 8, 1902; *Dallas Morning News,* November 8, 1902.

25. Gomer Gower to M.J.G., January 18, 1945.

26. Ibid., August 14, 1944.

27. Ibid.

28. *Annual Report of Texas & Pacific Coal Company, 1889,* p. 5.

29. C. W. Woodman to Ben L. Owens, April 22, 1940. Woodman wrote and negotiated all contracts with company employees in the 1903 labor troubles. Owens was a research assistant in the Department of Economics, University of Texas, at the time he received Woodman's letter.

30. V. Eoff, "A History of Erath County, Texas," p. 136 states "By 1920, thirteen mines had been opened in or near Thurber." The Texas Pacific Coal and Oil Company opened fifteen mines in and around Thurber. Gordon mentions the opening of fifteen mines in a letter to M.J.G., August 12, 1941. Gomer Gower explains the system for numbering the fifteen mines in a letter to M.J.G., June 24, 1944.

31. W. K. Gordon to M.J.G., June 23, 1944.

32. Ibid., August 12, 1941.

33. Erath County was organized in 1856, and the Johnsons began mining coal in Thurber in 1886.

CHAPTER 2

1. *Annual Report of Texas & Pacific Coal Company, 1889,* 1.

2. Hazel Miller, Stephenville, says she remembers playing with Wallis Warfield when she visited her cousins in Thurber. *The Strawn Tribune,* November 19, 1940, carries an article in which a former Thurber resident recalls the visit of Wallis. In a thesis, "Thurber, Texas, An Abandoned Coal Mining Town" (Southern Methodist University, Dallas), there is a denial based on a letter from the Duchess, stating that she never visited in Thurber, Texas.

3. Gomer Gower to M.J.G., July 14, 1944; *Who's Who in America,* Vol. 24, p. 2367 states that on January 1, 1932, Lawrence Tibbett married Mrs. Jonnie Marston Burgard.

4. *Annual Report of Texas & Pacific Coal Company, 1895,* p. 5.

5. Gomer Gower to M.J.G., July 14, 1944.

6. Gomer Gower to M.J.G., August 6, 1944.

7. W. K. Gordon to M.J.G., June 25, 1944.

8. Gomer Gower to M.J.G., July 14, 1944.

9. *Farm and Ranch,* January 22, 1898.

10. Gomer Gower to M.J.G., August 6, 1944.

11. Bill Lorenz, interview, July 14, 1944.

12. Gomer Gower to M.J.G., August 6, 1944.

13. Gomer Gower to M.J.G., August 6, 1944.

14. Ibid.

15. *Texas Mining and Trade Journal,* November 28, 1896.

16. *The Texas Mining and Trade Journal,* February 20, 1897.

17. *New York American,* April 19, 1918.

18. Gomer Gower to M.J.G., June 24, 1944.

19. W. K. Gordon to M.J.G, June 23, 1944.

20. *Texas Mining and Trade Journal,* March 6, 1897.

21. Ibid.

22. *Texas Mining and Trade Journal,* March 6, 1897.

23. *Annual Report of Texas & Pacific Coal Company, 1900.*

24. Bill Lorenz to M.J.G., August 8, 1939.

25. *Ranger Times,* Fiftieth Anniversary Edition, 1910–1934.

26. G. J. Gentry to M.J.G., interview, July 25, 1940.

27. *Fort Worth Press,* March 30, 1937.

CHAPTER 3

1. The Coalville Mines were located about eight miles northeast of Thurber.

2. Gomer Gower to M.J.G., August 14, 1944.

3. Gomer Gower to M.J.G., August 14, 1944.

4. *Annual Report of Texas & Pacific Coal Company, 1889,* p. 2.

5. All mined coal was thrown on a screen and the miners received no pay for the coal that fell through the screen. It has been estimated that when screens are used, the earnings of the miners would be reduced from twelve to fourteen percent.

6. Gomer Gower to M.J.G., August 14, 1944.

7. *Annual Report of Texas & Pacific Coal Company, 1889,* pp. 2–3.

8. Monthly Returns of Company B. Frontier Forces, for the Month Ending December 31, 1888, Adjutant-General's Papers, State Capitol, Austin. In Hunter's *Report* he states that the Rangers came after Christmas, a date which does not coincide with the one given by McMurry. Colonel Hunter was never very accurate about dates so in all probability the date given by McMurry is the correct one.

9. *Annual Report of Texas & Pacific Coal Company, 1889,* pp. 2–3.

10. *Fort Worth Daily Gazette,* January 21, 1889.

11. *Fort Worth Daily Gazette,* January 21, 1889.

12. [From] *Fort Worth Daily Gazette,* January 21, 1889.

13. [From] *Fort Worth Daily Gazette,* January 21, 1889.

14. McMurry to W.H. King, February 17, 1889. Adjutant General's Papers, State Capitol, Austin.

15. *Annual Report of Texas & Pacific Coal Company, 1889,* p. 3.

16. Gomer Gower to M.J.G., August 14, 1944.

17. McMurry to King, April 6, 1889, Adjutant General's Papers.

18. McMurry to King, May 23, 1889, Adjutant General's Papers.

19. Ibid., June 6, 1889.

20. Ibid., July 2, 1889.

21. Ibid., July 8, 1889.

22. Terence V. Powderly was the General Master Workman of the Knights of Labor.

23. *Annual Report of Texas & Pacific Coal Company, 1889,* p. 3.

24. *Report of the Adjutant-General, 1889–1890,* pp. 26–27.

25. Adjutant-General's Papers, State Capitol, Austin.

26. McMurry to King, July 12, 1890, Adjutant-General's Papers.

27. Hunter to W. H. Mabry, June 5, 1894, Adjutant-General's Papers.

28. McDonald to Mabry, June 13, 1894, Adjutant-General's Papers.

29. Affidavit filed by W. K. Gordon in the injunction brought by Bruce and Stewart against the T.&P. Coal Co. This affidavit, the threatening letter sent to Colonel Hunter and the circular advertising free beer are among the Adjutant-General's Papers, State Capitol, Austin. At the top of the threatening letter is a notice of the

reward which Hunter offered in connection with the letter. The writers were apprehended and tried in a federal court at Waco on the charge of sending such material through the mails.

30. Albert B. Paine, *Captain Bill McDonald Texas Ranger,* pp. 217–219.

31. *Monthly Reports, Company C,* Adjutant-General's Papers.

32. Gomer Gower to Ben L. Owens, April 12, 1940.

33. *Fort Worth Telegram,* September 14, 1903.

34. *Fort Worth Telegram,* September 14, 1903.

35. *Fort Worth Telegram,* September 11, 1903. Wilkins in "Thurber: A Sociological Study of a Company Owned Town," pp. 6–7 states: "Union labor was forbidden and the town kept closed to strangers until 1900. At this time the company's labor policy underwent a complete change. Unions were formed among all classes of workers." Thurber was unionized in 1903.

36. *Dallas Morning News,* September 11, 1903.

37. Ibid.

38. *Dallas Morning News,* September 11, 1903.

39. *Fort Worth Telegram,* September 11, 1903.

40. *Dallas Morning News,* September 11, 1903.

41. *Dallas Morning News,* September 11, 1903.

42. *Dallas Morning News,* September 13, 1903.

43. *Dallas Morning News,* September 14, 1903.

44. *Dallas Morning News,* September 14, 1903.

45. Bill Lorenz to M.J.G., August 8, 1939.

46. *Fort Worth Telegram,* September 15, 1903.

47. Ibid.

48. C. W. Woodman to Ben L. Owens, April 22, 1940.

49. *Dallas Morning News,* September 18, 1903.

50. *Dallas Morning News,* September 19, 1903.

51. *Dallas Morning News,* September 19, 1903.

52. Ibid.

53. *Fort Worth Telegram,* September 20, 1903.

54. *Fort Worth Telegram,* September 22, 1903.

55. *Dallas Morning News,* September 22, 1903

56. *Proceedings of the Sixth Annual Convention of Texas State Federation of Labor,* Fort Worth, Texas, November 16, 17, 18, 1903, p. 14.

57. *Dallas Morning News,* September 22, 1903.

58. Ibid., September 27, 1903.

59. Ibid.

60. Woodman to Owens, April 22, 1940.

61. *Dallas Morning News,* August 30, 1916.

62. *Thurber Journal,* August 19, 1916.

63. Ibid.

64. *Dallas Morning News,* August 30, 1916.

CHAPTER 4

1. *Annual Report of Texas & Pacific Coal Company, 1889,* p. 4.

2. *Annual Report of Texas & Pacific Coal Company, 1894,* p. 4.

3. Gomer Gower to M.J.G., January 18, 1945.

4. Daisy Varley Conn to M.J.G., September 22, 1944.

5. Texas & Pacific Coal Co. vs Thomas Lawson, p. 271.

6. *Texas Mining and Trade Journal,* May 29, 1897.

7. *Annual Report of Texas & Pacific Coal Company, 1897,* p. 4.

8. *Annual Report of Texas & Pacific Coal Company, 1900,* pages not numbered.

9. *Annual Report of Texas & Pacific Coal Company, 1902,* p. 15.

10. *Annual Report of Texas & Pacific Coal Company, 1903,* pages not numbered.

11. *Thurber Journal,* March 1, 1902.

12. Ibid.

13. Bill Lorenz to M.J.G., August 8, 1939.

14. Minutes of Department Managers Meeting, May 3, 1905. These Minutes are among the personal papers of Mose Miller and are in the possession of his wife, Mabel Miller, Stephenville, Texas.

15. Sadie Davidson to M.J.G., interview, June 15, 1941.

16. *Fort Worth Star-Telegram,* September 15, 1930.

17. Ibid.

18. Hazel Miller to M.J.G., interview, August 14, 1941.

19. Faye Nichol to M.J.G., interview, June 15, 1941.

20. Hazel Miller to M.J.G., interview, August 14, 1941.

21. Personal Papers of Mose Miller.

22. Fern Faggard Gibson to M.J.G., interview, June 20, 1941.

23. Texas & Pacific Coal Company vs Thomas Lawson, pp. 334–335.

24. Minutes of Department Managers Meeting, May 3, 1905.

25. Roy Miller to M.J.G., interview, October 22, 1944.

26. Bill Lorenz to M.J.G., August 8, 1939.

27. Texas & Pacific Coal Company vs Thomas Lawson, p. 307.

28. Texas & Pacific Coal Company vs Thomas Lawson, p. 322.

29. Ibid., p. 290.

30. *34 Southwestern Reporter,* p. 919.

31. Bill Lorenz to M.J.G., February 8, 1940.

32. Ibid.

33. Roy Miller to M.J.G., interview, July 4, 1940.

34. Bill Lorenz to M.J.G., February 8, 1940.

35. Ibid.

36. Personal papers of Mose Miller.

37. See Financial Statement, p. 121 [Table 2].

38. *Annual Report of Texas Pacific Coal and Oil Company,* 1933 (no page numbers).

CHAPTER 5

1. Wilkins, "Thurber: A Sociological Study of a Company Owned Town," p. 38.

2. W. K. Gordon to M.J.G., August 12, 1941.

3. W. M. McDonald to W. H. Mabry, June 16, 1894, Adjutant-General's Papers.

4. *Thurber Journal,* May 22, 1902.

5. This date was chosen because Thurber had reached the peak of its prosperity in 1920 as shown by the financial statement on page 121 [Table 2].

6. Daisy V. Conn to M.J.G., interview, July 20, 1942.

7. Bill Boyd to M.J.G., interview, June 21, 1944.

8. Bill Lorenz to M.J.G., August 8, 1941.

9. G. J. Gentry to M.J.G., interview, March 12, 1941.

10. G. J. Gentry to M.J.G., interview, January 5, 1940.

11. Bill Boyd to M.J.G., interview, June 21, 1944.

12. E. Buchanan to M.J.G., interview, July 20, 1943.

13. E. Buchanan to M.J.G., interview, July 20, 1943.

14. *Stephenville Empire,* June 11, 1909.

15. Bill Lorenz to M.J.G., August 8, 1939.

16. Faye Nichol to M.J.G., interview, June 15, 1941.

17. T. & P. Coal Co. vs Thomas Lawson, p. 269.

18. Bill Lorenz to M.J.G., August 8, 1939.

19. *Texas Mining and Trade Journal,* February 27, 1898.

20. *Thurber Journal,* April 25, 1907.

21. Bill Lorenz to M.J.G., interview, July 28, 1943.

22. Daisy V. Conn to M.J.G., September 22, 1944.

23. George Studdard to M.J.G., interview, July 28, 1943.

24. T&P Coal Company vs Thomas Lawson, page 269.

25. *Annual Report of Texas & Pacific Coal Company, 1891,* p. 3.

26. *Stephenville Empire,* February 13, 1892.

27. Bill Lorenz to M.J.G., August 8, 1939.

28. *Annual Report of Texas & Pacific Coal Company, 1896,* p. 3.

29. *Strawn Tribune,* November 29, 1940.

30. *Annual Report of Texas & Pacific Coal Company, 1896,* p. 3.

31. Bill Lorenz to M.J.G., interview, July 28, 1943.

32. G. J. Gentry to M.J.G., interview, January 20, 1944.

33. Ibid.

34. Personal Papers of Mose Miller, Stephenville.

35. *Thurber Journal,* April 6, 1901.

36. G. J. Gentry to M.J.G., interview, January 20, 1944.

37. T&P Coal Company vs Thomas Lawson, p. 329.

38. *Annual Report of Texas & Pacific Coal Company, 1896,* p. 3.

39. *Texas Mining and Trade Journal,* November 28, 1896.

40. Mrs. Joe Descavage to M.J.G., interview, May, 1935.

41. Texas & Pacific Coal Co. vs Connaughton, *50 Southwestern Reporter,* p. 173. Connaughton brought suit against the company charging that he was permanently injured because of inefficient medical service rendered by a company physician.

42. C. S. Campbell, Minutes of Meeting of Department Managers, May 3, 1905.

43. Ibid., May 17, 1905.

44. *Annual Report of Texas & Pacific Coal Company, 1889,* p. 3.

45. *Stephenville Empire,* January 9, 1892.

46. Information contained in a Scrap Book, Texas Pacific Coal and Oil Company, Fort Worth.

47. Sadie Davidson to M.J.G., interview, June 15, 1941.

48. Scrap Book, Texas Pacific Coal and Oil Company, Fort Worth.

49. Rev. D. D. Tidwell to M.J.G., January 25, 1940.

CHAPTER 6

1. *Texas Mining and Trade Journal,* October 24, 1896.

2. Ibid.

3. *Texas Mining and Trade Journal,* October 24, 1896.

4. Ibid.

5. Bill Lorenz to M.J.G., interview, July 20, 1945.

6. *Texas Mining and Trade Journal,* March 6, 1897.

7. E. Buchanan to M.J.G., interview, January 3, 1942.

8. Bill Lorenz to M.J.G., August 8, 1939.

9. Personal Papers of Mose Miller.

10. Daisy V. Conn to M.J.G., interview, January 3, 1942.

11. Bill Lorenz to M.J.G., August 8, 1939.

12. *Thurber Journal*, December, 1906.

13. Ibid., April 18, 1907.

14. *Texas Mining and Trade Journal*, January 2, 1897.

15. Personal Papers of Mose Miller.

16. *The Thurber Journal*, March 21, 1907.

17. *Texas Mining and Trade Journal*, October 3, 1896.

18. By-Laws, R. D. Hunter Fishing & Boating Club, 1904, Personal Papers of Mose Miller.

19. Reprint of an article from the *Dallas News*. *Thurber Journal*, June 13, 1907.

20. *Texas Mining and Trade Journal*, March 3, 1900.

21. George Studdard to M.J.G., interview, August 15, 1941.

22. Bill Lorenz to M.J.G., interview, July 20, 1943.

23. *The Thurber Journal*, January 26, 1901.

24. Ibid.

25. *The Thurber Journal*, May 22, 1908.

26. *The Thurber Journal*, May 22, 1908.

27. Bill Lorenz to M.J.G., interview, July 20, 1943.

28. *Texas Mining and Trade Journal*, March 3, 1900.

29. *The Thurber Journal*, May 22, 1908.

CHAPTER 7

1. Immigration Records, Office of District Clerk, County Court House, Stephenville, Texas.

2. S. P. Williams to M.J.G., interview, December 22, 1944.

3. Ernest Belcher to M.J.G., interview, December 22, 1944.

4. Bill Lorenz, interview, July 28, 1943.

5. Bill Lorenz to M.J.G., August 8, 1939.

6. Rita Buffo Studdard to M.J.G., April 10, 1940.

7. Mrs. Visentini to M.J.G., interview, July 23, 1943.

8. Rita Buffo Studdard to M.J.G., April 10, 1940.

9. Bill Lorenz to M.J.G., August 8, 1939.

10. Rita Buffo Studdard to M.J.G., April 10, 1940.

11. Ibid.

12. Daisy Conn to M.J.G., September 22, 1944.

13. Marjorie Venturi to M.J.G., June 6, 1944.

14. Bill Boyd to M.J.G., interview, July 29, 1943.

15. Rita Buffo Studdard to M.J.G., April 10, 1940.

16. Mrs. Visentini to M.J.G., interview, July 23, 1943.

17. Rita Buffo Studdard to M.J.G., interview, December 29, 1944.

18. Bill Lorenz to M.J.G., interview, July 14, 1944.

19. Rita Buffo Studdard to M.J.G., interview, December 29, 1944.

CHAPTER 8

1. H. H. Shaw to M.J.G., interview, December 29, 1939.

2. Bill Lorenz to M.J.G., interview, July 28, 1943.

3. G. J. Gentry to M.J.G., interview, August 29, 1943.

4. *Stephenville Empire-Tribune,* Anniversary Edition, January 31, 1936.

5. George B. Studdard to M.J.G., interview, August 15, 1941.

6. Leon Truesdell, Chief, Population Division, Bureau of Census to M.J.G., June 29, 1945.

7. Roy Miller to M.J.G., interview, October 22, 1944.

8. E. Buchanan to M.J.G., interview, July 31, 1945.

Bibliography

BOOKS

50 Southwestern Reporter, April 10–May 29, 1899. St. Paul: West Publishing Company, 1899.

Paddock, B. B., Editor, *History of Texas: Fort Worth and the Texas Northwest Edition,* Vol. II. Chicago: Lewis Publishing Company, 1922.

Paine, Albert B., *Captain Bill McDonald Texas Ranger.* New York: J. J. Little & Ives Company, 1909.

Powderly, Terence, *The Path I Trod, Autobiography of Terence Powderly.* New York: Columbia University Press, 1940.

Sullivan, W. J. L., *Twelve Years in the Saddle for Law and Order on the Frontier of Texas.* Austin: Von Boeckmann–Jones Company, 1909.

34 Southwestern Reporter, March 9–April 20, 1896. St. Paul: West Publishing Company, 1896.

Who's Who in America, Vol. 24, 1946–1947. Chicago: A. N. Marquis Company, 1946.

Who's Who in Commerce and Industry. New York: Institute for Research in Biography, Inc., 1938.

PERIODICALS

Graham, Llewllyn, "Wildcatters' Tribute," *Texas Parade,* June, 1939.

Senter, E. G., "A Pioneer Texas Industry," *Farm and Ranch,* January 22, 1898.

Official Publications

Annual Report of Texas & Pacific Coal Company, 1889–1892; 1894–1897; 1900–1903 (no publisher or date of publication).

Annual Report of Texas Pacific Coal and Oil Company, 1933, 1937 (no publisher or date of publication).

By-Laws of the R. D. Hunter Fishing & Boating Club (Revised 1904). Thurber: Printing Department of Texas Pacific Mercantile and Manufacturing Company (no date of publication).

Cummins, W. F., "Report on Geology of Northwestern Texas," *Second Annual Report of Geological Survey of Texas, 1890.* Austin: State Printing Office, 1891.

Dumble, E. T., "First Report of Progress," *Texas: Geological and Mineralogical Survey of Texas.* Austin: State Printing Office, 1889.

Dumble, E. T., "Report of Progress," *Second Annual Report of Geological Survey of Texas, 1890.* Austin: State Printing Office, 1891.

Proceedings of the Sixth Annual Convention of Texas State Federation of Labor, Fort Worth, Texas, November 16, 17, 18, 1903. Fort Worth: Press of Humphreys and Carpenter, 1903.

Report of Adjutant-General 1889–1890. Austin: Hutchings State Printer, 1890.

Tarr, R. S., "Report on Coal Fields of Colorado River," *First Annual Report of Geological Survey of Texas, 1889.* Austin: State Printing Office, 1890.

Public Records

Criminal Court Docket, Vol. D, Erath County Court House, Stephenville, Texas.

Minutes of the Commissioners Court, Vols. E, F, G, Erath County Court House, Stephenville, Texas.

Naturalization Records, Erath County Court House, Stephenville, Texas.

Texas & Pacific Coal Company vs Thomas Lawson, Office of the Clerk, Supreme Court, Austin.

Bibliography

MANUSCRIPTS

Adjutant General's Papers, 1888–1903, State Capitol, Austin.

Frontier Papers, State Library, Austin.

Personal Papers of Mose Miller, Stephenville, Texas.

Thurber Reunion Registers, E. Buchanan, Strawn, Texas.

NEWSPAPERS

Austin Daily American

Dallas News

Fort Worth Daily Gazette

Fort Worth Press

Fort Worth Record

Fort Worth Star Telegram

Fort Worth Telegram

New York American

Ranger Times

Stephenville Empire

Strawn Tribune

Texas Miner

Texas Mining and Trade Journal

Thurber Journal

Thurber Tiny Journal

THESES

Eoff, Vallie, "A History of Erath County, Texas," Master of Arts Thesis, University of Texas, Austin, 1937.

Floyd, Willie, "Thurber, Texas, An Abandoned Coal Field Town," Master of Arts Thesis, Southern Methodist University, Dallas, 1939.

Gough, Lula Cass, "The Vascular Plants of Erath County Not Including Poales," Master of Arts Thesis, University of Texas, Austin, 1923.

Smith, Linnie, "History and Development of Education in Erath County," Master of Education Thesis, University of Texas, Austin, 1940.

Wilkins, C. S., "Thurber: A Sociological Study of a Company Owned Town," Master of Arts Thesis, University of Texas, Austin, 1929.

LETTERS

Conn, Daisy Varley, September 22, 1944.

Davenport, Harbert, April 29, 1940; May 7, 1940.

De Loach, W. G., February 23, 1940.

Gordon, W. K., August 12, 1941; June 23, 1944.

Gower, Gomer, April 12, 1940; June 24, 1944; July 14, 1944; July 17, 1944; August 6, 1944; August 14, 1944; January 18, 1945; July 22, 1946.

Graham, Mrs. John S., January 31, 1940.

Lorenz, Bill, August 8, 1939; February 8, 1940; August 8, 1941.

Mancill, R. W., January 23, 1940.

Martin, R. E., January 23, 1940.

Ott, Pansy, November 14, 1939.

Patterson, A. B., August 1, 1939.

Studdard, George, August 12, 1939.

Studdard, Rita Buffo, April 10, 1940.

Thomas, D. L., October 31, 1939.

Tidwell, Rev. D. D., January 25, 1940.

Truesdell, Leon, June 29, 1945.

Venturi, Marjorie, June 6, 1944.

Woodman, C. W., April 22, 1940.

INTERVIEWS

Belcher, Ernest, December 29, 1944.

Boyd, Bill, June 21, 1944; July 20, 1943; July 29, 1943.

Buchanan, E., January 3, 1942; July 20, 1943; July 31, 1945.

Conn, Daisy Varley, July 20, 1942; January 3, 1943.

Creswell, Mack, December 30, 1944.

Davidson, Sadie, June 15, 1941.

Descavage, Mrs. Joe, May, 1935.

Gentry, G. J., January 5, 1940; July 25, 1940; March 12, 1941; August 29, 1943; January 20, 1944.

Gibson, Fern Faggard, June 20, 1941.

Lorenz, Bill, July 20, 1943; July 28, 1943; July 14, 1944.

Miller, Hazel, August 14, 1941.

Miller, Roy, July 4, 1940; October 22, 1944.

Nichol, Faye, June 15, 1941.

Shaw, H. H., December 29, 1939.

Studdard, George, August 15, 1941; July 28, 1943.

Studdard, Rita Buffo, August 15, 1941; December 29, 1944.

Visentini, Mrs. Erico, July 23, 1943.

Williams, S. P., December 22, 1944.

Woodman, C. W., December 30, 1940.

SCRAPBOOK

Texas Pacific Coal and Oil Company Scrapbook, Texas Pacific Coal and Oil Company Office, Fort Worth.

Index

ISBN-13: 978-1-58544-629-2
ISBN-10: 1-58544-629-7

Printed in the USA
CPSIA information can be obtained
at www.ICGtesting.com
JSHW021045021023
49102JS00002B/2